Two Hundred Years of
Muddling Through

Two Hundred Years of Muddling Through

The Surprising Story of Britain's Economy from Boom to Bust and Back Again

DUNCAN WELDON

Little, Brown

LITTLE, BROWN

First published in Great Britain in 2021 by Little, Brown

3 5 7 9 10 8 6 4

A CIP catalogue record for this book is available from the British Library.

ISBN 978-1-4087-1316-7

Typeset in Baskerville by M Rules
Printed and bound in Great Britain by Clays Ltd, Elcograf S.p.A.

Papers used by Little, Brown are from well-managed forests
and other responsible sources.

Little, Brown
An imprint of
Little, Brown Book Group
Carmelite House
50 Victoria Embankment
London EC4Y 0DZ

An Hachette UK Company
www.hachette.co.uk

www.littlebrown.co.uk

For Julia, Louise and Josie

Contents

Contents

Introduction

Men make their own history, but they do not make it as they please; they do not make it under self-elected circumstances, but under circumstances existing already, given and transmitted from the past. The tradition of all dead generations weighs like a nightmare on the brains of the living.

Karl Marx, *The Eighteenth Brumaire of Louis Bonaparte*

There is a very famous, and very old, Irish joke about a man asked for directions by a tourist and responding 'Well, if I was you, I wouldn't start from here.' While the joke may not have people rolling in the aisles it is a pithier way of expressing what Marx said. Both are making the same point: people do not get to choose where they begin, and that insight, whilst simple, is too often forgotten when discussing the economy and politics.

This is a book about how the British economy got to where it is today. The economy on the eve of the COVID-19 recession was strangely paradoxical: at the same time both one of the world's most successful and one of Europe's laggards. In terms of GDP per head Britain is a world leader but productivity levels (even before the last decade) are abysmally low compared to its advanced economy peers. The country contains some of the EU's richest areas but also some which are more akin to southern Europe than to Germany or France. It is really not too much of an exaggeration to describe the UK, in economic terms, as 'Portugal but with Singapore in the bottom corner'.

Economic history helps to explain how that happened. If this book has one theme, it is that path dependency matters.

Path dependency is perhaps best thought of as the idea that the route one took to arrive somewhere is just as important as the destination. In the social sciences (and especially in economic history) this notion can be crucial. Or, to put it another way, the past and history matter and sometimes in ways which, like the man advising the tourist, are not especially helpful in the present.

The idea has been widely applied in technological history and perhaps the most famous example that many economists instinctively reach for is the design of the standard QWERTY keyboard.

As traditionally told, the story runs something like this. When the typewriter was first invented in the 1860s, by Milwaukee-based printer and newspaper man Christopher Latham Sholes, he naturally laid out the keys in alphabetical order, and whilst that may look odd to modern eyes it intuitively makes a lot more sense than starting with the Q and then moving on to the W the E and the R.

But his early models suffered from mechanical problems and a tendency to jam if keys that lay next to each other were hit in rapid succession. So by the time he filed his patent in 1878 Sholes had rearranged the layout to get round this problem. Keys likely to be hit one after the other regularly were placed at opposite ends of the keyboard, and whilst this slowed down typing speed, that was a feature not a bug of the design. The whole point was to slow the process and prevent the expensive machines from constantly jamming.

Sholes went into business with gun manufacturer Remington, which given the end of the US Civil War in 1865, was presumably looking for new lines of business. By 1893 the five largest typewriter makers had all adopted the QWERTY standard and history was set in place.

Of course a modern computer does not suffer from the same mechanical faults as a nineteenth-century typewriter. Indeed, the argument goes, those mechanical faults had actually been eliminated on typewriters by the 1920s.

In 1936 August Dvorak patented an alternative layout, which in tests by the US Navy in 1944 (at a time when the ability to produce reports rapidly really mattered) apparently led to quicker typing. But despite a better design being available and despite the original rationale for the adoption of QWERTY no longer holding, it is still the industry benchmark.

By coming to market first the QWERTY board established a standard. Individual typists, who had trained on a QWERTY, were reluctant to switch to a new layout, and manufacturers, seeing no demand for alternatives, were happy to keep putting them out. The less efficient technology became baked in.

Or that is how the traditional story goes, anyway. And it serves very well indeed to demonstrate a practical application of the idea of path dependency. Sadly, like many good stories, it may not be entirely true: the Dvorak system has its sceptics. But whatever the actual truth of most economists' favourite example of the phenomenon, it remains very useful. And path dependency can be applied far more widely than in just technological history.

It certainly appears in what might be termed 'economic geography'. Ever since Adam Smith, economists have long noted the tendency for businesses to cluster. If, say, a thriving printing industry has developed in any one town or city it makes sense for other printers to open their businesses in the same place – the local labour market will contain skilled printers and the necessary suppliers of paper and ink will already be available. The reason why the particular industry originally grew up in that locale – maybe because of the presence of a certain skillset in the local jobs market, the availability of certain raw materials or something else entirely – may matter less than the fact that it happened.

One reason why the American publishing industry has historically been centred on New York is simply because it was where the fast boats arrived from the United Kingdom in the nineteenth century. This meant that the most recent Charles Dickens novels (in his day a writer with as much box office potential in the US as in Britain) hit New York first, where the local printers – showing a very poor regard for intellectual property rights – would pirate and reprint the text for the American market. (Concerns about the cross-border enforcement of copyright rules are truly nothing new.) Cross-Atlantic shipping schedules no longer have any relevance for the industry, but, having established itself in New York, once it was there it was there.

A depressing 2015 study by the think tank Centre for Cities looked at the growth and performance of British cities between 1911 and 2011. One important conclusion was that the proportion of 'knowledge workers' in a city's workforce was a significant determinant of a city's prospects in 2011. And the single most important factor explaining the number of knowledge workers in 2011 was how many knowledge workers had been present in 1911. The reason, the authors reckon, that Wigan did not have a booming tech centre in 2011 was that it was an industrial mill town in 1911. Central Manchester by contrast already had a core of highly skilled service sector workers a century before. History matters.

Another example is what some economists term 'hysteresis effects'. Derived from the Greek for 'that which comes later', hysteresis effects are simple effects which persist well after the initial catalyst or cause is gone. The two most common examples cited are in the labour market and international trade. It may be for example that a rise in the value of the pound makes certain British exports uncompetitive overseas and the firms in this industry respond by cutting back production and jobs. However if, a few years later, the pound falls in value and British exports are once again internationally competitive then production and employment may not return to their old levels. During the period of a highly priced pound and increased unemployment, British workers may have seen their skills degrade and other, foreign, firms may have taken up their market share. A rising pound thus may increase unemployment in one sector but the pound returning to its original level not eliminate the effect. This was the case in the mid- to late 1980s when a strong pound acted as catalyst to the decline of British manufacturing jobs. The weaker pound of the early 1990s failed to spur re-employment.

Similarly, some trade experts have found persisting hysteresis effects in international trading patterns. The argument goes that breaking into a new market requires large one-off sunk costs. Once a firm has chosen to commit the cash it may be reluctant to switch to another market, even if better-looking opportunities arise.

One recurring theme of this book is that the choices taken (and just as importantly those avoided) by one generation of politicians, policy-makers and business leaders usually shape the choices faced by their successors. None of this should be taken as an argument that history and the past will always decide the future but rather as an acknowledgement that the future will at least be *shaped* by what came before it.

Looking at many features of the British economy as it begins the 2020s it is all too easy to offer the advice 'Well, I wouldn't start from here,' but that is just about as useful to British policy-makers as the Irishman's advice to the tourist.

Path dependency is the central theme of this work, but it is not the only one. A look back over the last two centuries of British economic history reveals some other threads that return time and time again.

First, that political economy matters. Trying to understand the path an economy takes – especially over the longer term – without considering the wider political and social system is impossible. Britain's development over the last two hundred years has been shaped by the rise and fall of different (broadly defined) political interest groups. Second, that the *way* politics matters is often misunderstood. In the short term politicians overestimate their influence but in the long term they underestimate it. It is very rare that a long-standing economic problem has an easy, quick fix, and there is a limit to what any budget or set of political priorities can achieve over a matter of months and years. But over years and decades the big political decisions can have a major impact. Often well after those who made them have retired.

Political economy is really about the interaction of politics and the economy and the feedback loop between them. When growth is weak, politics is more polarised and distributional battles are more intense. In simple terms: when the pie is growing quickly, there is less fighting over the shares. When the economy is performing at its worst is when politics gets the most intense: the early/mid-nineteenth century, the decade before the First World War, the 1970s and post-2008 Britain have all been times of weak growth and vicious political battles.

The international economic-financial context matters. Britain, despite appearances, is not an island. Or at least not economically. The British economy has always been buffeted by head and tail winds from the world economy, and policy choices have often been constrained by international factors. The seemingly poor macroeconomic performance of the 1950s–1970s was driven by the (perceived) need to defend the value of sterling under the prevailing Bretton Woods system. A stable and growing world economy (plus the availability of cheap Chinese goods) explains much of the better performance of the late 1980s, 1990s and early 2000s. Domestic policy-makers tend to get too much credit and too much blame.

In policy terms, there are almost no free lunches. Most modern macroeconomic policy-making is about trade-offs, the terms of those trade-offs (say between inflation and unemployment, or in raising short-term revenue at the expense of longer-term growth) having varied over time. The trade-offs were particularly acute and unpleasant in the inter-war years, the 1970s and post-2008.

As this book canters over the last two hundred years many issues will recur frequently: the balance between economic openness and sovereignty, the question of whether the banks were too powerful/too big to fail, the failure of British voca-tional training, the supposed lack of scientific knowledge among the elite, the fear that German manufacturing was powering ahead, worries about the impact of new technologies on the labour market, fretting about rising inequality and the issue of how to help regions and cities that risked being left behind. One depressing conclusion is that little in UK public debate is ever that new.

Another, perhaps even more depressing theme is that all too often British policy-makers have chosen to avoid choos-ing. Presented with difficult decisions that have long-term implications, they've often taken the easy path of muddling on and hoping something will turn up eventually. Make do and mend has been a key aspect of economic policy for decades.

The Britain of the 2020s is a modern capitalist economy, and yet capitalism is not some sort of monolithic entity, it has a national character. Just as the Nordic model differs from American capitalism, so too does British capitalism depart from other advanced economies in important ways. These ways of arranging production and distribution have differing strengths and weaknesses: some are better at creating jobs and others at handling recession. It is tempting to ask which model is best, but that is a bit like asking which type of clothes is best, a raincoat or a pair of shorts? The answer of course depends on the weather. But, unlike garments, national models of economic development are not something which can be changed on a whim. Instead they take decades to achieve results and are rooted in path dependency.

But before one can really get into the story of how the British economy came to where it is today, one needs to understand how the modern economy itself began. Modern economic history began with the industrial revolution, and the industrial revolution began in Britain.

1

Before the Revolution

The story of human economic history is remarkably simple, having only two parts: the time before the industrial revolution and the time afterwards. As late as the eighteenth and early nineteenth centuries most people enjoyed, if enjoyed is not too perverse a word, a standard of living not only familiar to their parents and grandparents but to their ancestors living centuries before. As one eminent economic historian has put it: 'Jane Austen may write about refined conversation over tea served in china cups, but for the mass of people as late as 1813 material conditions were no better than their ancestors of the African savannah. The Darcys were few, the poor plentiful.' The workers toiling in the fields of Pemberley to provide Mr Darcy with his £10,000 a year would have produced and consumed much the same goods, slept in similar shelter and eaten similar food to peasants toiling in those very same lands five hundred years before. The dominant trend in the pre-industrial world was continuity, not change.

That is not to say the pre-industrial economy was simply static. Growth spurts occurred but they tended to be transitory affairs – a few good years or even a few good decades before the boom unwound and things returned to normal. After the industrial revolution growth was of a different character: sustained and persistent. That sustained and persistent growth drove income per head and living standards higher. Within a few short generations not only were the typical person's living standards above those of their parents or grandparents, but they expected them to be.

A few numbers illustrate the magnitude of the shift. Expressed in terms of today's money, average, or mean, income per head in England in 1300 was around £780 per year. Some 350 years later in 1650 it had risen to £977 per year. In terms of purchasing power, that essentially meant something not too far above subsistence level; a person can live off pottage without starving but they cannot enjoy an especially fun life. That might, at first glance, look like 350 years of miserably slow growth, but in reality the path was far from smooth. In a few good decades it had peaked above £1,200 per year and in the bad times sunk to a low of just £720. The big picture is that English incomes from the rule of Edward Longshanks at the turn of the fourteenth century to the rule of Oliver Cromwell in the 1650s were about £1,000 per head per year.

The next 350 years looked very different. By 1700 income per head per year had risen to £1,700 and by 1750 to just shy of £2,000. After centuries of stagnation incomes doubled in just one hundred years. And more was to come. By 1800 incomes were almost £2,500, and over £5,000 by 1900. By 2000 incomes had hit almost £26,000.

Numbers on a page can be deceptively dry. The sustained growth of the industrial economy was not simply a case of people getting a bit better off each year, it was utterly transformative. The industrial revolution was the beginning of the process whereby for most people on the planet life ceased being, in the words of Thomas Hobbes, 'nasty, brutish and short'. Life expectancy at birth, which had been around 35 years for the millennium or so before 1800, began its rapid rise, infant mortality rates collapsed in industrial countries, food got better and more plentiful, and leisure time not only increased but became vastly more wide ranging. The industrial revolution fundamentally changed the experience of human life. It was, in many ways, the single most important event in history. Certainly the most important human development since the beginning of farming and the end of the hunter-gatherer society in the Neolithic Age. And the fact that it happened first in Britain is still being felt some two hundred or so years later.

Dating any revolution is a tricky job. Did the French Revolution begin with the storming of the Bastille on 14 July 1789? Or with the calling of the Estates General the year before? Or indeed with the ousting of the King from power in 1792? Historians still debate this today. With an economic rather than a political revolution, the dating process becomes even more difficult. Painting in broad brush strokes, it is perhaps fairest to say that the industrial revolution occurred at some point between the 1750s and 1820s – although a case can be made for pushing the start date to as early as the seventeenth century and the end date to the 1840s. Indeed, whilst the impact was certainly revolutionary, the process itself was more a drawn-out economic *evolution* than a single *revolution*.

The question of exactly when the industrial revolution/ evolution began is of course impossible to answer unless one knows what one is looking for. The revolution cannot be dated to any of the particular inventions it is most commonly associated with – Hargreaves's Spinning Jenny, Watt's Steam Engine or Whitney's Cotton Gin – indeed for all the popular focus on steam power and coal, the early decades of the revolution relied far more on water power. The revolution was not really about any particular invention or innovation, it was a seismic change in the nature of the economy and of economic growth itself – it was almost the 'invention of invention', the beginning of a process of constant change, productivity growth and improvement.

The world before the industrial revolution was Malthusian (named for the Reverend Thomas Robert Malthus). It is a neat historical irony that Malthus's greatest work, *Essay on the Principle of Population*, was first published in 1798 just as the economic regime he described was in the process of ending.

Despite his clerical status the Reverend Malthus's attitude to the poor may appear, to modern readers, distinctly unchristian. He is often said to have been the inspiration for Dickens's Scrooge, which is hardly the most welcome of literary accolades. But unlike old Ebenezer, Malthus had no sudden revelation. If a pauper begged him for alms his instinct would be to refuse them. Not from a want of kindness, of course, but simply because feeding the poor would only, in the final analysis, lead to more poor people and ultimately more human misery. What might appear to the less educated to be simple cruelty, was actually driven by the very finest Christian virtues of kindness and charity.

Malthus believed the world to be governed by a brutal logic, a logic that stated that whilst human wants were infinite, human means were distinctly finite. Expressed in mathematical terms, human populations, when left unchecked, tended to grow 'geometrically' – that is to say they expanded by a constant ratio, 1, 2, 4, 8, 16, etc. But the means of human subsistence – land, food, consumer goods – grew 'arithmetically' – that is to say by a fixed amount rather than by a certain percentage – 1, 2, 3, 4, 5, etc. If the population grew geometrically and the means of subsistence only expanded arithmetically, then the two would regularly fall out of balance, the population outstripping the ability of the economy to feed it. This harsh calculus provided, for Malthus, an iron law of human development, what he termed the 'perpetual tendency' for mankind to 'increase beyond the means of sustenance'.

The balance between the two variables was maintained through the operation of two broad categories of Malthusian checks: positive and preventative. Positive checks (which despite the name are hardly 'positive') were those which Malthus saw as operating through nature: war, disease and (most common of all) famine. Preventative checks, as emphasised by the Reverend, were those designed to limit population growth in the first place and prevent the need for the positive checks to come into play: sexual abstinence or, at the very least, the delay of marriage to a later age.

The human suffering involved in plagues, famines and wars was something Malthus wished to avoid. His cold, although rational, argument dictated that the best way to achieve this was to limit population growth. Feeding the poor would only result in more poor people.

Whilst the morality of Malthus's solutions is certainly questionable, the basic thrust of his understanding of the dynamics between population levels and living standards in the pre-industrial economy is broadly correct: that world was indeed Malthusian. Economic output grew only very slowly and was only sustainable if it kept in line with population growth. As the population expanded but resources failed to keep up, income per head fell. If the population level contracted, then income per head rose. This was a horribly zero-sum way of living, where the death of a neighbour might cause you some fleeting grief but probably made you better off in the long run.

A long look back over English income per head and population levels before circa 1650 shows the relationship between the two was indeed inverse. Periods of rising births led to lower living standards, whereas periods with more death boosted the income levels of those remaining.

Of course, although Malthus was right in his diagnosis of the past, he was wrong not only about the future but also about his own time. At some point in the late seventeenth century England threw off the chains of the Malthusian trap: between 1700 and 1800, the English population grew from around 5.2 million to around 7.7 million without a consequent fall in incomes. But the lack of a fall of incomes was not immediately apparent to Malthus and his followers; what was obvious was that people were breeding rather more quickly than in the past. And that was just the start: between 1800 and 1850 the English population would double to more than 15 million and between 1850 and 1900 it would double again to over 30 million. This huge expansion did not, however, lead to famine, plague or falling incomes. The Malthusian checks were no longer needed, the relationship between population and incomes had broken down, something had changed drastically. The nature of economic growth had shifted, the industrial revolution had played out and modern productivity growth had begun. The importance of this cannot be overstated.

Few economists doubt that productivity matters. The Nobel Prize-winner Paul Krugman best summed this up with his often quoted remark that 'productivity isn't everything, but in the long run it is almost everything'. The problem, though, is that even compared to other economic variables it can sound pretty dry and uninteresting. A rise in unemployment or an increase in prices are the kind of thing that seizes the public and political imagination; they are what feature in newspaper headlines and political campaign posters. No one has ever put the latest productivity statistics on a billboard.

Simply put, productivity is the ability to get more economic output from any given level of inputs. Or, even more straightforwardly, the ability to make more stuff with the same number of workers. In the broadest of sweeps, the economic history of Britain – and indeed the wider history of Britain – since the late eighteenth century and the industrial revolution is the history of productivity growth. It was the take-off in productivity that allowed the population to expand and income per head to rise at the same time.

Even if most economists can agree that productivity growth is, in general, a very good thing, they have less idea about what really drives it over the longer term. New technology certainly plays a role but its adoption and spread can be uneven and patchy – and the question of what drives technology growth itself, what has recently been called 'innovation policy', remains something of an undiscovered Holy Grail in policy-making. Management practices and techniques are widely regarded as important, but what works in one firm or sector or country does not necessarily work elsewhere. Despite the exponential growth of management consultancy over the past few decades it appears that not every problem can be solved by a small army of bright recent graduates equipped with a decent knowledge of Microsoft Excel and the ability to make a PowerPoint presentation. Infrastructure and education no doubt play an important part – as do a hundred other variables from climate to contract law. Most economists, even those who make its study their primary area of research, can list the factors that influence productivity and many can come up with a handful of helpful (and, as is the way of much economics, often contradictory) proposals to push it higher, but no one has yet been able to conclusively say 'productivity is ultimately driven by *xyz*'.

In a fairer world Paul Krugman's famous (in economic policy circles anyway) dictum would be followed up with 'and yet sadly we still don't really understand it'.

If there is little agreement on what the ultimate drivers of productivity are today then it is perhaps no surprise that exactly what caused the first take-off in productivity growth to occur on an island off the northwest coast of Europe is still hotly debated.

2

The Great British Take-off

In the grand scheme of global economic history, the fact that the industrial revolution began in Britain is less important than the fact it began in Europe. In the early 1700s the world's two largest economies were India and China, with western Europe as a whole perhaps having roughly the same sort of economic weight as one or the other. In the next two hundred years the world's centre of economic gravity moved rapidly westwards. By 1900, western Europe represented around 35 per cent of global GDP, its offshoot the United States another 15 per cent or so and China and India only around 10 per cent each. The political implications of this economic 'Great Divergence' set the tone for nineteenth- and twentieth-century global history: the rise of the West, the expansion of Europe and the age of Empire. Only in the last few decades has the pre-industrial-revolution pattern of economic activity begun to slowly reassert itself.

Looked at from a global perspective, the question of 'Why Britain?' and not France, Germany or the Netherlands may appear insignificant. The crucial fact is that it began in Europe. But from the more parochial perspective of British history, the 'Why Britain?' question obviously matters more.

The fact that Britain was first gave it an immediate lead which persisted for decades, the fact that GDP per head was so much higher in Britain than in its more populous European rivals gave Britain a much larger economy than bigger countries.

In 1700 the total population of Britain and Ireland was around 8.7 million compared to 21.4 million in France. By 1800 the British and Irish combined population had risen to 15.6 million but was still dwarfed by France's 26.7 million or so inhabitants. But the decoupling of population and incomes created by productivity growth meant the dynamics of power had shifted. In 1700 the French economy was almost twice as big as that of Britain and Ireland but by 1800 their GDPs were roughly in line despite the French population being some 60 per cent larger. Britain was able to seize, compared to its population levels, an outsize world role (with all the advantages and disadvantages that entailed) that persisted well into the mid-twentieth century – and in many ways beyond that.

Britain did have some natural, geographic advantages. Being a relatively small island made access to the sea straightforward from most parts of the country and that, combined with a high number of large, easily navigable rivers, made transport and communications costs relatively low compared to what they were for, say, Germany or France. Before steam power, it was much cheaper to move goods on water than on land. Alongside the larger rivers, Britain was blessed with a plentiful supply of the sort of fast-flowing streams and brooks that were crucial to running water mills. As the industrial revolution progressed and water power gave way to steam, Britain was still more than self-sufficient in energy with easily reached coal seams to continue powering growth. For a small country, Britain's topography is unusually diverse, which allowed a variety of different sorts of agriculture to develop in different regions. The damp climate of northwest England may not have done much to support Blackpool's tourist industry in recent decades but was certainly helpful in processing raw cotton. All of this contributed, but the mystery of 'Why Britain?' cannot be solved through geography alone.

Just as the industrial revolution shaped subsequent British history, it itself was shaped by what had come before. It makes no sense to begin a history of the industrial revolution just as the revolution itself began, especially as on the eve of it Britain, and more specifically England, was already one of the richest regions of the globe.

Before the 'Great Divergence' of industrialisation came the 'Little Divergence', a shift of wealth and economic affluence within Europe. Many of the factors that help explain the industrial revolution and the Great Divergence can be traced back to its earlier cousin. Understanding the Little Divergence, or how Britain, in the few hundred years before the nineteenth century, came to be one of the richest regions of the world, is crucial to understanding what came afterwards.

At the turn of the first millennium in AD 1000 the richest areas of Europe were to be found just where they had been one thousand years before: in the Mediterranean basin. The Roman Empire might have fallen centuries before but post-Roman Italy and Moorish Spain remained the wealthiest parts of Europe. And yet by 1700 the continent's centre of economic gravity had shifted decisively from the warm shores of the Mediterranean to the colder climes of the North Sea. In terms of income per head, the economic leaders of 1700 were the United Provinces of the Netherlands and their commercial rivals across the sea in Britain.

Economic historians have identified two key turning points which drove this divergence. In economic parlance, these turning points would usually be described as 'shocks' and the first of them was certainly shocking: the Black Death.

The scale of the great plague is still staggering; the worst pandemic in human history killed somewhere between 75 and 200 million people in Eurasia. The global population took *two hundred years* to regain its pre-outbreak peak. And oddly enough, that outbreak was itself perhaps the result of an early form of proto-globalisation begun by, of all people, Genghis Khan.

The Great Khan united Mongolia by 1206 and by the time of his death in 1227 had built an empire covering 5.2 million square miles. By the time of his grandson Kublai Khan's death, just under seventy years later in 1294, the Mongol empire amounted to over nine million square miles stretching from modern-day Hungary in the west to modern-day China and Korea in the east and encompassing, along the way, central Asia, Ukraine, southern Russia, Iran and Iraq. The key to Mongol success was their control of around half of the world's horse population, and whilst Mongol armies rarely numbered much above 100,000, each warrior would have access to up to twenty remounts guaranteeing them fresh horses in a decisive battle and almost unprecedented mobility.

The political unification of much of Eurasia drove an economic integration. Mongol rule made travel along the old Silk Roads safer – as long as one was prepared to pay the tolls – and between 1250 and 1350 those roads were much busier than in the centuries before. Marco Polo may be the most famous European to have visited China in this era (or not: his account is disputed by some) but he was far from the only one. Land trade in bulky goods was still prohibitively expensive, but items with a high value-to-weight ratio began to move in greater numbers than before – spices, furs and, of course, silk. And ideas are less bulky still: European innovation in the 1300s received a large boost from the inflows of Chinese technology. Writing in 1620, Francis Bacon, the so-called father of modern science, argued that three great inventions had changed the world: printing, gunpowder and the compass. He probably did not know all three originated in China.

In the century before the Black Death people, goods and ideas began to flow across Eurasia. As Ronald Findlay and Kevin O'Rourke put it in their landmark history of the global economy:

> When did 'globalisation' begin? Whilst the answer depends on the definition used, a strong case can be made that it began with the unification of the central Eurasian landmass by the Mongol conquests and the reactions this aroused in the sedentary civilisations that they were launched against. Each civilisation previously had been aware of the others, but only as isolated entities, not as interactive components of a unified system.

But it was not only goods, ideas and people that were on the move. The political unification of Eurasia drove an economic integration which in turn created what one historian has dubbed a 'microbian common market'. Somewhere in the dry plains of Central Asia the Black Death began. Merchants, soldiers and travellers carried it down the Silk Road to the Crimea, where it boarded Genoese and Venetian galleys bound for western Europe.

In the space of five years somewhere between 40 per cent and 60 per cent of Europe's population died. Whilst obviously a human catastrophe, this was also perhaps the shining example of one of the Reverend Malthus's 'positive checks' operating, although even a man with as rational and logical a brain as the good Reverend might have struggled to see the advantages at the time.

In the Malthusian world of the mid-1300s an event which

killed millions of people but which did not devastate buildings or directly affect livestock or crops meant more resources and food for fewer people and stomachs. There might be fewer heads but income per head would rise.

Faced with the same economic and biological shock, the economies of the North Sea and Mediterranean regions reacted differently. In England and the Netherlands income per (surviving) head jumped and remained higher whereas in Italy the initial leap forward petered out within a century or so and in Spain the plague brought human suffering without the silver lining.

Spain in the 1350s was in the midst of its 'Reconquista', the 're'capture of the Iberian peninsula for Christian Europe. It was essentially a sparsely populated frontier economy where a drastic fall in population had the effect of snuffing out commercial networks rather than boosting the resources available to the survivors. Here the falling population meant not 'more crops for the survivors' but rather 'not enough people to till the fields'. In Italy, after a century or so of higher incomes per head, the Malthusian logic kicked in, and faster population growth dragged incomes back towards their pre-catastrophe level.

By contrast, in the North Sea area the economic gains of the Black Death were consolidated and built upon. The crucial differences between the two regions were to be found in the structure of their agriculture and in marriage ages and fertility patterns, alongside important differences in their politics and state structures.

North Sea agriculture was much more pastorally focused than Mediterranean agriculture – that is to say, more focused on the use of animals and livestock than crops and plants (though grains were of course grown throughout Europe). The typical Italian speciality agricultural products were olive oil and wine; the typically English products were wool and mutton. Just over half of the economic output from English agriculture in the 1350s came from milk, meat, wool, leather and other animal products rather than directly from the soil. This kind of agriculture usually requires more processing than arable farming and, although it does not produce more calories per head, it is higher in terms of 'economic value add', or in plainer words 'more profitable', than the kinds of farming found in the Mediterranean littoral.

It is also uses fewer workers than arable agriculture and is, in economic language, more 'capital intense'. 'Capital' being the standard economics term for anything other than people (labour) used in producing output, in this case the 'capital' is the livestock. Finally, this type of animal-focused agriculture was more extensive in its use of non-human energy – English farms made more use of horse (and bullock) power than manpower, when compared to their Italian equivalents. This type of high-value-add, capital-intense, non-human-energy-intense agricultural production not only coped better with the fall in the population after the Black Death but also provided the model for the production techniques which would spread from agriculture into the industrial and (later) service sectors which came to dominate modern economies.

In medieval Europe the age of marriage was a key driver of overall fertility. In general the younger women married the more children they would have, and in the Mediterranean region they got married younger – often much younger – than in the North Sea area. In 1965, the statistician and demographer John Hajnal identified what he termed the 'Western European marriage pattern' characterised by spouses marrying relatively late and being close in age, a significant minority of women remaining unmarried and newly married couples usually establishing their own household separate from that of the bride or groom's family. Outside of some areas of southeast

Asia this pattern was almost uniquely European until the late twentieth century. Even within Europe it was not universal, with Mediterranean families much more likely to consist of relatively older men marrying much younger women (or in many cases girls) and extended multi-generational homes being the norm.

The typical English bride of the Middle Ages was in her early twenties and marrying a man a year or two older, whereas a spinster of 21 in Italy would have been regarded as having missed her marriageable prime. At thirteen years old Juliet Capulet is a slightly, but only slightly, extreme example of the pre-industrial Mediterranean pattern; more common would be a bride of 17 or 18 marrying a man ten or twelve years her senior.

The later marriage age and lower fertility rates in the north of Europe allowed the boost to incomes from the Black Death to persist much longer than in the south of the continent. No doubt Malthus would have been pleased to hear that his 'preventative checks' appeared to be working.

The Black Death was the first shock that drove the Little Divergence. Hit by the same plague but with different marriage patterns and agricultural structures, the North Sea world received a permanent boost in incomes and caught up with the Mediterranean. The second shock came 150 years after the plague, in the 1490s, and in the subsequent decades pushed North Sea area incomes well ahead of their Mediterranean counterparts.

Adam Smith (who will play a large part in the chapter after next) wrote that 'the discovery of America, and that of a passage to the East Indies by the Cape of Good Hope, are the two greatest and most important events recorded in the history of mankind'. Whilst there is a fair degree of hyperbole in that declaration, Columbus's 'discovery' of the Americas and Vasco da Gama's voyage round the Cape opening a new sea route from Europe directly into the Indian Ocean were to have a huge impact on global economic and political history.

The two voyages – and Magellan's circumnavigation of the globe in the 1520s – not only changed the shape of the world but moved Britain to its centre. Any semi-decent map of the known world drawn up before the 1490s would have shown Britain as an island in the extreme northwest, with only desolate Greenland and Iceland being more distant. After the 1500s the map took on its familiar, Eurocentric shape with the British Isles holding a central position.

The following centuries saw the birth of the grim Atlantic commerce known as the triangular trade, whereby trade goods were shipped from Europe to Africa, traded for slaves and then those slaves shipped to the New World. The final side of the triangle was those ships returning from the new colonies to Europe, loaded with New World goods. Meanwhile, in the Indian Ocean Europeans armed with gunpowder weapons forcibly inserted themselves into the centuries-old trading networks that ringed the coasts of east Africa, western India and southern Arabia.

This expansion of global trade, trade done on terms very much in the Europeans' favour and backed by force and violence, had an impact every bit as important as that of the Black Death.

Given that da Gama's rounding of the Cape was sponsored by the Portuguese Crown, and the Genoese Columbus's expedition by the Spanish, one might expect the gains to have accrued to southern rather than northern Europe. But although the Spanish and Portuguese led the way, they were relatively quickly surpassed by the Dutch and then the British.

In purely economic terms, a major difference between the

North Sea and Mediterranean regions lay in what a modern labour market specialist would describe as the 'flexibility of labour supply'. That is to say, the willingness of workers to respond to higher demand for their labour by taking fewer holidays and working longer hours (or, looked at from the other end of the telescope – the ability of employers to compel workers to work longer hours). In the North Sea region the labour supply proved to be flexible, and around the Mediterranean less so.

The typical English worker of the 1400s or early 1500s worked something like 160 to 180 days a year, or under half of the year – which to modern ears sounds rather pleasant, until one remembers quite how poor these people were. The coming of the Reformation sliced the number of Saint's Days and other religious festivals that were typically taken as holiday, and pushed the working year up to around 260 days a year by circa 1600. Another wave of expansion came in the 1700s as the practice of 'St Mondays' (whereby workers would just fail to turn up on a Monday and declare they were celebrating St Monday's Day) came to an end.

This rise in the working year has been called the 'industrious revolution' and was both an important prelude to the later *industrial* revolution and a process that continued well into the nineteenth century. It was led by the Dutch and British, although later spread across most of Europe. The great sociologist Max Weber, writing in the early twentieth century, famously attributed it to religion. In *The Protestant Ethic and the Spirit of Capitalism*, he argued that the more worldly focus of Protestantism, and in particular that of Calvinists, was an important driver of industrialisation and modern capitalism. This thesis, though, is certainly far from universally agreed upon – Calvinism for example was never especially strong in England. A more common modern explanation is that the growth of global commerce and the rise of the early new industries created a wealth of new consumer goods that had previously either not existed at all in Europe or been entirely beyond the reach of ordinary workers. Eager to get their hands on tea, pepper, linen coats and porcelain plates, workers were prepared to work for longer to boost their incomes and their spending power.

Of course whilst the flexibility of labour supply can explain some of the rise in Dutch and English incomes between 1500 and 1750, it cannot explain the whole story of how global commerce came to be dominated by the North Sea countries. A full explanation needs to step away from 'pure economics' and look at the bigger, political, picture.

Economic historians have known for a long time a simple fact that many economists often ignore: politics matters. Nobel laureate Douglass North won his prize for his work on economic history and institutions, and provides the most useful framework for thinking through the role of the state and politics in the long history of economic development.

The really short version is that institutions are *a*, and sometimes *the*, key factor in explaining growth over the longer term. When economists and economic historians write of institutions, though, it is useful to be clear about exactly what they mean. Institutions in this sense are not necessarily what the non-specialist thinks of when they hear the word. An 'institution' does not have to mean an actual organisation with a front door that one can knock on. Rather it refers to what one might call 'the rules of the game' – the wider collection of actual institutions with doors that one can knock on, the legal framework, the governmental system and, just as crucially, the informal and often unwritten norms of behaviour and conduct which govern both politics and commercial transactions. An economy with a decent institutional structure is usually seen as one where two parties can enter into a transaction and be confident that it will not suddenly be reversed or the goods seized, where a banker making a loan knows there is a good chance it will be repaid and where the government is not likely to suddenly tear up the entire legal framework to appease one interest group or another. None of which should be taken as an argument that the ideal government should do nothing except make sure property rights are enforced and otherwise stand back with a laissez-faire, hands-off approach.

Take Philip II's Spain during that country's golden age of the late sixteenth century. Certainly Philip ruled over a global power and one, on a surface level at least, vastly enriched by the conquest of much of South America and its silver mines. And yet Philip has been called the 'borrower from hell', a sovereign who defaulted on his loans four times during his reign. The Netherlands, which revolted from Spanish rule during his time on the throne, lacked the riches and splendour of Spain and certainly lacked ownership of a vast New World empire teeming with slaves and silver, but it had a strong commercial culture, well-run guilds and functioning contract law. The economic institutions of the Dutch gave the Netherlands a stability that Spain lacked despite its seeming power.

Just as important as the institutional framework is the ability of governments to enforce it. State capacity – the ability of a government to ensure that what it says should happen actually does happen – matters. Good intentions may be better than bad intentions but they are next to useless if they remain only intentions.

There is a trade-off here: a state needs to be strong enough to enforce property rights but not so strong that it can rig the game in its own interest.

North outlines two types of settled state in the era since

the Neolithic revolution: 'limited access orders' and 'open access orders'.

Crucial to understanding these different social orders, and North's entire theory of social and economic development, is the concept of 'economic rent'. No one really likes paying rent, and especially not economists. But economists tend to use the word a little more widely than the lay person.

An *economic rent* refers not just to the price paid to lease an item – whether a car, a flat or a piece of machinery – but something a bit more technical. It refers to the excessive payment for land, labour or goods over what the owner would actually accept. To give a more grounded example: if a landlord were prepared to let a flat for £500 a month and got an offer of £550, they would obviously be receiving a rental payment of £550, but could be said to be earning an *economic* rent of £50 a month. Equally, if a worker was happy to take a certain job at £15 per hour and got that very same job at a rate of £18 an hour, they could be thought of as making an economic rent of £3 an hour.

In the ideal and absolutely impossible world of what microeconomists call perfect competition there would be no economic rents. In a world of perfect competition there are an infinite number of potential buyers and an infinite number of potential sellers and both are assumed to have perfect knowledge. If buyers and sellers of goods and services had perfect knowledge of how other buyers and sellers value every good or service then competition would force prices to a level where there was no rent involved. If a flat hunter knew a landlord would settle for £500 a month, then that is what they would offer. If an employer knew an employee would accept £15 an hour, then they would not offer the job at £18.

Of course, we do not live in a world of perfect information or perfect competition. No one ever has. The existence of market imperfections – whether the reality that neither suppliers nor buyers are actually infinite in number, or that no one really has perfect information – means that economic rents are a fact of life. And whilst few mind the odd worker being paid a pound or two an hour more than they would really settle for, the idea that flats can be let for hundreds of pounds a month more than is necessary tends to raise a few more hackles.

All of which might sound interesting from the point of view of a markets regulator but hardly relevant to the development of North's limited and open access orders. But it is the existence of economic rents which underpins much state development. Economic rents are a way of enriching oneself without actually producing anything extra. The landlord getting paid £50 a month more than they would accept is essentially getting £600 a year for no reason. The control and dishing out of economic rents has been crucial to how societies have developed, and for most of the last ten thousand years or so the control of economic rents has been won through violence.

In North's conceptual framework what he politely terms 'violence specialists' (the less polite word is 'thugs') are able to organise societies by promising to protect others from violence specialists such as themselves. Once the age of the hunter gatherer had ended and the age of settled farming had begun, it was only a short step to some bulkier humans realising that to take the produce of fields managed by someone less bulky was in some ways a much more straightforward job than actually growing wheat for oneself. The states which grew out of these groupings are North's 'limited access orders'. And until relatively recently, it was the dominant form of human organisation. Eventually the most successful 'violence specialists' gained titles such as Duke, Baron or King.

In such a state, violence is controlled, order and stability is (most of the time) provided and so greater production is achieved through economies of scale, greater specialisation and more trade. But the institutional set-up of limited access order is skewed towards the elite – towards the violence specialists and the descendants of the original thugs. The rules of the game were rigged.

The characteristics of such an order could be found in both the Roman Empire and *ancien régime* France, and most settled societies in between – the elite controlled the state through violence, rights to trade were limited and governed by an often complex set of rules, the property rights of the elite tended to be protected while those of everyone else were often weak. Such a system allows an economy to grow but is also the ideal vehicle for the creation of economic rents – granting a monopoly on certain goods to a favoured friend of the elite can almost guarantee them great wealth. Limited access orders work through using the control of violence to create seams of economic rent and then divide these up between the elite.

This may sound like a rather depressing view of the history of state formation but is generally consistent with actual reality. As one sociologist, only semi-playfully, once neatly put it: 'If protection rackets represent organised crime at its smoothest, then war risking and state making – quintessential protection rackets with the advantage of legitimacy – qualify as our largest examples of organised crime.' Medieval monarchs, in effect, were functionally similar to a mob boss extorting cash through threats.

By contrast North's open access societies are marked less by the creation and control of economic rents and more by competition – both political and economic. Such states are characterised by the rule of law applying to the elite, by there being ways of entry for outsiders into that elite and by the military (and its threat of violence) being politically controlled by a more formal framework than the whims of a ruler. The transition, in North's model, from a limited to an open access order is fraught and difficult. Not many states have managed it, but ultimately for North it is the driver of successful economies. The focus on genuine competition rather than the dividing up of flows of rent pushes firms and entrepreneurs towards innovation and improvement.

No one would seriously claim that the Dutch Republic of the 1600s and 1700s or the fledgling Great Britain after the Act of Union between England and Scotland in 1707 were what North would term an 'open access order'. But many would accept that the Dutch Republic and the Great Britain of the 1700s were certainly closer to such an order than, say, France or Spain. In both cases strong legislatures had developed which widened the circle of the elite (admittedly only from 'absolutely tiny' to still just 'tiny') and placed some constraints on executive power. In both cases merchant interests had the ability to exercise some say over wider questions of policy. English kings of course had never had total power – they had always had to keep the leading nobles on board – but by the early modern period that circle of necessary consent had widened to include the richest citizens of the leading cities, and especially of London, as well as rural magnates.

Britain, on the eve of the industrial revolution, was gradually transitioning from a limited access to an open access order.

Perhaps counterintuitively the more 'liberal' (although the word did not yet have this meaning) framework of the British state after 1688's Glorious Revolution, compared to France, actually made the state *more* powerful. The British state of the 1700s with its parliamentary checks and balances achieved a wider political buy-in and more legitimacy in the eyes of many of the elite than its French rival did across the Channel. The result was that 'liberal' Britain was able to develop a far more effective and powerful state than 'absolutist' France. In the 1750s the British state could extract the equivalent of 109 grams of silver per person in taxation whereas France and Spain managed less than 50.

Constraints on state action helped elites feel more comfortable with allowing the state apparatus to take more power – there was less chance of it being turned on them. From the 1650s onwards the British 'fiscal-warfare' state developed, building the world's strongest navy and paying for it both through an increasingly sophisticated tax system and through the ability to borrow on decent terms. This state focused its power not just externally through winning wars and colonies but internally too – internal barriers to trade were removed, creating a single large market across the British Isles. By contrast, a trader in France or Spain in the 1780s would still face internal customs fees when moving goods across the country. Such internal customs borders were excellent sources of economic rent for landowners but hardly conducive to driving forward growth or competition.

The state capacity and institutions that the Dutch and the English (and later British) developed allowed them to gain far more from the reshaping of the world after 1500 than the Spanish or Portuguese. And gain they did. Between 1689 and 1815 – the so-called 'long eighteenth century' – Britain rose to world power status. In those 126 years Britain was at war with France for 64 of them and, generally, it won. Although in population it was dwarfed by its rival, its capacity to maintain a lead in naval affairs coupled with the ability to pay generous 'subsidises' to continental allies proved decisive. The ability to borrow on good terms and raise revenue with relative ease mattered more than raw manpower.

The Britain of the late 1700s was relatively prosperous, it had developed a well-functioning agriculture sector, the process of urbanisation had begun and – most importantly – though it was not yet an industrial society it was certainly a commercial one. Money was in widespread use and the essentials of capitalism, the private ownership of property and the need for most workers to sell their labour for cash, were present. The dating of the birth of capitalism can be debated – but it certainly existed long before the move to factories and satanic mills.

The Malthusian shackles look to have been thrown off – or at least seriously loosened – against the backdrop of a workforce willing to work more days and hours than previously, and many of the key features of the era following the industrial revolution had begun to be established. After 1500 the flexibility of the labour supply and, crucially, a much more effective state allowed the Dutch and the British – and in particular Britain – to reap the benefits of the gains from the new trade.

That journey of three hundred or so years was just the beginning, however. The industrial revolution supercharged the existing trends, allowing income per head to really take off and British power to increase almost exponentially in the decades ahead. For a fleeting period in the mid-nineteenth century Britain was, arguably, *the* global power, and that power was built on the back of its industrial economy.

What caused the take-off and the transition to modern growth, the invention of invention, is hotly debated. The various explanations for the transition from the commercial economy of the 1780s to the industrial one of the 1830s can be broadly grouped into two competing schools of thought. Both attempt to explain why, after decades and centuries of limited productivity growth and fairly static ways of producing output, that all changed in these crucial years – why did innovation suddenly become the norm?

For some the key driver was culture and ideas. The enlightenment and subsequent 'Republic of Letters' that developed across Europe from the 1500s and 1600s was the crucial prelude to modern economic growth. Helped by the printing press and a fractured political system (compared to, say, China) that allowed rebel – and even 'heretical' – thinkers to find a bolthole from which to keep writing, science and reason flourished in Europe.

Early modern Europe created a continent-wide market place in ideas as thinkers, scientists and philosophers competed for patronage from monarchs and merchants, helping to embed a culture of learning, science and experimentation. Perhaps ten thousand European intellectuals belonged to this trans-national network where achievement and success were measured by originality and the ability to back up theoretical propositions through actual experimentation. The institutions that developed around the ideas that flowed from Erasmus, Bacon and Newton saw the establishment of the modern university and the standard procedures of academia such as the appeal to evidence development. It was against this background that European science, notably behind that of China, India or the Muslim world in 1500, leapfrogged ahead by 1800.

The addition of the commercial culture of the Netherlands or England – where money-making was no longer seen as distasteful and in fact something to welcome, even something virtuous at times – created a climate in which it was only a matter of time before innovation would take off. A culture of valuing learning and originality plus the potential to make an income from providing it may have been the necessary ingredients for a sudden increase in inventiveness.

A more materialist school places greater emphasis on a traditionally economic look at incentives and cost structures than on developments in culture. The Britain of the 1780s had a combination of historically unusual features: relatively high wages compared to its neighbours, easy access to cheap energy (both coal fields and water power), cheap borrowing and capital costs (the result of British institutional development) and a large market not beset by internal barriers.

The early breakthroughs of the late seventeenth century were hardly 'scientific'; they were more straightforward engineering problems that needed to be solved. And solving them did not require advanced knowledge but it did require time and financing.

Materialists argue that many of the key early inventions of the industrial revolution were biased towards substituting capital (machines) for labour to produce goods. For entrepreneurs who were looking at a high wage bill but cheap capital (and cheap energy) anything that used more capital and more energy whilst cutting back on labour costs made sense. That combination of costs existed in Britain but not elsewhere. This is a theory of 'induced innovation' which argues that the industrial revolution happened simply because the incentives aligned in that way. Neither the spinning jenny nor the water frame – crucial breakthroughs in cotton production – came about because of some deep scientific thinking flowing back to Erasmus but simply because cotton manufacturers desired a way to make cotton more cheaply and had the money to finance experimentation.

One can attempt to reconcile the two competing ways of thinking by arguing that culture and ideas drove the supply of new inventions but that it was material conditions and incentives in Britain that drove the demand for them. What is not really in doubt is that the preceding years mattered – the rise in incomes after the Black Death, the marriage and fertility patterns, the strength of the British state and its role in the global commerce of the 1600s and 1700s.

Historians will be debating what caused the industrial revolution for centuries to come and it is doubtful there will ever be a single answer. In the final analysis, though, what really matters is that the revolution happened and that it began where it did. The world changed and Britain changed first. The consequences can still be felt.

3

Booms, Busts and the New Working Class

Between the turn of the nineteenth century and the Great Exhibition of 1851 Britain underwent a change in its economic and social structure unlike any it had experienced before. The United Kingdom of Great Britain and Ireland that had been created by the Act of Union of 1801 had a population of around 16 million. The release from the Malthusian shackles (outside of Ireland at least) saw that population soar to over 27 million by the middle of the century. The population was not just larger, but fundamentally changed. People lived in different places, they did different jobs. In 1801 only around one third of the population was urbanised but by the census of 1851 more than half lived in towns or cities with populations above 2,500. A third of workers in 1801 were directly employed in agriculture, but in 1851 that proportion had fallen to just one fifth. The percentage employed in industry and mining rose from less than 30 per cent to more than 40 per cent.

Cotton was the cover star of the early industrial revolution, the industry that experienced the first rapid transformation.

Starting in the late eighteenth century, cotton spinning and weaving processes were radically altered by the application of new techniques and modern machinery. Textile manufacture moved from a skilled task done at home to an industrial process performed in mills. Exports had been running at around 150 million yards per year in 1800 but grew by a staggering 1,000 per cent in the next fifty years to hit 1,500 million yards. Metal working drove the second stage of industrialisation. New metallurgy processes and the fillip to demand given by the need for more cannons in the long wars with France saw iron output rise by 1,000 per cent in those five decades. Coal production leapt up from 11 million tons per year to more than 50 million. Steam power was gradually applied to new sectors of the economy. Industry after industry was affected by the invention of invention and saw output numbers pick up sharply.

The best modern estimates suggest that the total size of the UK economy in 1851 was around two and half times as large as it had been just fifty years earlier. Compared to anything that had come before, this was spectacular growth. But that progress had been far from smooth, in fact it was anything but.

The industrial revolution marked the birth of the modern economy. The abrupt shift from economic continuity to economic change. Early to mid-nineteenth-century Britain was a country transitioning to something that looks like a modern macroeconomy but without any of the tools that are used to stabilise a modern macroeconomy.

Nowadays, to a greater or lesser extent, politicians and policy-makers see the business cycle as something to be managed. The Bank of England can lower and raise interest rates and the Treasury can raise and lower taxes and spending to impact on economic demand. An economy that looks in danger of overheating can be deliberately cooled, and when spending pressures are weaker, lower borrowing costs or lower taxes can try to perk things up. These tools are imprecise and using them in practice is much harder than the theory suggests. Recessions do, after all, still happen. But the business cycle of the nineteenth century was much more volatile. The kind of modern macroeconomic thinking which informs policy-making today simply did not exist. In the last fifty years the UK has experienced six recessions; in the first fifty years of the 1800s it experienced fourteen.

With a large share of the economy still devoted to agriculture, crop failures and natural blights still had the potential to have an economy-wide impact. But alongside the traditional, now came the modern. The first stages of the industrial revolution were marked by a series of classic over-investment booms followed by equally classic busts. New technologies and new production techniques offered potentially great riches to their owners and many people were keen to get a piece of the action.

Take the railways as an example. The Liverpool and Manchester Railway opened in 1830, connecting the great cotton boom town to the great cotton exporting port. It was the first recognisably modern rail line – steam-powered throughout with no horse-drawn traffic allowed, double-tracked in its entirety and with a modern-style timetable. Designed and built by steam power pioneer George Stephenson, it was profitable from the get go. It was also the first railway to lead to a fatality when Liverpool MP William Huskisson managed to wander into the path of an oncoming train at the opening ceremony.

Despite this unfortunate beginning, shares in railway companies became the dot com stocks of the 1840s. Here was a brand new technology that offered the promise of a genuine transformation of both the economy and people's lives.

Ever since the great South Sea Bubble of the early 1700s, Britain's politicians and wider elites had been wary of speculative manias. In that case a deeply corrupt company had misled the public about its true value, engaged in outright bribery and fraud and seen its share price rise by over 1,000 per cent, sucking in other investors who feared missing out on spectacular returns. When the share price came crashing down many were bankrupted. Sir Isaac Newton was one loser, commenting afterwards, 'I can calculate the movement of heavenly bodies, but not the madness of men.'

The Bubble Act of 1720 had essentially banned firms from having more than five shareholders. The repeal of that Act in 1825 was an important stepping stone on the road to modern financialised capitalism. The limited liability company, which has its own legal identity and which can borrow in its own name, is a core institution of the contemporary world.

Freed from previous restrictions those with savings were keen to pour them into new railway companies, and the growth of newspapers provided an easy way to promote such share schemes. Building a railway meant both raising the cash and getting a bill through Parliament which granted the permission for a proposed route. As MPs were often investors in the underlying companies, few such bills failed. In the so-called railway mania of the late 1840s 442 Railway Acts made their way onto the statute book in just three years. While MPs were technically not supposed to consider the merits of rail bills in which they themselves had vested interest, there was a great deal of 'you scratch my back and I'll scratch yours' in play, together with aggressive lobbying from firms. As one cabinet minister put it, 'I saw before me the results of active canvass by powerful companies . . . members [of Parliament], few of whom had read a word of the evidence . . . were prepared to vote on other considerations than those of the merits of the questions.'

The railway booms of the 1830s and 1840s, and an earlier canal boom of the 1790s, all took a similar form: the initial promise of high returns sucked in investors and began by

building genuinely useful and profitable economic infrastructure. But as more money flooded in seeking those high returns,
projects were embarked on that were either plain unprofitable
or, worse, actually unbuildable given existing engineering
techniques. This would lead to a sudden bust in which investors lost their cash and economic activity slowed as building
work came to a sudden stop.

This boom/bust pattern, driven by agricultural developments, the course of foreign trade and investment cycles,
marked the first few decades of post-industrial revolution
Britain. But behind the volatile economic cycles was a structural shift. The underlying growth in productivity which had
begun to seep throughout the economy meant that the overall trend of growth was upwards. Although that ascent was
marked by sudden reversals, the direction of travel was clear.

None of which should be taken to mean that the first few
decades of the nineteenth century were a pleasant time to be
alive for most people.

National income per head, or GDP per capita, rose by
almost 50 per cent between 1801 and 1851 from about £1,700
per person annually (in modern money) at the time of the Act of
Union to around £2,500 by the time of the Great Exhibition.
In theory the average Briton could now afford meat a few times
a week and enjoy the odd trip to the pub rather than subsisting
on vegetables and bread. They might even have some shop-
bought as opposed to homemade clothes for special occasions.
But whilst national income per head is the best cross-country,
and cross-time, measurement of economic development it does
not always give the full picture.

National income might have been rising in the first half of
the nineteenth century but it remained extremely unequally
distributed. The industrial revolution was creating great fortunes but for mill owners not mill workers.

The economic history of inequality in the industrial revolution is inseparable from the political history of the industrial revolution. Politics, then as now, was shaped by the interplay of economic and political factors. Just as the industrial revolution restructured Britain's economy it also restructured Britain's politics.

As discussed in the last chapter, by the turn of the nineteenth century Britain had already developed from a completely closed access order, dominated by the descendants of medieval violence specialists, to a slightly more open access order, in which the voices of a narrowly wider commercial and rural elite were heard. The order reflected the economic structure of the day.

According to modern estimates, in 1688, on the eve of the Glorious Revolution, which established the constitutional order for the next century and a half, the landed elite represented around 1.8 per cent of all British families and what Marx would term the bourgeoisie made up around 3.4 per cent of all families. That landed class plus limited parts of the bourgeoisie comprised the ruling elite. Think in terms of landed families – both aristocrats and more junior gentry – coupled with a privileged few lawyers, merchants and bankers in the towns. These were the people that dominated public life for centuries. Families such as the Cecils and the Russells pop up time and time again in British history from early modernity until, well, now. Owners of either vast tracts of agricultural land or prime real estate in London or indeed both, their country houses near London have often effectively acted as seats of government.

A useful way to think about how the spoils of economic growth are divvied up is the concept of factor shares. How much of total national income flows back to each of the factors of production, namely land, capital and labour? Take the example of a factory producing one million pounds' worth of output: if the factory owner pays his or her workers £600,000 a year in total and his or her rent on the ground space is another £100,000, then that leaves £300,000 in profit. If this factory was the entirety of the economy, the factor shares would be 10 per cent to land, 60 per cent to labour and 30 per cent to capital.

In 1688, 24 per cent of national income flowed back to land in the form of rents, most of which ended up in the pockets of the landed 1.8 per cent (which is a less catchy term than 'the 1 per cent' but more accurate). Another 18.8 per cent of national income was taken by capital, much of which was also owned by the landed families but some of which was in the hands of the bourgeoisie. A huge proportion of national income flowed to a very small circle of families.

Fast-forward to 1846, though, and the structure of the economy had changed radically. The growth of new industries had changed the sources had changed the constituents of GDP and with that the factor shares. Land now took only 10.2 per cent of national income while capital took 33 per cent. The road to riches was to be found not in controlling great rural estates but instead increasingly in the new mills, factories, mines and railway lines that were changing the face of Britain. In terms of population structure, the landed elite had slipped back to 1.3 per cent of the total, whereas bourgeois families now made up 8.6 per cent of the population. The share going to labour was relatively constant although now divvied up between a smaller proportion of the population as the middle classes grew.

The changing shape of the economy changed the shape of Britain's class structure in important ways. The landed elite were still fabulously wealthy compared to the rest of the population, but their position was much less dominant than it had been in previous centuries. The new bourgeoisie, the growing middle class of towns, was taking a much larger share of national income than previously and also growing in number. Meanwhile urbanisation and the growth of industry were creating a new class of industrial workers grouped together near their places of work and earning a wage from the owners of capital for their income.

Stripped back to its basics, much of the political history of the nineteenth century was the interplay between these three political economy interest groups. A constitutional order which had very gradually evolved in the six hundred or so years after the signing of the Magna Carta in 1215 and become more formalised after the Glorious Revolution of 1688, suddenly underwent rapid change. That process mirrored economic developments, where again the picture is of hundreds of years of gradual evolution followed by structural transformation.

The fault lines between the old landed gentry and the new middle class are the subject of the next chapter. The rest of this chapter is concerned with the divide between the new working class and just about everyone else.

Concurrent with Britain's economic revolution was France's political one. The French revolution and its legacy would play an important role in Britain's own political transformation. The first stages of events across the Channel had won some support from parts of the British elite, but the early promise of a less absolutist, more open France was soon drowned out for most elite British observers by the execution of the monarch and the Reign of Terror. Although written in 1859, some sixty years after the revolution, Dickens's *A Tale of Two Cities* is no bad guide to how many earlier nineteenth-century Britons perceived events. Writing in the mid-twentieth century George Orwell took issue with Dickens's portrayal, accusing him of exaggerating the scale and effect of the Terror. 'To this day,' he wrote, 'to the average Englishman, the French Revolution means no more than a pyramid of severed heads.' Of course, the thing about a pyramid of severed heads is that it's the kind of thing that tends to stick in one's mind, especially if one is a great landowner and the heads in question belong to fellow nobles.

Britain never saw, outside of Ireland, that kind of full-throated violent revolution, but the fear of revolution was something that kept the elite awake at night all the way to the 1840s. Every major economic downturn that brought rising unemployment, depressed living standards and rural or urban unrest was taken as a possible herald of more widespread violence.

In the stop/start environment of early British industrial growth such downturns were common. Unemployment spiked with cyclical slowdowns and recessions much more frequent than in the past, and the (very nascent) welfare system known as the Poor Laws failed to cope. That system, codified during the reign of Elizabeth I, made parishes responsible for their 'paupers'. Local Poor Law overseers were seen as best placed to judge whether an individual was deserving or not of support. But with the population on the move to new cities and bouts of unemployment becoming more common, the system proved totally inadequate. A rural parish might be able to corral the local gentry into providing some alms if a crop failed; in an urban environment with a much larger and more transient population that system was not fit for purpose. Unemployment frequently meant not being able to eat. In the 1800s, the 1810s and the 1830s downturns saw serious unrest.

The most famous bout of worker unrest is that associated with General Ludd. Ned Ludd may or may not have actually existed, but he was said to be an apprentice weaver who had smashed his weaving frame in retaliation for his master beating him. As the cotton industry mechanised, many skilled weavers found that their specialist artisan skills were being devalued by the introduction of mechanical processes. The response of many in areas such as Nottinghamshire, Derbyshire and Yorkshire was to smash the new machines to preserve their own livelihoods and their existing way of life.

Modern economic theory would say that these fears were misplaced and would probably have explained to the angry crowds of machine breakers that things would be fine in the long run. The Luddite fear that new machines capable of doing the work of many people would result in fewer jobs over-all is one that has recurred time and time again in economic history. The fears of cotton weavers in the early 1800s were not radically dissimilar from those of industrial workers seeing robots appear on factory lines in the later twentieth century or how many white-collar workers view the growth potential of artificial intelligence today.

The introduction of any new labour-saving technology has two economic impacts: the displacement effect and the compensation effect. The displacement effect is the one that tends to set nerves on edge and is the simple fact that any decent labour-saving technology does precisely what it says on the tin: it displaces some workers.

But, over the longer run, the compensation effect is more important. Because fewer workers are now producing the same total output the individual productivity of each worker will have risen. So, if a factory is producing fifty widgets (widgets are always the go-to economic example, no one knows what they actually are) each day with ten workers then the output (in widgets) of each worker can be thought of as five. If a new technology allows the same level of widget production but with half as many workers, then output per worker (or productivity) will have doubled.

As each worker is now more productive, the factory owner should be able to pay them more and their compensation levels should rise. Finding themselves with a higher income, the retained workers can go and out and spend their cash on other products and services, creating demand that should create new jobs. So, although some workers are displaced by the new technology, the economy as a whole generates new sources of employment. Machines, in other words, don't actually steal anyone's job. Or rather they do sometimes, but they also indirectly lead to new jobs.

This all sounds nice in theory but is much messier in reality. Labour market interactions are rarely the bloodless interplay of a supply line and demand line on a nicely drawn graph. It would be a brave economist indeed who offered to explain displacement and compensation effects to a torch-wielding mob about to smash up some looms.

The standard theory is, so far at least, correct over the longer run. As yet mankind has failed to invent a new technology which has reduced employment overall. But the short run can last a long time, a generation even. And for the displaced weavers of the 1810s the fact that it would all work out eventually was cold comfort.

Crucially this theory relies on the idea that the higher productivity of the retained workers would mean that they got some sort of pay rise. And they might, or they might not. In the early nineteenth century they almost certainly did not.

Between 1780 and 1840 output per worker in Britain rose by 46 per cent but real wages (that is wages adjusted for changes in prices) rose by only 12 per cent. In other words the structure of the economy might be changing but precious few of the benefits were flowing to the workforce in general.

One of the keenest observers of this trend was the son of a German businessman sent to help manage the firm's operations in Manchester; his name was Friedrich Engels. Young Friedrich had been expressing increasingly radical political beliefs and his parents hoped that keeping him busy and immersing him in the running of the family business operations would help knock that youthful rebellion out of his system. If that was the intention, it backfired spectacularly. If anything was likely to radicalise the proto-anti-capitalist further, it was being sent to live in the rapidly expanding and somewhat squalid heart of the new urban, industrial capitalism.

Engels's *The Condition of the Working Classes in England* was published in 1845, although it didn't appear in English until forty years later. A deeply researched work, packed with statistics, it argued that the new industrial workers were materially worse off than their pre-industrial peers. In particular the death rate, among adults and children alike, was substantially higher in the new towns and cities than in the countryside.

Some have dubbed the era 'Engels' pause', a forty-year period when rising productivity and output per worker was not matched by rising real wages. While some modern historians argue that workers' wellbeing was gradually rising in the 1820s and 1830s, the sheer amount of unrest suggests that Engels was on to something. His was not some polemical outlier compared to other early to mid-nineteenth-century commentaries. As early as 1804 Blake's 'Jerusalem' was already referring to 'those dark satanic mills'.

For many in the new industrial workforce, going to work in one of those mills, whether satanic or not, was very different from the working life they had previously led. Workers had previously set their own hours, worked at their pace and taken days off whenever they chose, but moving to larger workplaces changed that. Marx quotes a cotton-mill owner as saying, 'When a labourer lays down his spade, he renders useless, for that period, a capital worth eighteen pence. When one of our people leaves the mill he renders useless a capital that has cost £100,000.' Factory work meant factory discipline. Hours and behaviour were regulated, with sanctions ranging from fines or dismissal to occasionally corporal punishment. The working week by the 1840s was some 65 hours long.

The number of children in work soared at the end of the eighteenth and the beginning of the nineteenth century, partly because some of the new tasks in factories required smaller hands and partly because the generalised squeeze in real wages forced families to send their children out to work at an early age to make ends meet. Children working was nothing new in Britain but the character of that work shifted. Whereas previously children would usually have worked with their parents, they were now more likely not to. The average age of starting work dropped from around eleven years old to closer to eight. In 1819 a Factory Act, which applied only to cotton mills, banned children under nine from working and set the maximum working day as 12 hours – for those aged nine to sixteen. As the Act did not authorise any inspections to check on compliance, it was regularly flouted. It would be the 1850s and 1860s before more meaningful legislation actually had the teeth to enforce such rules.

The new industrial cities packed workers in tightly in often quickly and shoddily built accommodation. Sanitation was often lacking and frequent outbreaks of cholera were one early result. It was the 1830s and 1840s before the authorities began to take public health more seriously. The 1832 Cholera Act and the 1848 Public Health Act were belated responses to a half-century of urban growth.

This was the backdrop to the Luddite machine smashing of the 1800s and 1810s and the Swing Riots of 1830, when agricultural workers sought to destroy new threshing machines. Neither campaign was entirely, or even primarily, about the fear that new machines would destroy jobs. Both were grounded in a reality whereby the economy was changing rapidly, wages were generally stagnating and living conditions in the new cities were undeniably grim. And there appeared to be little that working-class people could do to remedy these facts of life.

Any demands for economic or political reform, no matter how modest they sound to modern ears, were greeted as a potential Jacobin plot that could lead to revolution.

The classic example occurred in August 1819. The late 1810s were a tough time for the economy and for industrial workers in particular. The end of the Napoleonic Wars in 1815 saw a drastic reduction in the size of the armed forces. Meanwhile, in what is now Indonesia, the volcano Mount Tambora experienced a major eruption that threw up enough ash to radically change weather patterns over the entire globe: 1816 was known as 'the year without a summer', and heavy rainfall led to crop failures across Britain and Europe. The unemployment rate spiked to over 10 per cent by 1819, while the purchasing power of weekly wages fell by 9 per cent between 1815 and 1819.

The crowd that assembled in St Peter's Fields near Manchester to hear Henry Hunt rail against the injustices of the age had a lot to complain about. Magistrates ordered the (peaceful) gathering to disperse and then, in a somewhat confused turn of events, the assembly was charged by the local Yeomanry followed by regular army Hussars with sabres drawn. Eighteen people were killed, and the *Manchester Observer* coined the portmanteau word 'Peterloo', combining the location with the memory of Waterloo, to describe the massacre.

The outrage over the killings saw protests spread across the north and midlands, and the response of the government was to pass the so-called Six Acts clamping down on public freedoms, censoring radical papers and banning large public meetings. The industrial revolution was far from bloodless.

Labour market interactions often come back to a question of power, and in the early to mid-nineteenth century power was firmly held by the employers not the employees. Attempts by workers to organise themselves to bargain for higher wages were fiercely resisted. The Combination Acts of 1799 and 1800 had explicitly made trade unions illegal with fears expressed that worker organisations would be the harbinger of revolution.

The law was loosened in 1824 with trade unions being legalised as long as they confined themselves to bargaining for higher wages and better working conditions and stayed out of wider political questions. But even the adoption of this more liberal approach did not mean life was any easier for working-class organisers. In 1833 six agricultural labourers from Tolpuddle in Dorset formed a Friendly Society to resist wage cuts. Convicted under the obscure Unlawful Oaths Act of swearing secret oaths to each other they were sentenced to transportation to Australia. This, though, in the slightly calmer atmosphere of the 1830s, was a step too far. After a public and political outcry the so-called Tolpuddle Martyrs had their convictions quashed and were returned to England.

The 1830s may have seen a more liberal approach to trade unions but for many poorer workers the transformation of the Poor Law was a more pressing concern. The old Elizabethan system, as previously noted, was struggling to cope with economic change, rising demographics and the movement of the population. The costs of administering the system had doubled between the late 1780s and the early 1830s.

Guided by Malthusian principles – the notion that being too generous to poor people would only lead to more poor people – along with the work of early political economists such as David Ricardo, the system was reformed by the 1834 Poor Law Amendment Act. The new Poor Law was based on a report written by Oxford's first professor of political economy.

One present-day economic historian has described it as 'the mother of all welfare reforms'.

Under the old system anyone in need of support could appeal to the local Poor Overseers for help. The cutting edge of economic thought in the 1830s believed this system to be disastrous – it increased the fertility of the poor leading to more poor people, it discouraged people from looking for work and it harmed labour mobility by encouraging people to stay where they were rather than moving to look for a job. The guiding principle of the new system was still to provide support to so-called paupers but make that support as unpleasant as possible. Hence was born the workhouse. Those with no other choice could enter such an institution, where they would be subject to strict discipline (including the separation of family members) and endure hours of largely pointless work such as smashing stones in return for meagre food and somewhere to sleep.

This was the Britain that Engels and Marx were observing when they penned the *Communist Manifesto*. The first industrial nation looked like a vision of the future, and the three decades of data that they meticulously analysed in their study of scientific socialism suggested that workers were losing out. Capitalism seemed to mean miserable conditions for most people and rising profits for the capitalists. Against such a backdrop political revolution seemed the inevitable result of the economic revolution. Capitalists would continue to eat up the gains of rising productivity growth and push workers' living standards to breaking point. Eventually something would have to give.

Something did give, but not in the way they expected. Just as Malthus wrote his great work on the dynamics of population growth at the point when the world he was describing changed, so too did Marx and Engels put pen to paper just as economic relations began to shift.

Engels' pause ended in the 1840s. Between 1840 and 1900 output per worker rose by 90 per cent and real wages rose by 123 per cent; the relationship of the last forty or so years of rising productivity but stagnation of wages was broken. The next fifty or so years of industrial capitalism would be a very different time for workers.

4

Capital, Land and the Reshaping of British Politics

Economic change often drives politics. In a modern democracy, recessions and rising unemployment or high inflation are the kind of things that see governments voted out of office. 'It's the economy, stupid' as the campaign strategists often note. The first half of the nineteenth century saw a wide-ranging restructuring of British politics and the British constitution: the further downgrading of the role of the monarch, a lessening of the old agricultural elite's previous tight grip on power, the rise of the new middle class to political influence and the (very slow) expansion of democracy and the vote. There is sometimes a tendency to view this process as inevitable, the so-called Whiggish view of history as gradually moving towards modern, liberal, democratic forms of government. The alternative way of looking at this is through an economic lens. Viewed this way the reforms of the period were not driven by progressive historical forces but were a reaction to how the structure of the economy itself had been reshaped by industrialisation. It's the political economy, stupid.

In the first decades of the nineteenth century the newly enriched and growing urban middle classes challenged the position of the older, entrenched, aristocratic and landed elite. In terms of North's framework Britain moved further towards an open access order, but only gradually so. The key flashpoints in this decades-long struggle came in 1832, with the passing of the Great Reform Act, and 1846, with the repeal of the Corn Laws. Both are best understood in political economy terms.

The British constitution that evolved over the six hundred or so years before 1832 was based on maintaining a balance of interests, and the interests that were to be balanced were the Crown, the aristocrats and the commons. The commons in this case not meaning 'the people as a whole' but instead a small subset of people with a 'stake' in society: property owners.

By the 1370s a parliamentary system had developed whereby the Lords and the Commons sat separately with the Commons having its own speaker. Notable and prosperous towns, the Boroughs, had the right to elect (generally) two MPs from amongst their propertied classes, and Parliaments were summoned whenever the monarch needed cash, which generally meant when they were fighting a war. The basics of the political economy settlement were that the monarch and the traditional landowners held most of the power, with the consent of some of the wealthiest commoners being needed when the monarch wanted to raise additional taxes.

This division of power was sustainable in a world where a tiny proportion of the population controlled most of the land, and land was the primary driver of wealth; a very privileged elite thus had a disproportionate amount of power. The reshaping of the economy and with it the reshaping of the factor shares called this old balance into question.

The power of monarchs had been waning for centuries

in England and later Britain. The execution of Charles I in 1649 and the ousting of James II in the Glorious Revolution of 1688 were both good indicators of the direction of travel. The monarch did still have power, however; the government of the day was very much 'the King's government'. Indeed, the death of a monarch was always followed by an immediate general election until 1837. King William IV (who ruled from 1830 to 1837) still felt able to dismiss Prime Ministers and appoint new ones. Queen Victoria interfered much more actively in the actual work of government than any modern ruler would attempt to do. But things had moved a long way from the 1600s. Real power now lay in Parliament, and whilst the monarch could technically refuse to give Royal Assent to a bill, that had not happened since the early 1700s.

The House of Lords in the 1830s was a much more exclusive club than today. It numbered around 250 voting members. Primarily made up of the descendants of the great medieval magnates, its members often explicitly spoke about representing 'the landed interest'. It was of course possible for a commoner to get ennobled and join its ranks, but this was most likely to follow government or military service (think Wellington and Nelson) rather than through having been successful in industry or commerce. Winning battles could get one a peerage, owning a lot of mills did not.

Cabinets were still mainly drawn from the Lords, two thirds to three quarters of government ministers in the early nineteenth century being aristocrats.

The pre-reform House of Commons was a strange beast. Each county elected two MPs and in addition a number of boroughs had, over the years, been granted a royal charter entitling them to elect their own members to the House. The point of enfranchising boroughs had been to ensure that the kind of towns which were asked to make large financial contributions when the monarch needed them were represented in Parliament. But, and this is a big but, once a borough had been granted the right to elect MPs it never lost it. And no new grants had been issued since the late 1600s. The result by 1832 was a mess.

The House was made up of 176 MPs representing the counties, 5 from the Universities (a state of affairs that lasted until 1950) and 467 from the boroughs. The actual franchise varied by seat. So, in an English county seat, every freeholder with 40 shillings of property (that is, house or land with an annual rental value of £2, which in 1832 meant a moderately sized urban dwelling or a substantial rural farm rather than a small holding) had a vote, but this excluded the vast majority of the population, who were tenants rather than property owners. The end result was that almost all county seats were held by either the landed gentry or the relatives of members of the House of Lords. In many counties the major landowners would simply agree between themselves on who to appoint, and contested elections were rare. Nottinghamshire, for example, saw no actual elections in the century before 1832. Indeed it was usual for only around 30 per cent of seats to be contested at any given vote.

The borough franchises varied, from the relatively democratic 'householder boroughs' where essentially all male householders not in receipt of poor relief held a vote, to 'burgage boroughs' where only the owners of certain prescribed properties held that right.

The transformation that the economy had undergone in the late eighteenth and early nineteenth centuries was not reflected at all in the distribution of seats. So Manchester and Birmingham, with respective populations of around 180,000 and 140,000, elected no MPs. Meanwhile Old Sarum, a desolate hill two miles from Salisbury that had once been a site of settlement but was long since abandoned, still elected two MPs despite having no permanent residents. Eleven local property owners made up its electorate. Dunwich, once a prosperous market town north of Ipswich, had mainly, and literally, fallen into the sea by the 1830s. This 'town', which also elected two MPs, was described as having a population of 232, 44 houses and 'half a church'.

The fact that parliamentary seat distribution had not kept up with the changing demographics of the country should come as no surprise, for that change was happening at a rapid pace and many institutions were left behind. In 1800, for example, the Church of England maintained seven hundred parishes in agricultural Norfolk, but only seventy in rapidly industrialising Lancashire.

There was no secret ballot until the 1870s and public voting plus tiny electorates made for predictably unfair elections. Outright bribery and intimidation both played a role. Boroughs with small electorates were often thought of as 'pocket boroughs' or 'rotten boroughs' which could be controlled for the right price. The 'old corruption', as it came to be known, was the name given to the generalised system whereby votes and seats were bought and sold, and government offices and sinecures handed out in return for support.

At least the system of outright bribery made for some interesting experiments in game theory. Take the case of Thomas Cochrane, later a Royal Navy admiral. He fought and lost a by-election in 1806 for the Devon seat of Honiton and afterwards paid ten guineas to each of the 124 voters who had backed him as a reward for their loyalty. This of course created the expectation that anyone voting for the generous Mr Cochrane would be well rewarded in the future. At the subsequent general election, just four months later, he swept to victory only for his wallet to then remain closed.

The growth of the new industrialised towns and the movement of the population meant that Britain, by 1832, was less
democratic than it had been on the eve of the English Civil
War in 1640. Perhaps 3.2 per cent of the population held a vote
in 1831, down from 5.2 per cent in 1715.

The party system, in as much as it can be called a party
system, was, to modern eyes, underdeveloped. Many MPs sat
as independents or declared no party affiliation; party identity was fluid, with leading politicians often serving in both
Whig and Tory cabinets at different times in their careers.
Generally speaking the Tories stood for the defence of the old
institutions of the land – the monarchy, the established church
and the rights of rural gentry. Their Whig opponents stood
for the supremacy of Parliament over the monarch, supported
Protestant non-conformers and increasingly drew more support from the emerging commercial and industrial middle
classes. That said, the leading Whigs tended to come from the
grandest of aristocratic families. Both Tories and Whigs generally viewed the five to ten or so Radical MPs, who supported
such seemingly crazy ideas as universal voting, as dangerous
demagogues.

The Great Reform Act of 1832 brought a change in the
structure of the Commons. It rationalised and standardised
the franchise requirements (including specifically debarring
women from voting for the first time) and it redistributed seats
to eliminate the notorious rotten boroughs whilst granting
MPs to growing cities such as Leeds, Manchester and Sheffield
for the first time.

The ending of the pocket boroughs that had often been
controlled by wealthy landowners and the enfranchisement of
the new industrial towns and cities represented a fundamental
change in the nature of Britain's governing elite. The era of
almost total dominance by the landed elite was over; for the

next century those old aristocratic families would have to share power with the new middle class. The reshaping of the economy had reshaped the structure of wealth, and this was now reflected in the governing of the country.

Of course the division between those earning their income from the ownership of land and those earning their income from the ownership of capital was not stark and absolute. Landowners had been early investors in many of the new industrial enterprises and railways. A middle-class capitalist who did particularly well would usually seek to buy some land, build a large country house and generally ape the manners of the rural gentry.

And, importantly, the interests of both groups seemed to align on not agreeing to any further expansion of the franchise. (To treat the Act as the first step on some road to democracy is oversimplistic. In one third of the boroughs that retained their seats the number of electors was actually reduced. There was overall a net increase in the franchise, yet even so, only around one in five adult men held a vote.) The 1832 Act can be thought of as expansion of Britain's governing elite to reflect the alteration of the economy, but it was a limited expansion that specifically did not include the workforce suffering through Engels' pause. This was a rebalancing of Britain's previously unbalanced constitution to once more reflect what was still a very unequal economic reality.

Given the changing balance of economic power, the balance of political power was sure to shift eventually. In the run-up to 1832 a series of chance events allowed the right political coalition to be formed to push through reform. The Tory party, which was more opposed to electoral reform, and had dominated the previous two decades of politics, found itself badly split over the question of granting rights to Catholics, and a Whig government came to power. Prime Minister Lord

Grey was able to scrape a one-vote victory in the Commons in favour of a reform bill, but realising that would not be enough to push the bill through the Lords, fought a general election which essentially acted as a referendum on the question.

That election saw a Whig majority elected. It came against the backdrop of the agricultural Swing Riots, and recent work by economic historians has shown that the closer a parliamentary seat was to areas affected by those disturbances, the more likely it was to elect a reform-minded member. This seems to bear out the notion that the fear of wider revolution played a role in the gradual reform of Parliament. The best way for the existing quasi-autocratic agricultural interest that dominated Parliament to secure its position was to do a deal with the commercial and industrial middle-class interest.

This was the co-option of the new economic elite into joint rule with the old, not the birth of modern democracy.

Perhaps even more important than the general election of 1831 was the decision by the House of Lords in 1832 not to veto the bill. The King had eventually promised Grey that if the Lords continued to oppose reform, he would create enough new Whig peers to drive it through. As they would do again in 1846 and 1911 the Lords accepted short-term political defeat in order to retain their joint hold on power.

It is really striking how even as Britain rose to become the world's leading industrial nation and one of its most urbanised, the older rural, landed interest retained such a large say in government.

Voices calling for a wider electorate were nothing new. The Levellers had been urging universal male suffrage as early as the 1640s and the crowd at Peterloo in 1819 called for the same. The Chartist Movement calling for wider democratic reform would be an important feature of the 1830s and 1840s, although most of their demands were not met until 1918.

The next three and a half decades were dominated politically by the Whigs, who gradually took on the name of
Liberals. The reform of the Poor Law discussed in the previous
chapter was a classic Liberal/Whiggish policy of the time –
driven by the latest in 'modern' political economy thinking,
reform-minded, aiming to save money and not especially
working in the interests of the wider populace even if it did
appeal to those wealthy enough to be enfranchised.

Thinking through early to mid-nineteenth-century economic policy means realising that much of the modern
conception of economic policy simply did not exist. Although
the census had begun in 1801 and the government was certainly collecting plenty of data and statistics, the very concept
of GDP would have been totally alien to any 1840s Chancellor.
The state itself was, by modern standards, incredibly small. In
1821 the entire staff of the Foreign Office consisted of 28 men.
During the Napoleonic Wars the percentage of GDP made
up of government spending had been around 20 per cent,
but post-war it fell back to closer to 10 per cent, compared to
around 40 per cent in the late twentieth and early twenty-first
centuries. Even that 10 per cent figure is misleading as over
half of it went on debt repayments and interest bills. In effect
actual government spending was more like 4 or 5 per cent of
the economy and a big chunk of that was on the military. The
footprint of the state remained very small until the twentieth century.

In as much as governments had an 'economic policy' it was
what has come to be known as 'mercantilism' or the 'mercan-
tile system'. This type of thinking informed government policy
across Europe in the centuries before the industrial revolution. Broadly put, mercantilists believed in a zero-sum world.
Something which made one state better off was something
that made another rival state worse off. In an era when the

currency was still (most of the time) based on notes backed by precious metals, the acquiring of precious metals made a state richer. A positive trade balance was a way to enrich one's own nation at the expense of another. Commerce that enriched a nation was seen as good; commerce that led to an outflow of money abroad was bad. In short: exports were something to be welcomed and imports something to be avoided unless absolutely necessary.

Mercantilist policy focused on building up colonial holdings whose trade could be controlled. In Britain a series of Navigation Acts and other restrictions in the 1600s limited the ability of foreign merchants to trade with the British.

Mercantilist thinking leads to some seemingly odd results. During the Napoleonic Wars the French Emperor sought to enforce the 'continental system', to run an effective blockade on Great Britain. But the aim of the policy was not to deprive the UK of key imports needed for its war effort – as a modern wartime embargo would – but to prevent British exports to Europe that were seen as enriching Britain and increasing its power. In 1809 and 1810, when Britain suffered poor harvests, imports of grains from France – a country it was at war with – actually increased. It was the flow of money from Britain to France to pay for those grains that was seen as important in Paris. Both sides believed this, as evidenced by Napoleon's army often marching in boots and coats made in Leeds and Northampton.

The beginning of the end of mercantilism in Britain as a dominant economic theory can be dated to the 1770s. The loss of the American colonies undermined much of the system but what history tends to emphasise is a work published in March 1776, a few months before the Declaration of Independence. Adam Smith's *The Wealth of Nations* has a good claim to being the most influential work published on economics of all time.

Adam Smith was a moral philosopher turned political economist, a particularly shining example of the late eighteenth-century Scottish enlightenment, who wrote widely on all manner of issues. Later followers of his, like the later followers of almost all economists, are wont to pick and choose which bits of his message they retain.

Today Smith is sometimes seen as an apologist for capitalism's worst excesses, but his concern was always with consumers, not with banks or manufacturers. It was the same Smith who wrote the *Theory of Moral Sentiments* as penned *The Wealth of Nations*. Taken together, his work is about the freeing of mankind from rule by often arbitrary government and, that most crucial of all philosophical questions, how to live a good life?

In economic terms, though, Smith's impact could be felt in two ways. Firstly, his rejection of the mercantilist framework for thinking about trade. Smith wanted to tear down the restrictions and tariffs that prevented foreign trade in favour of a more open, free-trading world. Such restrictions might or might not aid governments in their desire for power but they also harmed consumers and individuals in the interests of businesses and special interest groups. Smith recognised that many of the aspects of the mercantilist system were really about generating and dividing up economic rents among a relatively closed elite. For Smith freer trade would enrich all nations and consumers.

On a more micro level, Smith is best remembered today for his notion of the 'invisible hand', the idea that each individual acting in their own self-interest can contribute to a better outcome for society as a whole. But, for Smith, such outcomes could only arise in a free market; in the kind of protected and regulated economy implied by mercantilism this invisible mechanism would break down. A free market, according to Smith, would not just see lower prices for consumers but reward the best firms with higher profits, allowing them to expand to meet consumer demand and hire more workers, often at higher wages. To let mankind flourish, the state had to step back from interfering too much in the market place.

This laissez-faire approach to regulation was to dominate British government thinking for much of the following century. Imposing itself into economic relationships was not the business of the state.

The infrastructure of British mercantilism was gradually dismantled in the first half of the nineteenth century. The Navigation Acts were repealed in 1849. But the major battle was over the Corn Laws. The new industrial and commercial middle classes had been brought into government in 1832 and by 1846 they would triumph over their rural partners with a decision that would shape the next century of British economic history and development.

The Corn Laws were a protectionist measure adopted in 1815. Faced with falling agricultural prices in the immediate aftermath of the Napoleonic wars (the impact of Mount Tambora's eruption had not yet been felt in Europe), an agricultural interest that dominated Parliament moved to do something about it. As one Scottish MP commented in 1814, 'No set of men cry so loud or so soon as the farmers,' a sentiment that many modern politicians might echo.

A tariff on imported grain was set so high as to essentially keep it out. This could of course be dressed up as a national security measure – ensuring the self-reliance of Britain on domestic food. But given wheat imports from France had not been stopped in 1809 and 1810, that justification looked somewhat flimsy. This was, in reality, the self-interested policy-making of the landed elite. Keeping out foreign grain might ensure higher bread prices for everyone and more profits for them.

Standing against the Corn Laws were not just workers desiring lower living costs but also much of the new commercial and industrial middle class. The stage was set for a classic political economy battle over whether agriculture needed special privileges or not.

Ideas, as they always do, played a key role in framing this battle. Smith's doctrines already had reasonably widespread approval from British opinion formers, and David Ricardo, with his theory of comparative advantage, further reinforced their intellectual armoury.

Ricardo made many contributions to the growing science of political economy but the most crucial was his theory of comparative advantage (a name coined by J. S. Mill some years later). The essence of the theory is that countries should specialise in the goods and services in which they most excel. Ricardo, himself with Portuguese ancestry, drew on the example of England and Portugal. Like all economists he started with a relatively simple model, imagining a world where the only two goods were cloth and wine.

In his thought experiment, he imagined that Portugal could produce both cloth and wine more efficiently than England (he did not comment on the quality or respective merits of English wine, this is a thought experiment after all). But whilst England was actually relatively more efficient at producing cloth than wine, Portugal was relatively more efficient at producing wine than cloth. On Ricardo's numbers, if England were to specialise entirely in cloth production and Portugal in wine production and they traded cloth for wine, both countries would be better off.

But the case for repealing the Corn Laws relied on more than simple economic models and some straightforward maths.

For Richard Cobden, Stockport MP and the real evangelical of British free trade, repealing the Corn Laws would solve

four problems in one go: it would provide an outlet for British
manufacturers as Britons buying foreign grain put money in
the hands of potential new customers; it would relieve 'the
condition of England' in the era of Engels' pause by reducing
food costs; it would make English agriculture more efficient
when faced with foreign competition; and it would also herald
a new era of international peace based on mutually beneficial
trading relationships. This was a powerful intellectual case.
And Cobden was not a man who tended to mind his language.
According to him the only people in favour of the Corn Laws
were the 'bread taxing oligarchy, unprincipled, unfeeling,
rapacious and plundering'.

Attempts at repeal in the 1820s went nowhere fast. William
Huskisson made some attempts when President of the Board
of Trade but opposition in an almost totally landowner-
dominated Parliament was too intense.

The 1832 Reform Act reopened the door to repeal. With the
commercial and industrial middle classes now directly represented in Parliament it seemed as though change was possible.
Possible but still tricky. A Tory government led by Robert Peel
was once again in office in the 1840s and firmly committed to
defending the interest of the gentry. The balance of the House
of Commons had shifted radically towards the commercial
and industrial interest but rural interests remained disproportionately over-represented. And the Lords was a bastion of the
landed classes.

The campaign for reform was organised by what became
one of Britain's most successful political pressure groups of
all time: the Anti-Corn Law League. Founded in London
but soon finding its more natural home in Manchester, the
League pulled in large donations from the new manufacturing bosses.

The League benefited from the concentration of cotton

businesses in the northwest of England. This geographical concentration made organisation and fundraising amongst the most interested parties more straightforward. But it also benefited from the wider diffusion of exporting firms in other industries across the UK. These firms might not place repealing the Corn Laws at the top of their list of demands but they were broadly supportive.

The money raised was put to good effect in a propaganda war of pamphlets and newspapers. The League was generally successful at drawing on cross-class support, arguing to industrial workers that repealing those laws would mean lower food prices and thus effectively a wage rise. Despite the reasonable enough suspicions of Marx that manufacturing capitalists hardly had the workers' best interests at heart, the League proved adept at turning attention to their opponents: Cobden's 'bread taxing oligarchy'.

Pamphlets and public meetings played a role, but the League's real success was in its mastery of the opportunities created by Britain's new electoral system. Much effort was spent going through the rolls of voters constituency by constituency and attempting to get known protectionists struck off and new free-traders added. Cobden urged the parents of free-traders, if they had the money, to give their children the forty-shilling freehold required to become a county elector. Several thousand new electors were created in key constituencies.

The new commercial and industrial class was pouring cash and organisational ability into changing Britain's electoral landscape. The League's efforts to map voters gave it a much better picture of what was happening on the ground across the nation than had the actual political parties, whose own organisational base was still very much a work in progress in the 1840s.

In the end, though, this strategy for changing Britain's political geography was not required; repeal came not following a victory for the Whigs/Liberals but under a Tory government. Robert Peel in 1846 split his own party to vote in favour of repeal.

The question of course is why a party which relied on support from the very rural classes that would be hit by repeal would choose to carry it, when the main short-term winners were the supporters of their opponents?

It is sometimes argued that the Irish famine played a role in shaping the British debate. Ireland unlike Britain had not industrialised in the first half of the nineteenth century. The country remained agrarian and poor. Much of the land was held by absentee British landlords who managed it badly and creamed off much of national income in the form of rents. Irish inheritance laws had seen much subdivision of Irish-owned plots, leaving farming relatively unproductive. Small land plots encouraged a focus on farming potatoes, one of the few foods that could feed a family from such small holdings. The potato blight of the mid-1840s had an impact across Europe, but nowhere more so than Ireland. Perhaps 100,000 people died outside of Ireland compared to one million there.

Around half of the crop failed in 1845 and three quarters in 1846. Landlords still tried to extract their rental payments, and the government, dominated by the advocates of laissez-faire, failed to provide any relief. The numbers imprisoned soared as people committed crimes solely in order to be placed somewhere they would be fed. Emigration was one solution, with the population of Ireland falling from 8.5 million in 1845 to 6 million a decade later. Ireland remains one of very few geographies with a lower population density today than it had in the mid-nineteenth century.

The idea of keeping out foreign food even as a famine was raging across part of the UK may seem repellent to modern readers, but the direct impact on the Corn Law debates in Parliament was relatively limited.

Reconstructing Peel's decision-making in the mid-1840s is not straightforward. He had certainly read his Smith, Ricardo and Malthus and was well versed in the intellectual case against the Corn Laws. He was the kind of politician that sought to build a party with cross-class appeal. His Tamworth manifesto of 1834 was all about the need for dealing with legitimate grievances and not standing in the way of necessary reform. Only around one third of his own MPs voted with him for repeal. Some recent work by political scientists notes that the Tory MPs who became Peelites tended to represent less strictly agricultural districts; the Tory party was not by 1846 a simple agrarian interest group even if much of its wider leadership wished it to be.

In the end Peel's decision to revoke (and the crucial decision of the House of Lords, which was utterly dominated by the landed interest, not to oppose revocation) was part of his strategy to preserve Britain's existing political economy and constitution. Peel, as one recent social scientist has noted, 'characterised repeal as a means to preserve the traditional institutions of the British government – and in particular, the aristocracy'. By compromising with the commercial and industrial interests Peel sought to preserve a role for the agricultural interest in government. As in 1832, accepting a short-term defeat allowed that landed interest to preserve its longer-term role in British government.

For all the fuss, though, the shorter-term direct impact of the repeal of the Corn Laws in 1846 proved fleeting. Not until the 'American grain invasion' of the 1870s would food prices really drop sustainably.

What mattered more than the economics was the politics. The ideology of free trade had won a great battle, the last vestiges of mercantilism had been torn down. Free trade appeared to offer cheap food to workers, overseas markets to manufacturers and the promise of international peace. The ideology of free trade would dominate British economic life for the next seventy or eighty years.

5

Global Britain, from the Corn Laws to the Great War

There is a tendency in popular political and economic writing to emphasise the new. Presumably, volumes offering to break new ground attract more readers than those slogging over old terrain. The late twentieth century and early twenty-first saw many books heralding the new era of 'globalisation' but little of what was published would have been totally unfamiliar to a middle-class London resident of 1914. Writing in 1919 John Maynard Keynes (always Maynard to his friends) looked fondly back to the old world before the Great War. What is most striking about his reminiscences is just how modern they sound to a reader in the early twenty-first century. 'The inhabitant of London could order by telephone, sipping his morning tea in bed, the various products of the whole earth, in such quantity as he might see fit, and reasonably expect their early delivery upon his doorstep; he could at the same moment and by the same means adventure his wealth in the natural resources and new enterprises of any quarter of the world.'

Globalisation, if defined as the process of increasing

international economic integration and the cross-border movement of goods, services and capital, is nothing new. The world has seen several cycles of globalisation and deglobalisation, driven by both politics and technological change. The current bout, which began in the late 1970s and accelerated after the fall of the Berlin Wall, is just the latest example. The globalisation of the late nineteenth and early twentieth centuries was extensive and much more akin to that of the late twentieth century than the proto-globalisation seen along the Silk Roads in the era of Genghis Khan. Britain was at the forefront, a uniquely globalised and globalising country.

Britain's repeal of the Corn Laws in 1846 was a hard-fought battle domestically, but the victory that the ideology of free trade won was almost total. Tariffs became a taboo subject in sensible British political discussion for several decades. Britain's free trade was unilateral – it enforced no distortionary tariffs on goods imported from other nations regardless of whether they applied charges on British exports. Britain was open to the goods of the world whether the world wanted British goods or not. Late Victorian statemen (and they were all men) regarded this as an easy win for British firms and British consumers. Few other states went as far, even though Cobden took his gospel overseas, preaching the benefits of freer trade around Europe. The 1860s did see a Europe-wide movement towards lower tariffs and a series of bilateral trade deals (Cobden himself negotiated much of the Cobden-Chevalier treaty with France) but this proved fleeting. By the 1880s tariff walls were once again climbing.

It is all too easy to assume that tariff levels are a key driver of globalisation and deglobalisation cycles. In reality, though, they are just one factor, and in the 1880s and 1890s global trade flourished even as tariffs rose. The driver of nineteenth-century globalisation was technology rather than politics.

Technology made it much easier to move goods quickly. Tariffs could throw some grit in the mechanism but they were not enough to seriously slow down the process of market integration. Take trans-Atlantic crossings as an example. Columbus's voyage revolutionised the global economy but it took around two months. By the 1700s more efficient ship design and better navigation had cut the journey time to around six weeks. By the 1840s steam-powered vessels could cross from Europe to North America in just two weeks. But progress did not stop there: journey times fell to closer to a week by the 1880s. The *Titanic*'s ill-fated maiden voyage from Queenstown in Ireland to New York in 1912 was scheduled to take just under six days. The opening of the Suez Canal in 1869 effectively lopped 4,000 miles off the seaborne distance between Europe and Asia, reducing the distance between London and what was then known as Bombay by about 40 per cent. Alongside faster shipping times came the global expansion of the rail network. Around 125,000 miles of track was laid globally by 1870, a figure which leapt to over 400,000 miles by 1900 and over 620,000 miles by 1913. Jules Verne was best known as an author of science fiction, but his *Around the World in 80 Days*, published in 1873, would have felt plausible to contemporary readers and it is no coincidence that Phileas Fogg's journey began in London, the centre of the globalised world. Faster travel was accompanied by much speedier communication. The first telegraph lines appeared in Britain in the late 1830s. The technology quickly went global with a working trans-Atlantic submarine cable in place by 1866 which cut the time taken to send a message from London to New York from a week or so to just minutes. India was connected to Europe by 1870 and Australia by 1872. In the 1890s two thirds of global cables were owned and operated by British firms. Refrigerated shipping, which really began in the 1860s and 1870s, added to the range of goods which could move long distances. Rapid increases in communication speeds and falls in journey times created an impression of a world that was shrinking. Few, if any, of these developments had been foreseen when Britain ditched the Corn Laws, but the timing turned out to be extremely opportune. As one historian of the period has put it: 'the annihilation of distance was a late Victorian cliché'.

Rapid technological change had huge economic impacts. The cost of shipping grain from the American midwest to Britain was the equivalent of about 33 per cent of the price of the crop in 1870, but by 1910 that had fallen to 7.4 per cent. That is to say, the cost of purchasing and moving £100 worth of grain fell from £133 to less than £108. The fall in what economists tend to call freight factors was equally dramatic for some other commodities and routes. Getting rice from Rangoon to Europe, for example, incurred a freight factor of about 74 per cent in 1880 but only 18 per cent by 1910. These sort of falls in transport costs swamped variations in tariffs.

Perhaps the best way to measure market integration is to turn to the economic theory known as the law of one price. Simply put, this is the notion that, in the absence of the kind of complicating factors that the real world usually throws up, there should be a single price for each good. In other words, identical items sold in different places should be priced the same, otherwise there would be an easy profit to be made by buying goods where they are cheap and selling them where they are dear. The price difference should be arbitraged away by intermediaries. Of course, in reality, there are all sorts of frictions that prevent the law of one price from holding. In international trade the two biggest ones are usually tariffs (which can artificially raise the price of a good in one country compared to another) and transport costs. Much of the margin from buying rice cheaply in Rangoon in 1880 and hoping to sell it where it was more expensive in Europe would be eaten up by the transport costs. But as transport costs fell, price differentials for internationally demanded goods began to narrow sharply. Take wheat as an example. Between 1800 and 1840 the price differential between American and British wheat was around 100 per cent, that is to say British grains were sold for about twice as much as their US equivalents. But as tariffs were removed and, more importantly, transport costs collapsed, that differential narrowed sharply – down to around 10 per cent by 1900. Over the same period British imports of US wheat jumped from close to zero to an annual 1.8 million tons.

Driven by a combination of lower transport costs, relative international peace and better communications, global trade took off in the 1850s. The total value of goods crossing borders, as a percentage of global GDP, rose from around 5 per cent in the mid-1840s to 12 per cent by 1900 and peaked at 14 per cent by 1914 – a level that would not be reached again until the early 1980s. It wasn't just goods crossing borders either: people and money were also on the move. Annual cross-border migration amounted to around 0.36 per cent of the global population in the 1850s but 0.96 per cent in the 1880s, a trebling of the share of the world's population on the move each year. By the eve of the First World War it had reached 1.67 per cent – in that year around one in sixty people migrated across borders. Only after the War did passports and quotas become the norm. International free movement was one early casualty of 1914.

Money moved along with people and goods. Cross-border capital flows, in the form of either overseas lending or direct investment, rose from a value of about 7 per cent of global GDP in the 1860s to about 20 per cent by 1914 – again a level that would not be surpassed until the 1980s.

Whether measured by goods, prices, migration or financial flows, the world economy of 1914 was more globalised than that of 1979. The economically dominant power in this globalised world was Britain. The early lead gained by being the first country to industrialise was exploited to the full. In 1870 more than 40 per cent of all global exported manufactured goods, by value, were made in Britain. Even after western Europe and the United States had begun to emerge as serious industrial competitors, the share remained high. By 1912 it was still about 30 per cent. For context, compare these figures to contemporary China's market share. In recent years there has been much talk of the People's Republic as a manufacturing export superpower, but its share of global manufactured exports in 2018 was *only* around 13 per cent.

British dominance stretched well beyond manufactured exports, though. Alongside what Victorians called 'visible exports', which moved in crates on railways and ships, were the 'invisible exports' of services, which typically made up about one quarter of total British exports. By 1914 London was the home of global finance; some two thousand or more foreign banks maintained a presence in what was the global centre for cross-border lending and investment. The vast majority of global trade was conducted in sterling values and financed by bills of exchange payable in London. A Swiss exporter, for example, selling goods to an Italian importer would likely receive their payment in the form of a bill drawable in London. Companies and governments around the world came to London to raise cash. The London Stock Exchange was the world's largest and most liquid and accounted for about 40 per cent of the total value of all listed stocks globally. Around a quarter of all the government bonds issued globally in the decade before 1914 were traded in London. Over the course of the nineteenth century rival financial centres such as Paris and

Amsterdam had fallen by the wayside, and while New York's star was rising, London's prominence at the centre of global finance was undisputed as never before or since.

To finance and manufactured goods can be added cross-border services such as shipping, where the British merchant marine controlled about a quarter of global capacity by 1913, insurance and cross-border legal services. Just as important was Britain's share in the global energy market. Coal was the key energy commodity of the late nineteenth and early twentieth century and Britain had plenty of easily tapped seams. US production surpassed that of Britain in the late nineteenth century but in the first decade of the twentieth the UK remained the world's second biggest miner of coal and was the world's largest exporter. British coal powered industry and transport across Europe and as far afield as South America.

Putting it all together, the Britain of 1914 was the dominant manufacturer of exported goods, the centre of international finance and the world's largest net energy exporter. In the last great cycle of globalisation Britain combined the roles that China, the United States and Saudi Arabia play in the current cycle. Free trade and an open global economy certainly suited Britain well and it is no wonder that many foreign observers took to viewing the UK's support for ending tariffs with a pinch of salt. What was all well and good for the country with, say, the world's largest textile industry was not necessary ideal for less developed states, which feared that free trade for them simply meant being swamped with British goods.

Of course, not every British trading partner had a great deal of choice over how that trade was governed. The globalisation of the nineteenth and early twentieth centuries moved hand in hand with imperialism. In the latter half of the nineteenth century about 10 per cent of the world's surface area was added to the British Empire, which by 1914 covered about a quarter of the world's land surface and governed about a quarter of the globe's population. The decades from 1870 to 1900 are sometimes referred to as a 'high age of imperialism' but in reality the acquisition of overseas territory by Britain was fairly evenly spread over the whole century. What was newer in the final third was the growth of competition from other European powers in the so-called 'Scramble for Africa'. The Great Divergence between European and North American economies on the one hand and those of Asia and Africa on the other, set the stage for nineteenth-century imperialism. With higher GDP per head, more access to military technology and more effective state structures, the more advanced economies were able to use force to impose their will.

The British Empire was a strange mismatch of governance struggles and models. By the late 1860s, the settler colonies – such as Canada and Australia – were part of the empire but effectively self-governing in most regards. Until 1858 India was ruled by the East India Company, which had begun as a trading company in the 1600s. Deploying soldiers as often as spreadsheets, by the mid-eighteenth century it had established itself as a powerful player in subcontinent politics. As the previously dominant Mughal empire fell apart, the company's rule had extended across modern-day India, Pakistan and Bangladesh. The Indian War of Independence of 1857 to 1858 (known at the time as the Mutiny or the Sepoy Revolt) put an end to all that. Suppressing that major insurrection required the deployment of thousands of British soldiers, and the Government of India Act of 1858 was perhaps the largest nationalisation ever carried through Parliament. The company was dissolved, and direct rule by the Crown instituted in the form of the British Raj. The Colonial Office in theory oversaw the governance of large parts of the globe other than the dominions and India but, in reality, much power was devolved to what came to be known as 'the man on the spot'.

Perhaps as important as the formal Empire was its informal equivalent. At various times China, other parts of Asia and much of Latin America found itself pushed into lopsided economic treaties with Britain, often backed up by the threat of force. The British sphere of influence stretched well beyond the parts of the atlas coloured pink. Between the Crimean War of the 1850s and the First World War of 1914, Britain remained aloof from European military conflicts but it was rare for a year to pass during Queen Victoria's long reign from 1837 to 1901 without her soldiers being in action somewhere in the world. Gunboat diplomacy was very much a tool of British commercial policy during Britain's heyday as the champion of global free trade. And if a gunboat was not enough, the government was usually happy to commit full naval squadrons and army regiments. The two Opium Wars fought against China in the 1840s and the 1850s were the most egregious examples.

The roots of those particular conflicts dated back decades. During the eighteenth century demand for Chinese luxury goods – such as silk, porcelain and tea – led to the country running a trade surplus with its neighbours, including British-controlled India. Tiring of the flow of precious silver to China that was paying for these goods, the authorities encouraged the growth of an Indian export that could narrow the trade gap with Qing China: opium. The drug had long been used in traditional Chinese medicine but its use for non-medical purposes surged in the 1830s. Cheaply grown in Bengal and smuggled into China by British and Indian merchants, the narcotic's widespread sale reversed China's trade surplus. When the Chinese emperor moved to restrict opium usage and seize stockpiles in China, the British reacted with force in the name of free trade. Two wars and several thousand deaths later,

Britain had taken control of Hong Kong and forced China into a series of unequal treaties giving commercial privileges to European traders.

Britain, particularly come the late nineteenth century, was far from unique in its imperialism. The leading European powers, and increasingly the United States too, all engaged in serious empire-building. This should not be surprising; imperial rule has a long history. But the Britain of the 1850s to 1900, as any glance at a map of the Empire reveals, was unusually successful in its endeavours. Nineteenth-century technology – telegraphs, steamships and Maxim machine guns – allowed for much wider-ranging territorial acquisitions than did eighteenth-century or earlier gear. Britain, as the world's leading economy and the world's leading naval power, was well placed to take advantage.

That of course assumes there was an advantage to take and, in economic terms, that is a debatable proposition. Leaving aside fraught contentions about the economic impact on the conquered territories themselves (and the short version is: 'being a British colony was probably better for your long-term development than being a Spanish or Belgian one, but that is not a high bar to get over'), it is all too easy to assume that the Empire was an economic asset to Britain, but even this is something that has been argued about by economic historians ever since. Certainly, the ability to dictate the terms of trade was helpful to British exporters. The Indian railways, for example, bought British locomotives rather than those of rivals, and that procurement did not exactly follow a competitive tendering process. But India is not as typical an example as many assume. The Dominions, which, with their much higher GDP per head, were in many ways more attractive export markets, were much less enthusiastic about free trade than the policy-makers in Westminster, and with self-government increasingly came tariffs, tariffs usually applied just as much against British manufacturers as American or German ones. Nonetheless, despite the vast population differential, between them Canada and Australia consumed just as many exports as India. More broadly, imperial markets were less important to British exporters during the so-called high age of imperialism than is often supposed. In 1870, only around one quarter of exports went to the Empire, and by 1900 that had risen only to one third. Europe remained the UK's key export market right down to the beginning of the First World War.

Depending on the assumptions used, one can come up with a range of estimates of how big an impact the existence of the Empire had on British exports in the years before 1914. But even with punchy assumptions, such numbers are rarely more than about 6 per cent or 7 per cent of the total size of the pre-war economy. A sizeable amount but not enough, on one level, to suggest that late Victorian Britain minus its empire would be, economically speaking, a radically different place. That said, while Britain generally ran trade deficits with Europe and the United States (importing more than it exported) it usually ran a surplus with the colonies and India.

The Empire of course also incurred costs, but again not as high as is often assumed. Like so many things in history, Britain attempted to build its empire on the cheap. The idea that colonies should be, as soon as possible, self-financing was a core principle of British imperialism. Local taxes and duties were used, wherever possible, to pay for local administration and defence. In the case of India, things went further. The large Indian Army – generally British officered and Indian manned – was paid for by the Raj and regularly used well beyond its borders in imperial actions across Asia and east Africa.

The most striking feature of Britain's global standing

between the 1870s and 1914 was its role not as the world's ruler but as its banker. British overseas investment in the decades before the Great War was on a scale that had not been seen before and has not been matched since. As other parts of the world followed Britain down the path towards industrialisation in the later nineteenth century, it was British investors who financed a hugely disproportionate share of this.

Understanding the wider picture means delving, briefly, into the somewhat mysterious world of the balance of payments accounts. Balance of payments accounting, like national income accounting, is all too often shrouded in a layer of misleading and counterintuitive terms. But the basic principles are relatively straightforward to grasp. Simply put, the balance of payments is a way of measuring, at the level of the whole economy, how countries financially interact with each other. The first thing to note is that balance of payments consists of two sets of accounts which, as the name suggests, balance. On the one side is the current account and on the other the capital account (which is, and this is when it starts to get murky, sometimes called the financial account). The current account, which is the account that tends to feature more heavily in the twentieth-century economic history of Britain, measures short-term flows between one country and the rest of the world. It starts with the more familiar trade balance, which is a straightforward measure of a country's exports of goods and services minus its imports of goods and services. The current account, however, is a broader measure which adds to the trade data financial flows such as official government payments sent or received overseas and, crucially, flows of profits across borders. It is perfectly possible for a country to be running a positive trade balance (that is to say exporting more to the rest of the world than it imports, in terms of goods and services) but a negative current account if, say, there are many foreign-owned firms operating within its borders which remit some of their profits back to their parent companies each quarter. The current account is fundamentally a measure of whether a country is a net borrower or a net lender to the rest of the world. A current account deficit, which is usually measured as percentage of GDP, means that the households, firms and government of a country, taken together, are borrowing from the rest of the world, while a surplus means they are net lenders.

The counterpoint, and the other side, of the balance of payments is the capital account. And it is the capital account that really matters when thinking about the economy of late nineteenth-century Britain. This measures change in the ownership of assets. A country running a current account deficit will, by definition, be running a capital account surplus. As it is essentially borrowing from the rest of the world, other countries will be running up financial claims on its output either in the form of loans or direct stakes. The Britain of the 2010s for example, ran a relatively large current account surplus – borrowing from overseas each year – and funded that with a capital account surplus by borrowing from abroad and selling assets (a combination of property, shares and firms) to foreigners. The terms 'deficit' and 'surplus' are in some ways unhelpful. A surplus sounds like something healthy while a deficit suggests something to avoid, but of course a deficit on one side of the balance of payments means a surplus on the other. Whether or not a country should be running a current, or capital, account surplus or deficit depends on many things, not least its stage of development. Economists tend to find their eyebrows rising when confronted by a large deficit or surplus within the balance of accounts, as it is often, but not always, suggestive of some underlying imbalance in the wider economy: why exactly is it that a country needs to lend so such abroad or borrow so much from other states?

One way to think about the balance of payments, one highly relevant to nineteenth-century Britain, is as a measure of the balance between national saving and national investment. In macroeconomics, the terms 'savings' and 'investment' are used slightly differently from their everyday usage. National savings refer to the portion of total income of households, firms and governments which is not immediately spent on consuming goods and services. Those savings have to go somewhere and that is to investment. Investment, in a macroeconomic sense, means the acquisition of goods which are not immediately consumed – typically that would be machinery, plant and buildings that will be used to produce more goods in the future, but it could just as well be the building of new houses or transport links or the building up of inventories of goods for later sale. Savings, in a closed economy, equal investment. If the national savings rate is 10 per cent of GDP (i.e. in total, firms, households and governments are saving a tenth of their income) then the national investment rate will be 10 per cent. Of course, once the assumption of a closed economy is dropped, then things become a touch more complicated. Domestic savings and domestic investment can decouple. An economy might have an investment rate of, say, 10 per cent but national savings might be only running at 8 per cent. The difference, 2 per cent of GDP, would be found from accessing the savings of another country. That would mean a capital account surplus of 2 per cent as money was borrowed and a corresponding current account deficit of 2 per cent. A 2 per cent of GDP surplus or deficit on the current or capital account is firmly within the range of what might be considered normal.

Late nineteenth-century Britain, though, was far from normal. Being the first country to industrialise created some unique circumstances. To start with, it allowed for a far higher national savings rate than had been seen in the past. Saving is, after all, a luxury only the relatively affluent can afford. A subsistence farmer does not run much of a surplus. In the late nineteenth century Britain ran a national savings rate of around 10 to 15 per cent of GDP each year. By the standards of a century later that is not an especially high level for an advanced economy, but it was much higher than was typical in the 1870s or 1880s. Investment, though, was usually between 6 and 10 per cent of GDP. The result was current account surpluses/capital account deficits that were frequently around 5 per cent of GDP and got as high as 8 per cent of GDP on the eve of the First World War. In other words, a great deal of British money was flowing overseas.

Britain had the savings to splash around the globe just as demand for them was rising. Between 1865 and 1914 almost 70 per cent of those outflows went into railways, docks, telegraphs, gas and electrical plants – the kind of social overheads that Britain had already developed and which other countries now sought to replicate. By 1914, about 40 per cent of this overseas investment was in the Empire, with 60 per cent being non-imperial.

Of course this was not charitable giving; such investments overseas came with a return and it was an attractive one at that. Net payments from abroad, either as interest on debt or dividends from shares or profit remittances from joint ventures, amounted, after subtracting comparable payments sent overseas from Britain, to about 1 to 1.5 per cent of GDP each year in the 1840s. By the 1880s that had grown to between 4 and 6 per cent of GDP each year and by the decade before 1914 to between 6 and 8 per cent of GDP each year. In 1913 for every £11 of output produced by the British economy, it received another as payment for money lent overseas in the past few decades. Britain was a creditor economy with financial claims stretching across the globe. The simple reason why so much

British capital flowed abroad was that the available returns were consistently higher, even accounting for the greater risk. The annual return on investment in a British railway, for example, between 1870 and 1914 was 4.33 per cent. Not at all bad, but well below the 8.41 per cent in the USA over the same period.

The Britain that went to war in 1914 was a country that had truly embraced globalisation. Goods imports, as share of GDP, rose from about 20 per cent in the mid-1840s to 30 per cent by 1913. It was a country that preached unilateral free trade and was happy to import the products and commodities of others; its national standard of living was topped up by the fruits of previous overseas investment. The first industrial country at the beginning of the nineteenth century had transformed itself into the lynchpin of an increasingly integrated global economy by the beginning of the twentieth. The lasting domestic causes and consequences of that globalisation make up a large part of the story of mid-Victorian to Edwardian Britain.

6

The Successful Failure

When Queen Victoria died in 1901, she was ruling over the wealthiest country on earth. And yet much debate at the time focused on Britain's economic failures rather than its successes. In truth the early lead over its rivals, in terms of GDP per head, that Britain had clawed out in the first half of the nineteenth century was never something which would last for ever. As other countries industrialised, the gap began to narrow. The Great Exhibition of 1851, in the purpose-built Crystal Palace in Hyde Park (later moved to south London), had been a showcase of Britain's industrial leadership, but by the time of the Paris Exhibition of 1867 it was already obvious to British manufacturers that the future would be more competitive. American, German and French industrialists were not only catching up, but in some sectors surpassing British achievements. Alongside the evidence of rising foreign industrial ingenuity came what the Victorians would call the Great Depression – renamed by later historians the Long Depression, after the 1930s had claimed the top (or depending on how one looks at it, bottom) spot – of the 1870s to early 1890s. There was certainly a sense of decline and decay pervading much of the economic commentary of the time, and Parliament formed a Royal Commission to 'inquire into the depression of trade and industry' in 1886, alongside two inquiries into agricultural distress and a broader examination of whether the UK's currency system was harming the economy.

The Victorian sense of failure was one echoed by many historians in the 1960s and 1970s. Whenever the contemporary mood is gloomy, there is a tendency to project the failure back into history. But more recently that attitude has begun to shift. The best modern estimates of economic growth in the 1870s and 1880s show little evidence of depression. It is all too easy to take for granted the regular production of accurate (or at least semi-accurate) economic statistics. But the kind of data which modern policy-makers rely on was unavailable to their Victorian peers; the very concept of GDP and national accounting is really a mid-twentieth-century notion. Indeed, the main argument for Parliament assembling a Royal Commission to investigate the supposed depression was to find out whether one was actually happening.

With the benefit of later years of scholarship, the economic historical record looks clearer. Late nineteenth-century Britain did not undergo a depression lasting two decades in the sense of a contracting economy, but it did experience a shift in relative prices which redistributed income around the economy and may have felt depressing to the losers.

The growth of output per head did slow somewhat, from around 1.3 per cent per annum in the 1850s and 1860s to closer to 1 per cent in the 1870s to early 1880s – although it then picked up again until the end of Victoria's reign. Compared to earlier nineteenth-century growth rates, let alone those of the eighteenth or seventeenth century, these sorts of advances were none too shabby. But other countries managed faster growth. As Britain itself had demonstrated between 1750 and 1850, moving workers from relatively low productivity sectors to higher productivity ones such as manufacturing could give a rapid fillip to growth rates. The problem of course is that this is very much a once-only trick and one that Britain had already played. In 1870 a mere one in five Britons worked in the fields, whereas around half of Germans and Americans still did. Over the next forty years that would fall to around one third. As other countries followed in Britain's footsteps its lead narrowed. GDP per head in Britain in 1850 was around 2.1 times that of the countries that would become Germany. But by 1900 that ratio had fallen to 1.25 times. Britain was still the richer country, but the gap was much smaller. British and American levels of GDP per head tracked each other closely for most of the nineteenth century before the US pulled ahead sharply in the late 1870s. By 1900 America's output per head was some 10 per cent above Britain's.

The changing balance of the international economy came at a time of rapidly shifting prices. When the Britons of the 1870s or 1880s bemoaned a depression, what they really meant was falling prices, especially agricultural ones. This was globalisation at work. The technological advances in transport of the 1870s and 1880s allowed the grains and meat of the New World to flood into the old. In the decade before the repeal of the Corn Laws, foreign grains had accounted for only around one twelfth of consumption but that began to rapidly change in the 1870s. By the first decade of the twentieth century more than half of all bread, fruit, butter and cheese was imported, along with 40 per cent of meat and 30 per cent of eggs. The relative winners were Britain's consumers and the relative losers its agriculturalists and rural landowners.

Thankfully, there were fewer farmers about. The move to the cities and towns that had begun in the first half of the nineteenth century continued into the second, accelerated by the ability to import more food. The number of workers employed in farming fell from over two million in 1851 to one and a half million by 1901, while the number working in manufacturing rose by more than two million to five and a half million over the same period. By 1901 the migration from the countryside was mostly complete, with male workers moving into manufacturing and trade and over two million women working in domestic service. The service sector, from domestic staff to transport workers, grew especially quickly.

Whereas the impact of the late twentieth-century globalisation on British workers still provokes debate, the results of globalisation in the late nineteenth century seem more clear-cut. Workers got both cheaper food and the chance for emigration while landowners saw the returns from agriculture drop. Broadly put, the globalisation of Britain acted to reduce inequality at the margins. Which is not to say that inequality did not remain staggeringly high, with the wealthiest 1 per cent of the population holding perhaps 70 per cent of the economy's total assets in 1900.

Britain's manufacturing performance in the late nineteenth century remains especially contentious. On the one hand Britain remained the world's leading manufacturing power, but on the other its share of the global manufacturing trade fell from more than 40 per cent in 1850 to just over 30 per cent by 1900. The loss of foreign markets, especially as tariffs rose in the 1880s across Europe, was a particular bone of contention for many businesspeople. As was the easy availability of foreign-made goods in British stores. Ernest Edwin Williams's diatribe *Made in Germany* was a best-seller in 1896. Many Victorian commentators looked at the foreign manufactures filling up British retail stores and, rather than celebrating the fact that consumers now faced a wider range of cheaper goods, asked themselves what had gone wrong. Sloppy British workmanship, a lack of ingenuity or a supposed failure of industrial training were named as common culprits. German-manufactured toys and haberdashery were particularly singled out for criticism. The fact that British manufacturing had chosen to concentrate on other markets, such as shipbuilding and textiles, was often ignored. A *Daily Mail* headline of 1900 sums up much of the mood: 'American furniture in England. A further indictment of the trade unions'.

The shifting structure of the global economy, and in particular the rise of successful German and American industrial firms, began, by the 1890s, to shift the calculus of Britain's own domestic political economy. In the 1840s, faced with no serious foreign competition, supporting free trade had been an obvious step for Britain's commercial and industrial elite. The case for repealing the Corn Laws had united the interests of mill owners and mill workers; the results of importing more food were likely to be lower bills for workers and new markets for industrialists. But that coalition began to fray as manufacturers realised that free trade was not always an unalloyed benefit for them. By the Edwardian period, the battle over free trade versus tariffs would be re-joined in full, although with the opposing sides and interest groups somewhat rejigged.

While the so-called staples of British manufacturing – textiles, iron, steel and shipbuilding – continued to perform well in the last third of the nineteenth century, Britain did fall behind its German and US rivals in the new sectors such as chemicals and electrical engineering. In chemicals, for example, British firms managed an 11 per cent market share by 1913 compared to 34 per cent for the US and 24 per cent for Germany. Modern global chemicals giants like Germany's BASF or the US's Dow Chemicals emerged in the Victorian period, whereas their British rivals remained of a much smaller scale. The name Nobel is nowadays associated not with the

Scottish manufacturer of explosives Nobel Industries (later part of ICI), but with the prizes established by its Swedish founder. The notion of a British failure to innovate, during what is sometimes called the second industrial revolution, is usually backed by an argument that Britain's domestic investment rate was low. The headline figures suggest there is something to this. Between 1855 and 1914, total investment in the British economy averaged 9.0 per cent of GDP each year. By contrast in Germany it was 19.8 per cent and in the US 21.9 per cent. But care is needed with this number. Both Germany and the US invested substantial sums in housing during this period compared to Britain – which may have led to better living conditions but likely did little for their manufacturing prowess. Similarly both spent a great deal on the kind of rail and transport networks which Britain had already developed in the first half of the nineteenth century. Looking at just investment in producers' equipment the differences are much less stark. Britain averaged 3.2 per cent of GDP a year between 1855 and 1914, while Germany and the US were at 5.1 per cent and 5.3 per cent respectively.

Right from the Victorian era itself, there have been arguments that attempt to tie together Victorian Britain's vast outflow of savings abroad and its supposed failure to keep pace in terms of economic growth. Britain's financial system, some contend, failed Britain's industries by choosing to channel funds to foreign railways rather than upgrade British manufacturing. The City of London is often identified as the culprit for underinvestment in British manufacturing. The problem with this argument is that, while relatively low investment in manufacturing equipment coupled with a large outflow of national savings are established facts, there is little evidence that British manufacturers were seeking funds and had been denied them. The contrast with the US is instructive.

American manufacturing received more investment and was certainly more capital intensive than its British equivalent. But American industrialists in the late nineteenth century faced different constraints and incentives: their biggest problem was a shortage of skilled labour, necessitating the replacement of human muscle with machine power. In Britain, where there was no shortage of skilled manufacturing types, the endowment of assets favoured more craft-based techniques.

To the economist John Hobson, Britain's capital account surplus was indeed a very real problem but not because it meant manufacturing was poorly served. He drew a link between wealth inequality, the capital account, imperialism and ultimately war. Hobson, who would later influence the thinking of Lenin in the 1910s and Keynes in the 1920s and 1930s, developed what he termed the under-consumption argument. Simply put, he theorised a limit to what any individual could realistically spend in any given year. All things being equal, the rich would save a greater share of their income than the poor. That remains uncontroversial. Savings rates are, by and large, positively correlated with income – the more someone earns each year, the higher the proportion of it they save. For Hobson, the inequality of late Victorian and Edwardian Britain was a driver of what he saw as over-saving and under-consumption. With a more equal distribution of income, he assumed, more of it would be spent. In Hobson's mind the sheer volume of British saving was a driver of British imperialism. There simply were not enough profitable domestic outlets for the flow of available funds. This over-saving, in his view, pushed Britain to seeking overseas outlets to invest in. Britain acquired a larger empire, according to this model, because the wealthy needed somewhere to park their cash.

His link between inequality and imperialism – one which would later be seized on by Lenin – is superficially attractive but does not quite match the pattern of British overseas lending. While the Empire took a great deal of Britain's capital, Europe and the United States generally took more. Equally, his argument that inequality was the primary driver of the capital account surplus suggests that inequality was rising throughout the late nineteenth century, which does not seem to fit the data. Hobson's work, while perhaps oversold, did bring out the important role played by the structure of inequality in macroeconomic developments and, what is more, in the economic interactions between countries. Echoes of his view that under-consumption could drive excess saving and lead to large current account surpluses/capital account deficits can be found in twenty-first-century concerns about the role of China and Germany in the global economy.

A stronger candidate for Victorian failure can be found in human capital rather than physical capital. The various parliamentary and Royal Commissions of the 1880s were often quick to diagnose a lack of the kind of technical skills required to work in the new industries such as chemicals. Victorian education policy certainly looks, to modern eyes, rather strange. Literacy among adults, which had been around the 50 per cent mark for a century before 1850, did then rise sharply to around 75 per cent by 1870, but the state cannot claim much of the credit. The dominant theme was voluntarism rather than compulsion. In the late 1860s around half of children had no access to schooling, around a quarter attended voluntarily run schools (often associated with the church) and another quarter attended state-aided primary schools. The Education Act of 1870 required the setting up of new state-aided schools (which would charge a fee, but one that was generally subsided) in areas lacking them but, like much Victorian social legislation, it left the decision as to whether attendance would be compulsory up to locally elected politicians. By 1876 parents had a duty to ensure their children attended school but there was no real way to enforce this. By 1880 schools were required to ensure attendance from the age of five to ten and empowered to fine the parents of absent children. Only in 1891, though, did the government agree to pay primary school fees of up to ten shillings, effectively making universal primary education free. The prevailing attitude was that education was a matter for self-help, and as Robert Lowe, an 1870s Chancellor, put it: 'I hold it as our duty not to spend public money to do what people can do for themselves.' British education spending in the late nineteenth century (expressed as a share of GDP) was regularly about half that of Germany and the United States. It was not just that Britain was late to embrace universal primary schooling, but that secondary schooling – where many technical skills were developed – remained a minority pursuit and, according to many critics, Britain also lagged in university education.

It was certainly during the 1880s and 1890s that Britain developed its fascination with German technical education, something which would reappear during other periods of supposed decline. Many a pamphlet was written on the Trade Continuation Schools that taught technical skills to teenagers or the Technical High Schools that existed alongside the university sector. Too often, though, the evidence was cherry-picked to make the case for failure. German success in, say, chemistry, was celebrated whilst British advances in physics were ignored. British universities did begin to expand in the later nineteenth century, with new institutions such as Imperial College in London and the Manchester Institute of Science and Technology being very much up to the standard of their continental peers. Mass primary schooling was rolled out late but the problems of the 1850s to 1880s had been mostly overcome by 1900.

British investment levels in manufacturing did lag behind those of some rivals in the latter half of the nineteenth century and British education did fail to keep pace with international best practice. But the dominant factor in the relative economic decline of the 1850s to 1900 was that Britain had already made the decisive shift away from being a primarily agrarian economy. Victorian Britain had more than its fair share of declinists, who often looked to pin the blame for a declining economic edge on some or other feature of society or policy. Often, like the declinist writing of the late twentieth century, these complaints would be marked by what one modern historian has dubbed the problem of the 'pernicious other'; best practice overseas would be compared to the British experience but the home of the example would regularly change – Britain was not being fairly compared to an individual rival but to a hodgepodge of features taken from a half-dozen countries. British successes – whether in finance, shipping or services – were often left out of the story.

As Britain continued to urbanise and its economy to grow in the second half of the century, there were shifts in other aspects of its society, too. Life expectancy at birth, which was stable at about 40 from the 1820s to 1860, rose to 50 by 1900. Birth rates fell, with the average number of births over her lifetime per woman dropping from 5 in 1800 to 3.5 by 1900. While rising life expectancy is evidence of rising prosperity, perhaps as many as one in six Britons still lived in absolute poverty in 1900. The failure of many volunteers to meet the fitness and health standards required by the Army during the Boer War at the turn of the twentieth century provoked a wide-ranging debate on poverty and national efficiency.

It was also during the Victorian period that the roots of some of Britain's regional inequalities can be found. A quick glance at the distribution of the population of England tells much of the story. In 1801, around 27 per cent of the population of the country lived in the broadly defined north – the northeast, the northwest, Yorkshire and modern-day Humberside. At each census until 1901 that proportion rose until peaking at about 37 per cent. For the last 120 years the ratio has been declining and is now back to around 28 per cent.

In the early years of the industrial revolution many of the key developments happened outside of London. Manchester was the great industrial centre, Liverpool the great cotton port, coal mining and iron and steel working thrived in Wales, Scotland and the English north and midlands. Although calculating regional estimates of historical GDP per capita is even trickier than calculating the national-level figures, the broad facts seem clear. London's lead as the UK's richest region already existed in the mid-nineteenth century but rose sharply in the three decades before 1900. In both the northwest and the west midlands, GDP per head was above the national average before 1870 but below it by 1900. East Anglia – the most farming-dependent region – experienced a relative decline in the late nineteenth century far more dramatic than any that resulted from late twentieth-century deindustrialisation. Whereas London had been responsible for 20 per cent of income tax receipts in 1871, by 1901 that was 25 per cent. Even in the heyday of the great staple industries, employment growth was faster in London than in other then high-income areas such as Lancashire or Clydeside. In the first half of the nineteenth century the growth of new industries pulled wealth – and people – towards the regions best placed to meet rising demand for these new products. But as those industries matured and demand for services – long London's strong point – became a more important driver of the overall economy, the capital's lead began to extend once more. The existing cluster of service and commercial businesses in

London made operating there easier than beginning afresh in Bristol or Newcastle for many firms.

Despite these varying economic fortunes and rapid societal change, politics moved slowly. Compared to modern politicians, mid- to late Victorian statesmen (and they were almost all men) spent extraordinarily little time on the bread and butter macroeconomic issues of employment and growth that make up much of modern politics. There was the occasional commission or inquiry into the performance of the economy alongside factory legislation, some slum clearance and educational reform but politics tended to be dominated by questions of social reform, the role of the established church, the nature of the governance of Ireland or expansion of the Empire. The conception of both economic policy and the role of the state remained far more limited than in the twentieth century.

But despite the differences in the debate, the form of British politics did become more modern. The makeup of Parliament itself continued to shift towards a better reflection of where economic power lay and away from the old landed interest. Two further reform acts, in 1867 and 1884, widened the franchise so that by the 1890s two in three men aged over 21 (about one fifth of the population) had the vote. A crackdown on vote-buying and the introduction of the secret ballot removed some of the more blatant corruption from the system but elections remained raucous and occasionally violent occasions. Until 1918 general elections took place over a four-week period rather than on a single day, in part to allow the police to spread their resources and control the fallout. Violent jostling of one's opponents, smashing the windows of their offices and hurling rotten vegetables as they made their canvassing trips were all very much par for the course. The atmosphere on election days in a tight seat can be compared to a football derby match in the 1970s or 1980s.

The makeup of the Commons shifted away from the sons of landed aristocrats to take in more of the commercial and industrial middle class. The year 1874 even saw the election of the first two working-class members (both elected as Liberals, in mining seats), despite the inbuilt barriers: the role of MP remained unpaid and took up an increasing amount of time, so for a working-class man to even consider standing for Parliament he generally needed to find a financial sponsor. The composition of the Lords, too, began to alter with the arrival of more business owners – still at this point granted hereditary rather than life peerages. Despite these changes, however, cabinets continued to be dominated by peers and the sons of peers until the end of the century. In part this was to do with the age at which people entered politics: for a successful factory owner or lawyer Parliament would usually be a second career begun in their late thirties or, more likely, forties or fifties, those with aristocratic ties could still find themselves in Parliament in their mid- to late twenties.

The structure of the party system certainly began to feel more modern. The number of independent members declined and MPs began to vote more along party lines. While governments of the 1850s would think nothing of losing a dozen or two divisions a year, by 1900 the government could usually rely on its whipping to pass its bills. By the 1860s a two-party system was in place, with the Whigs, Peelites and Radicals coming together as the Liberal Party, opposed by the Conservatives. The broadening of the electorate necessitated the growth of the party apparatus in both cases.

Broadly put, the 1850s to 1870s were dominated by Liberals and the later decades of the century by the Conservatives. There is a tendency to talk of late nineteenth-century politics as the age of Gladstone and Disraeli, but the age of Gladstone, Disraeli and Salisbury would be a fairer description. For the

34 years from 1868 to 1902, with a brief 18-month exception in the mid-1890s, the office of Prime Minister was held by one of these three. Each had, in his own way, a lasting impact on the political economy of modern Britain.

William Ewart Gladstone, a Tory turned Peelite turned Liberal, had served two long terms as Chancellor in the 1850s and 1860s before assuming the leadership of the Liberal Party in the late 1860s. He was to dominate the party for the next three decades and, by the end of his career, was not only the party's only plausible leader but also its opponents' most prized electoral asset. Gladstonian Liberalism combined a lofty tone of moralising with a harder-edged focus on reform and retrenchment; if a cost could be cut Gladstone was generally in favour of cutting it. He was in many ways a classic Liberal, espousing policies of laissez-faire free markets, low taxes and small state but combined with the righting of obvious wrongs to allow more freedom of opportunity. He rarely seemed so happy as when presented with some mission or cause to campaign on. The treatment of Christians in the Ottoman Empire, the case for Home Rule in Ireland and the inequities of British imperial policy in Africa all provided grist for his mill. The last two decades of his career were marked by frequent retirements from public life, only to be called back when some moral issue or another presented itself. While the main beneficiaries of his opening up of institutions tended to be distinctly middle class, the People's William – as he was occasionally known – did win widespread working-class support. 'Peace, economy and reform', as his earlier platforms were described, may not seem a particularly popular pitch to working-class voters by twentieth- or twenty-first-century standards, but the context was vastly different. In an era when taxation was mostly based on indirect charges levied on products rather than direct deductions from income, the burden fell disproportionately on the poor. Meanwhile the vast bulk of government spending was either on the armed forces or the interest on debt run up fighting previous wars. Retrenchment, for the British working class, generally was taken to mean a smaller military, which for them would mean lower prices for goods. When the state consisted of little more than the ability to fight wars, cutting it could be considered a left-of-centre position.

Ernest Bevin once joked that he had heard Gladstone was at the Treasury from 1860 to 1930, and in many ways his spirit certainly was. It was in the nineteenth century that the Treasury emerged as the strongest and most central department of Britain's government machinery. Victorian fiscal policy, though, was not about supporting economic growth or smoothing the economic cycle, it was instead concerned with the management and repayment of government debt. Britain had played a central role in organising, and financing, the six coalitions that fought against France between 1792 and 1815. That victory had not come about cheaply and nor had defeat in the American War of Independence in the 1770s. Government debt to GDP peaked in the UK in 1815, at around 210 per cent of GDP. By 1850 that had been reduced to 130 per cent and by 1900 to just 35 per cent. Of course, to Victorian policy-makers the very concept of GDP would have been alien. They thought of the debt not in comparison to some abstract notion of the size of the economy but instead as an absolute number, a sterling value that had to be serviced and eventually repaid. Most of the fall in the ratio of debt to GDP between 1815 and 1850 was driven by rising GDP rather than falling debt. The national debt stood at around £820 million in 1815 and was still at around £770 million in 1850. Given that total annual tax revenues only amounted to £57 million, this was thought a colossal sum. The answer, according to the Treasury of the time, was to keep spending on a tight leash. A lower debt burden would mean lower interest payments, freeing up more space for cutting taxes and encouraging growth.

Taxation, while usually bemoaned by politicians of all parties at the time, was by modern standards exceptionally low. Of the 27 million inhabitants of the United Kingdom in 1851 only around half a million were liable for income tax and even then it was charged at a rate of just 2 per cent. Income tax had been introduced, as a temporary measure, in 1799, to finance the war with Napoleon. It was indeed repealed in 1816 but reintroduced in 1842 to help service government debt. Both Gladstone and Disraeli promised to abolish it once more in their manifestos for the 1874 general election, although like many electoral pledges over the years that one went unfulfilled.

Gladstone himself, and generations of nineteenth-century Treasury officials who imbibed his views, saw a great danger in politicians competing for votes by promising spending on certain projects. To avoid this threat Gladstonian Liberalism, building on the principles of his reformist Tory mentor Peel, emphasised the neutrality of the state in economic matters. Taxes on agriculture should, for example, be balanced against taxes on industrial activity. So, any increase or decrease in income tax, which would generally affect the pockets of prosperous industrialists, would be balanced by changes in death duties and estate taxes, the burden of which fell most heavily on landowners. The state was certainly not in the business of redistributing income between the classes. Control of spending was viewed as crucial to maintaining this class neutrality and preventing the return of the 'old corruption'. The result was the Treasury assuming a significant role in domestic policy-making, much more expansive than many of its contemporary finance ministry peers. Departmental spending plans not only had to be agreed with the Treasury in advance but voted annually through Parliament. Tight control of the purse strings gave the Treasury influence across Whitehall.

The state did gradually expand in other areas from the middle of the century. State intervention in education was discussed earlier in the chapter. The modern police force developed between the 1840s and the 1860s; the Royal Mail (which introduced uniform penny stamps in 1840 and post boxes in 1852) was handling 2.3 billion letters annually by 1900. But the state remained small. Employment is perhaps the best measure: some 1.7 per cent of workers in 1890 served in the Army and Navy and just 0.7 per cent worked for central government. Local government employed another 1.2 per cent, and it was there that some more wide-ranging expansion took place. Permissive central government social legislation usually took the character of allowing local authorities to take certain actions but not requiring them to do so. Given that such policies would have to be paid for by local ratepayers, the results were often patchy.

Birmingham was the great innovator. Under Joe Chamberlain, father of Neville and perhaps the most consequential British politician never to serve as Prime Minister, it pioneered what some have termed municipal socialism. Chamberlain, though, was no socialist, he was instead that rarest of creatures: a successful businessman who managed the transition to politics. He became Mayor of Birmingham in 1873 and quickly pushed through educational reform and slum clearance. More significantly he took the city's gas and water works into public ownership, helping establish a model for municipal ownership of so-called natural monopolies (essentially the utilities) that was replicated in many other cities and towns. Radical Joe, as he was known in the 1870s and 1880s, became a national figure in Liberal politics, urging a more interventionist approach than allowed by the Gladstonian orthodoxy. His Radical Programme of 1885 called for land reform, higher direct taxation and universal free education, and yet, in one of British political history's great ironies, he soon found himself in government with the Conservatives. Splitting with Gladstone over his pursuit of Home Rule for Ireland, Chamberlain led a ragtag bunch of former radical Liberals and grander Whigs to cross the floor and form the Liberal Unionist Party, which not long after joined a coalition government with the Conservatives. While insisting that they remained a separate party, the Liberal Unionists gradually merged into the Conservatives; as Lady Bracknell put it in Oscar Wilde's *The Importance of Being Earnest,* 'Oh, they count as Tories.' The simple fact that the supposed radical left of the Liberal Party could choose to sit with the Conservatives because of their views on Irish Home Rule says a lot about the nature and primary concerns of late Victorian politics; economics was not a central feature.

In fact, in terms of their economic policies – in as much as any existed – both main parties were broadly liberal with a small *l*, and both were, in political economy terms, parties of capital. If anything the Tories were the more interventionist. Disraeli, who had not been a notably successful Chancellor, has often been fondly invoked by his successors as the architect of 'One Nation Conservatism', a somewhat slippery term that has meant different things in different eras. Disraeli being most associated with a slippery phrase is no surprise; he was after all the most slippery of politicians. Always quick with a joke, he was the kind of figure who would no doubt have been fun to follow on Twitter and have made a name for himself on TV panel shows had he been born a century and half later. But being born in 1804, Benjamin Disraeli had to content himself with writing novels to fill the time outside of politics. *Sybil, Or the Two Nations* was his 1845 take on the condition of the English working class and had far fewer numbers in it and rather more jokes than Engels' efforts at the same time. One Nation Conservativism is typically taken to mean support for traditional institutions coupled with a sometimes almost paternalistic focus on improving the conditions for workers.

That approach certainly suited the Conservatives as Britain moved, ever so slowly, to something resembling mass democracy. One might have expected a party that was traditionally seen as the defender of the landed interest and more at home in the countryside to have struggled in a rapidly industrialising and urbanising country, where economic power was slipping away from its core support. One would be wrong. The Conservative Party proved itself to be incredibly flexible in its programme and able to build a solid cross-class electoral coalition. Indeed, by many measures it has been the most electorally successful party in any democracy for a century and a half. Building on Disraeli's insights, Lord Salisbury – himself a true aristocrat – pulled together an electoral base that ranged from landowners such as himself to the increasingly numerous suburban population of Victorian Britain and also a fair chunk of the working class. 'Villa Toryism', with the 'villas' in this case being the kind of large Victorian terraces which sprang up in the 1870s and 1880s, was a popular programme based on support for the Empire, a general sense of John Bull patriotism and some modest measures – such as factory acts and slum clearance – to alleviate working conditions. It never quite grew to the stature of an ideology or even, in many ways, a set of ideas, but was rather a mood and a sense. It was always the Liberals who were more associated with ideas; John Stuart Mill went so far as to call the Conservatives 'the stupid party'. (Mill himself lost his parliamentary seat in 1868 to the Conservative candidate – and later cabinet minister – William Henry Smith. As *The Times* put it, the electors preferred the unknown Conservative who sold books to the famous Liberal who wrote them. British politics has not always been kind to intellectuals.)

Mill may have lost his seat in 1868 but it is hard to say he lost power. His more 'radical' ideas (such as giving women the vote) were mostly ignored by the political consensus, but his broad economic approach of laissez-faire liberalism dominated British policy-making throughout Queen Victoria's reign. By the turn of the twentieth century Britain had experienced a century of historically unprecedented growth, it had built a large empire and was a, if not *the*, leading political and financial power in the globe. That success seemed to have been built with a relatively hands-off approach to state management. While the governments of continental powers and the United States assumed an increasingly active role – via state-owned banks, tariffs and nascent forms of corporatism – in growing their economies (often explicitly aimed at aping Britain's path), the Tory governments of the late nineteenth century took a Gladstonian or Millian approach. Free trade and free markets seemed to bring success. In the first decade of the twentieth century that would begin to change.

7

Edwardian Interlude

In hindsight the thirteen years or so sandwiched between the death of Queen Victoria and the start of the Great War certainly benefit from coming before the horror of the Somme, and this period has often been portrayed as some sort of more innocent time. A kind of perpetual Downton Abbey summer party. But for those who lived through it, it was often far from tranquil. The economy went through a difficult patch and, as has often been the case in hard times, politics became more fractious and fraught. Britain's political economy shifted considerably during the period with seeds first planted during the long Victorian era beginning to flower. The state grew larger while workers became more organised and began to thrust their way into politics. The wider Edwardian crisis involved a constitutional stand-off, an increasingly militant campaign for votes for women and a near civil war in Ireland. All of this came alongside a wave of trade union activism, a major dispute on taxation and the reopening of the tariffs versus free trade debate. This was not one long drawn-out summer party.

While the Edwardian era has gained a decent reputation in popular culture, economic historians have been more downbeat on the decades before the Great War. Indeed many scholars have taken to writing of an 'Edwardian climacteric', borrowing a term from medicine usually more associated with the drop in fertility during the menopause to describe the supposedly sluggish state of the British economy. As economic historians are prone to use different dating chronologies from their non-economic peers, their Edwardian climacteric stretches back to the late 1880s, well before Edward took the throne. The traditional way to account for the slowdown has been to argue that the late nineteenth and early twentieth century coincided with a gap between the end of the steam age and the birth of modern electricity. For an advanced economy such as Britain, right out on the edge of the technological frontier, the gains from steam (in terms of boosting productivity and hence income per head) had petered out, and it would be a while before mass electrification drove a similar productivity boom across industries. One of the Bank of England's Deputy Governors reached for the terminology of climacterics in 2018 when seeking to draw a parallel between Britain's weak productivity growth of the 2010s and the performance of the early 1990s. More recent scholarship argues that the slowdown in British growth, taken for granted by earlier historians, was less severe than once believed. Less severe perhaps, but still there in the data. And certainly something which dominated much of politics at the time. The world-beating British economy of the Victorian era seemed to have lost its oomph, and the two major parties of the time competed on various visions of how to restore it.

Edwardian politics and economic policy-making make more sense if placed in the context of a national crisis in confidence. Headline growth had slowed, British manufacturing was being forced to compete not just with the Americans and Germans but increasingly with the French. Newspapers brimmed full with stories of foreign goods packing British shops. Something seemed to have gone wrong with Britain's previous world-beating model: not only was it not producing healthy economic numbers nor was it producing healthy people.

The Edwardian period is the missing link between the old world of Britain's Victorian economic model, one in which laissez-faire dominated the approach to markets and the state kept as much as possible out of the direct management of the economy, and what came after: a growing state, more redistribution and more regulation. It took the crisis of the First World War to catalyse the change but many of the trends which accelerated in 1914 to 1918 were already visible in 1900. It was during this time that labour, the broad way of describing the workers of the country, became Labour, an organised political force. Early Victorian politics had been dominated by a fight between the landed interest and the new middle class; towards the end of Victoria's reign formal party politics was essentially fought between different wings of capital. In the late Victorian and Edwardian era, labour began to make its vast economic weight felt politically.

Craft unions, very much akin to medieval guilds based around specific skills, grew throughout the early to mid-Victorian period. The Trades Union Congress, an umbrella organisation, was formed in 1868 in Manchester. Initially dominated by engineers' unions and the like, it very much represented the so-called 'aristocracy of labour', generally those with a trade (the clue was in the name really) that took years of training and apprenticeships to master. And like petty aristocrats, the craft unions were rather keen on maintaining distinctions. More locomotive drivers, for example, joined the rather grandly titled Associated Society of Locomotive Engineers and Firemen than the positively plebeian-sounding General Railway Workers' Union, which admitted all comers, from highly skilled engineers to porters. The Cardiff branch of the Amalgamated Society of Carpenters and Joiners in the 1860s was described as 'nicely decorated with evergreens and over the head of the president's chair was a design portraying the friendship existing between employer and workman, by their cordially shaking hands'. This was a different type of trade unionism from what would follow.

In those pre-welfare state days, the unions were about much more than simply bargaining with employers – they provided sickness benefits and life insurance, organised clubs to pay funeral costs and had a social element too. It was very much this model of unionism that the members of a Royal Commission into trade unions carried out in the late 1860s had in mind when they drew up the Trade Union Act 1871, which put industrial organising on a firmer legal footing. These were, after all, sensible sorts of chaps (and they were indeed mainly men) with a stake in their community, indeed many of them were exactly the kind of men given the vote in the second and third reform acts.

The character of British trade unionism underwent a profound shift during the 1880s. Workers had had a terrible time during the early decades of the industrial revolution, the time of Engels' pause, but then enjoyed a decent few decades of catch-up growth. As that growth petered out and real wage growth started to sag, they began to, quite rightly, push for more. The new unionism of the 1880s was not just more confrontational towards employers but drew in a whole different set of previously unorganised workers – the semi-skilled and unskilled, not to mention women.

The London Matchgirls' strike is a case in point. Victorian Britain used an estimated 250 million matches a day and making them was both big business and grim work. Much of the work was done at home to avoid falling under the provisions of the various Factory Acts, and the mainly young and female workforce were expected to put in ten-hour days six days a week, dipping the matches in sulphur and applying the white phosphorus. The pay was low and workers were subject to a variety of fines for breakages which reduced it further. Alongside their small pay packets many of the workers received an unwelcome bonus in the form of 'phossy jaw', a facial disfigurement brought about by inhaling phosphorus. The advice of many employers to their staff was simple: if your teeth start to develop aches, get them all removed. The London establishment of Bryant and May saw unsuccessful strikes throughout the 1880s until eventually a strike in 1888, initially following the sacking of a worker, led to higher pay and fewer fines.

If the matchgirls of Bow could win concessions, then so too could the dockers of London, then the world's largest port. The dock strike of 1889 saw around 100,000 mainly unskilled workers refusing to work for almost a month until the employers agreed to increase their basic rate to sixpence an hour (the docker's tanner). More significant, though, than the strike itself were the new unions of dockers and labourers that emerged from it and joined the TUC over the following decade.

British trade unions grew faster between the 1880s and 1914 than at any other point in their history. The core demand for much of that time was for an eight-hour working day, which, in the standard six-day working week, would amount to 48 hours. This still sounds long to modern ears but, given that the average working week in 1900 stood at almost 57 hours, was seen by employers as an unreasonably radical demand.

By 1900 some two million Britons, representing just under 10 per cent of all workers, had joined a trade union. By 1913 that had risen by four million to more than one in five employees. The industrial-organisation muscle of small-*l* labour was slowly transforming into political muscle. Two working men had, as previously noted, been elected in 1874 as so-called Lib-Lab MPs, working men backed by their union but sitting as Liberals. In 1892 trade union organiser Keir Hardie managed to get himself elected as the MP for West Ham South after the Liberals stood aside to give him a clear run against the Tories – although without offering direct assistance. The next year he formed the Independent Labour Party. The bulk of the trade union movement, however, held back from supporting the new ILP, preferring to stick with the more established Liberals. The TUC established the Labour Representation Committee in 1900 to bring together the ILP and more middle-class left-leaning groups such as the Fabian Society, and provide them with trade union backing, with the aim of establishing a group of MPs who would take their own whip and press for the voice of workers in Parliament. The early days did not go well: fewer than half of the TUC member unions chose to affiliate to the new grouping and only two MPs were elected at the 1900 election.

Things changed more rapidly after a misstep by the courts. Following a strike by the Amalgamated Society of Railway Servants, the Taff Vale rail company decided to sue the union for damages. To the surprise of many jurists the company won. That verdict was overturned by the Court of Appeal only to be upheld by the House of Lords. The union was ruled liable for the financial pain the company had suffered and asked to cough up £23,000 (closer to £3 million today) in compensation. In effect the courts had overruled the 1871 Trade Union Act: yes, workers had a right to go on strike but if their employer could then sue their union for the costs, then the right to strike might exist in principle but was not there in practice. Seeing the potential impact on their own organising efforts, union after union ditched the Liberals to join the LRC. The number of affiliates doubled and 29 MPs were returned in

1906 (following a secret electoral pact with the Liberals). The new grouping renamed itself the Labour Party and generally supported the broad programme of the Liberals all the way to the First World War.

The 1906 Trades Dispute Act, passed by the new Liberal government, reversed the Taff Vale precedent and unions were once more free to organise and go on strike. This they did in droves. The best measure is to look at the number of weeks lost in strikes per worker across the economy. So if an economy has ten million workers and half a million of them go on strike for one week, the ratio would be 0.05 (half a million weeks of strike action from a total of ten million workers). If that half a million stay out for two weeks, or if one million workers are on strike for one week, the measure would show 0.1. In the late 1890s this number had generally been around 0.02 or 0.03; in other words strikes were very rare events. On the eve of the First World War it was up to 0.07 – strikes were happening two to three times as often. In 1912 the ratio hit 0.30 – a rate that would only ever be surpassed in the General Strike of 1926 and almost twice as high as the 0.17 hit in 1979 and the 'winter of discontent'. Trade unions were at their most consistently militant in the years before the First World War. When British statesmen in early 1914 spoke ominously of the 'Triple Alliance' they were just as likely to be referring to the new grouping of railway, transport and general workers' unions as to the military alliance of Germany, Austria and Italy that they would soon be at war with.

The early Labour Party should not be thought of as especially ideological; while it certainly contained socialists it was not by any stretch a socialist party. When the 29 MPs were asked in 1906 to name their favourite authors none chose Marx or Engels although Adam Smith was picked four times. Only John Ruskin and Charles Dickens managed to garner more support than the Bible. The old saying that the party owed more to Methodism than Marxism has the ring of truth to it. Public ownership was not endorsed until 1918 and the party was firmly in favour of free trade. In as much as the party had an ideology it was what might be termed Labour-ism, the notion that working men should have a voice in Parliament and that legislation should be gradually tilted towards improving working conditions. Crucially for the later twentieth century the British trade union view – shared by the party they created – of bargaining was, on one level, a fundamentally free market one. Free collective bargaining meant that haggling over wages and conditions should be carried out at company level between the bosses and the union. The kind of wider sectoral or national agreements that many European countries would later experiment with ran deeply against the grain of British unionism.

It is against the backdrop of the rise of political organised labour, of slower economic growth, of a rising tide of labour unrest, all amid a general loss of confidence, that the gradual Edwardian expansion of the state should be viewed. To which can be added the increasingly militant campaign of the suffragettes for votes for women, and Ireland sliding further towards a violent solution to its ongoing constitutional travails.

Gladstone's death in 1898 had allowed the Liberals to reinvent themselves, and the party that won the 1906 election by a landslide was a quite different beast from its Gladstonian incarnation. Although led initially by Henry Campbell-Bannerman, it was dominated by successful younger men, often middle-class lawyers, such as Henry Herbert Asquith and David Lloyd George. The party swept back to power on the back of the reopening of the free trade debate (on which more later) but once in office embarked on a series of reforms which came to be known as New Liberalism. Nowadays this is often seen as the birth of Britain's welfare state. The steps were small but the direction of travel clear. As Winston Churchill, who himself had defected from the Conservatives over the issue of free trade and served as a Liberal minister, put it when speaking of one of the new benefits, 'It's not much unless you have not got it.'

The model for many was Germany. The new second Reich which Bismarck had pulled together in 1871 was around twenty years ahead of Britain in terms of social policy. Faced with rising working-class discontent in the 1880s, the German Chancellor had responded in a two-handed manner, on the one hand with tough anti-socialist legislation, but on the other attempting to alleviate working-class suffering via an increased role for the state in social insurance. In the early twentieth century a fair few members of Britain's elite saw things in similar terms – workers could be bought off relatively cheaply, and if no action were taken, then the consequences could be much more dire. For most Liberal politicians, though, the choice was not so cynical. The Liberals risked being a victim of their own success; the great struggles that had animated the party in the nineteenth century had mostly been won. Universities had been opened up, the franchise extended, religious tolerance had grown. The gradual reform of Britain's economic model to give more security to workers seemed the obvious next step, and it had the side benefit of helping to contain the new Labour Party as a peripheral player in British politics.

The Old Age Pensions Act of 1908 granted small payments to the over-70s, administered via the Post Office. The National Insurance Act of 1911 introduced not only statutory sick pay and healthcare cost coverage for workers covered by the programme but also unemployment benefits. These were large changes in the nature of what the British state did. The notion that the state should be administering a scheme to provide unemployment benefits or paying pensions to those who had not saved for themselves ran completely counter to a Gladstonian view of the role of government. But what had not changed from the Gladstonian era was the notion that the budget should remain balanced. It was on the revenue side of the government's ledger that the real drama of Edwardian politics occurred.

Pressure to raise revenues came from two directions. Old age pensions and National Insurance were profound changes from what had gone before but, initially at least, the costs were manageable. Social transfers (pay from the government to citizens) rose from about 2.3 per cent of GDP in 1900 to closer to 3 per cent by 1914 – a big proportional rise but still small in absolute terms. Having said that, in the context of a state which raised only around 10 per cent of GDP in taxes, even this small rise would mean relatively large increases in the overall tax burden. But it was not just social spending that was on the rise, it was defence spending too. Some British policy-makers might have looked with admiration towards Germany's nascent system of social insurance, but few took a benign view of its growing naval strength.

Britain had been the dominant global naval power since at least the Napoleonic Wars, and continuation of that lead had been formalised in the 1889 Naval Defence Act, which established the two-power standard. The British fleet, it was decided, should always be at least equal to the combined strength of the second and third global powers. At the time, this law was most likely to be targeted at some combination of the USA, France and Russia, but within a decade the Admiralty was nervously glancing across the North Sea towards Germany. A series of German naval laws, beginning in 1898, began to turn the country's industrial might into a battlefleet.

Britain's lead, of course, would still be commanding until military innovation took its course and reset the race. HMS

Dreadnought was launched in 1906. An 'all big-gun ship', she was armed with 12-inch guns that could outrange anything else afloat, and equipped with engines that made her faster than any opponent she would likely face. The combination of speed and range effectively made all existing battleships obsolete overnight. From then on naval strategists would talk of 'pre-Dreadnoughts' and 'Dreadnoughts', and it was the latter that counted. Britain's lead was reset to one ship. She was also expensive, costing around twice as much as the previous generation of capital ships. Dreadnought building continued at an increasing pace until the war came. In December 1908, for example, the Admiralty requested six dreadnoughts be laid down in the financial year of 1909/10. The Cabinet pushed back, arguing that four could be laid down in 1909/10 and another four at the start of the next financial year. The Conservative opposition, and much of the press, objected with the punchy slogan 'We want eight and we won't wait', pushing the Cabinet in the end to relent and order the full eight for 1909/10. Only in the hyper-paranoid atmosphere of Edwardian Britain would eight be an acceptable compromise between four and six. As it turned out, Britain's lead over Germany was never seriously challenged, despite a few scares. Britain mustered 32 dreadnoughts in 1914 to Germany's 19; the United States was a distant third at just 10.

With expenditure rising under the pressure of both a naval arms race and a growing domestic role for the state, the question became how to pay for it. Joseph Chamberlain, by now a leading figure in the Conservative/Liberal Unionist coalition, had one potential answer: tariffs.

Tariffs seemed to Chamberlain, always an enterprising politician, to solve many problems in one step. They would, it was hoped, revitalise British manufacturing by preventing foreigners from 'dumping' cheap goods on British markets and undercutting domestic firms; they would bind the Empire together through a system of 'Imperial Preference', a common external customs border uniting Britain with its colonies and dominions; they would raise the revenue to fund an expansion in social spending and, most of all, they would help Chamberlain build a cross-class political coalition. Manufacturers would benefit from protection from overseas competition, thus binding them into the Conservative Party, while workers would reap the rewards through higher social spending.

Things had certainly changed since the 1840s. Britain's position in the global economy had shifted since she was the sole real manufacturing power of note. Whereas Manchester and its mill owners had been core supporters of free trade in the middle of the nineteenth century, there were now many firms open to the argument that maybe tariffs had their place in policy. The general rise in tariff levels globally since the 1870s had certainly left Britain, a unilateral free trader, looking out of step.

But for all the supposed logic that went into this calculation, it backfired spectacularly. The Conservative Party itself suffered defections (not least the young Winston Churchill), and while some manufacturers were won over, the bulk of the working class was not. The debate of the 1840s was reheated with new vigour, and campaigners (both Liberal and Labour) emphasised that what tariffs really meant was dear food. The iconic symbol of this was the free trade loaf, a prop which was waved at rallies and compared to the smaller tariff loaf which, free traders argued, would be all workers could afford if Chamberlain got his way. The politics of food occasionally ran in advance of the evidence – more than one free trader took to claiming that the German taste for horsemeat sausages reflected not a different set of culinary sensibilities but the impoverishment of the German working class by the evils of protectionism.

At the 1906 general election the Liberals won almost 400 seats to the Conservative and Liberal Unionists' 156. The 29 Labour MPs and the 82-odd Irish nationalists could be relied upon to vote with the Liberals in most matters. The Lords, though, remained firmly Tory, and that would have consequences in the years ahead.

If tariffs were ruled out as a revenue source, that left taxes, and it was towards them that the Liberals turned. Campbell-Bannerman stood down as Prime Minister in 1908, replaced by Asquith, a successful London barrister who liked a drink (hence the slang 'Squithy' for 'drunk') and the company of young women. He proved a relatively easygoing PM; a clubbable sort who seemed to enjoy the pace of pre-war administration, he was the stereotypical New Liberal of the era. His slogan might as well have been 'Progress, but at steady pace'. His Chancellor Lloyd George was another lawyer, although in this case a Welsh solicitor. Lloyd George too had a penchant for younger women, but there the similarities ended. A great orator who had made his name campaigning against British conduct in the Boer War, the Chancellor had more radical instincts and he was not one to duck a fight. Especially a fight against the landed gentry.

Lloyd George's solution to the budgetary shortfall was not only to raise taxes but to raise them especially high on the rich. This of course was another break with the Gladstonian orthodoxy, which firmly believed the state had no business getting involved in redistribution. Viewed from more than a century later, Lloyd George's People's Budget of 1909 looks ridiculously modest in its aims. The standard rate of income tax moved from 3.33 per cent to 5.8 per cent, while the new top band was to be levied at a rate of 8.33 per cent only on income above £5000, the equivalent of half a million pounds in modern money. Death duties too would increase and the value of landed estates would be taxed annually at 2 per cent. This was all too much for the House of Lords, which rejected the finance bill, provoking a constitutional crisis which ran throughout 1910.

Lloyd George was happy to rise to the fight, quipping that 'a fully equipped Duke costs as much to keep up as two dreadnoughts; and Dukes are just as great a terror'. It is unclear what his ministerial colleague, and then friend, Winston Churchill, himself the grandson of a Duke, made of all this. While the Lords were in theory entitled to reject a budget they had not done so in two centuries.

It took two general elections in 1910 and the eventual threat by the King to create enough new Liberal peers to swamp the Tory majority in the upper house before, just as in the 1830s and 1840s over the Great Reform Act and the Corn Laws, the Lords backed down. A new Parliament Act limited the power of the upper chamber to block (as opposed to delay) legislation coming from the Commons and, while most of the tax rises went through, the taxes on land value never quite made it.

The tumultuous economy of the Edwardian era gave rise to political turbulence. The rise of organised Labour as a political force pushed government spending up, and the ruling out of tariffs forced the necessary revenue adjustment to come from tax. Fiscal policy, even while it provoked a constitutional standoff, remained anchored to Victorian principles. The budget, outside of war at least, had to remain balanced. If more spending was desired then that meant more taxes or more tariffs.

Lloyd George in his first bout of prominence as an economic policy-maker might be a (relatively) big spender and high taxer but he was fundamentally traditional in his view on deficits and their dangers. As was the young Labour Party. The active management of the economy via government policy, even in the defensive manner of just trying to lean against recessions, was not the business of the state. Fiscal policy was about balancing the books while monetary policy was the job of the (then still privately owned) Bank of England. But the active use of monetary policy to manage the business cycle by raising interest rates to cool booms and cutting them to drive expansions was still decades away. Instead, monetary policy was still bound by the gold standard (on which more later). The job of the Bank was to protect the value of sterling relative to gold by raising interest rates to attract inflows when the value looked to be sagging and cutting them when it rose. Senior British officials thought of this trinity of free trade, the gold standard and balanced budgets as creating a 'knave-proof' economic constitution for the nation. A government which could not run deficits nor fiddle with trading arrangements nor seek to manipulate interest rates had few of the tools of economic management that are nowadays taken for granted by policymakers, but was, it was hoped, a government that could not muck up too badly. It would be the Great War which destroyed the knave-proof system and the forlorn task of the 1920s to attempt to put it together again.

8

Smashed. Britain's Economy and the Great War

Historians are wont to debate periodisation. Eric Hobsbawm's 'short twentieth century' lasted from 1914 to 1991, while others date the start of the contemporary era to as early as the 1870s or as late as 1944. Others of course prefer to stick to literal interpretations; there is a vivid simplicity after all in a twentieth century that runs from 1901 to 2000. However one cuts it, though, the First World War was a decisive break in British history in general and in its economic history in particular. The British economy of the 1920s was almost as distinct from the economy of the 1900s as the post-industrial revolution economy was from its predecessor.

The war was unlike anything else the British state, or the British economy, had faced, and economic strategy, like grand strategy in general, evolved as the war progressed. There was a consensus among most of the Liberal ministers, at least initially, that the war was best managed in a way which interfered as little as possible with the rest of the economy, and that the whole affair would not last long. The business world was inclined to agree, the journal of the London Chamber of Commerce hopefully noting that 'the majority of our trade routes – with the exception perhaps of the North Sea – are open and it may not be unreasonable to hope that very shortly trade with markets outside of Europe will be flowing in normal channels'.

Neither view – that the war would be over relatively quickly or that running the economy as normal was the best aid to victory – was as odd as it looks in retrospect. The European great-power wars of the latter half of the nineteenth century had been rapid affairs. France had defeated Austria in a matter of weeks in 1859, the Six Week War of 1866 between Prussia and Austria had that name for a reason, and the conventional stage of the Franco-Prussian War of 1870–71 had lasted only months. Britain had remained aloof from European conflict since the Crimean War of the 1850s but it had long experience to draw on and the lesson of that experience, according to many policy-makers, was that Britain's strength lay in its naval power and its economic and industrial clout. Britain had in 1914 a world-leading economy and the globe's strongest fleet, but a relatively weak army. The strategy expected by many politicians was the strategy that had seemed to work in the long wars against Napoleon a century earlier: for Britain to support its allies on the continent financially and economically whilst enforcing a naval blockade of its opponents, contributing ground forces only when absolutely necessary. If this was how the war was to be fought by Britain then preserving as much of its existing economy as possible would indeed prove useful.

The Army, though, had other ideas; staff talks with the French before the war had led to a commitment to supply an expeditionary force to guard the French left flank. And once battle was joined in France the British found themselves increasingly drawn in. Lord Kitchener, brought into the

Cabinet as Secretary for War at the beginning of the conflict, rapidly oversaw an increase in the size of the armed forces to around 2 million men by January 1915. A six-division-strong British Expeditionary Force (BEF) was sent to France on the outbreak of the war; by 1918 70 divisions were in the field – an unprecedented expansion in the size of the armed forces.

In August 1915, after a year of conflict, Britain finally had to face up to the choice of what kind of war it was due to fight. Kitchener was then pushing his 70 division plan and was opposed by the Treasury and Trade, who argued that such a large army would draw too many men out of industry, impacting both production and Britain's ability to financially support its allies. Kitchener won and the course to conscription and a very different kind of war was set. The war was, in a term popularised by the German General Erich Ludendorff, a total one, requiring not just the mobilisation of a country's armed forces and people, but the complete commitment of its economic, industrial and financial resources to the quest for victory. In the long run, industrial and economic factors proved crucial to the war's course.

Britain's generals were not the donkeys of legend unimaginatively sending their men in to die in ill-thought-out attacks, but soldiers faced with a new situation: an enemy of roughly equal strength, equipped with modern weapons and, as the trench lines stretched from the coast to Switzerland, with no obvious flanks to turn. Over the course of the war the Army's tactics evolved along what some have termed a learning curve. By 1918 the allies had a better grasp of the nature of modern warfare, which itself had moved rapidly. The BEF had gone to France in 1914 with mounted cavalry regiments to handle its reconnaissance. By 1918 it was equipped with tanks and backed by aircraft. But the decisive factors by the end of the war were not events on the battlefield. It was the weight of allied materiel on the Western Front, together with a collapse of the German economy under blockade, that forced Germany to surrender.

Slowly at first, but then faster, British policy-makers accepted the total nature of the conflict, and the idea of 'business as usual' went out of the window. Not only did the state spend more, but its powers expanded and it took more control, both directly and indirectly, over vast areas of the economy. A state which had been experimentally introducing limited social insurance in 1911 found itself conscripting and directing labour by 1916. All of which would prove too much for many of the original Liberal members of the Cabinet.

One of the war's earliest casualties was the doctrine of Treasury control of expenditure. In the first months there was no co-ordination at all between naval and army spending plans, resulting in the two services pushing up munitions prices even faster as they bid against each other to secure supplies from limited capacity. Both wanted shells and they wanted them quickly so they simply placed enormous orders with a domestic armaments industry unable to keep up. The Treasury initially proposed a joint standing committee with representatives from all the armed services but the War Office simply declined to take part. Once Lloyd George moved on from the Treasury to become Minister of Munitions he was replaced by a relative political lightweight in the form of Reginald McKenna, further undermining the department's clout. On Lloyd George's assumption of the post of Prime Minister the Treasury received a minister with real heft in the form of Conservative leader Andrew Bonar Law, but one for whom controlling expenditure in wartime was an extremely low priority.

The demand for arms and munitions on the Western Front in particular was exceptional. Britain produced 120,000 rifles in 1914 but manufactured 1.2 million in 1917. Machine gun production rose from 300 to 80,000 over the same period. But from 1915 on, the nature of trench warfare meant it was artillery that came to dominate the battlefield and industrial production. The country's existing armaments industry had pumped out half a million shells in 1914 but by 1917 output was almost 90 million. To achieve all this the pre-war arms companies such as Vickers and Armstrong ramped up production while civilian factories found themselves repurposed. The Lincoln-based tractor manufacturer William Foster and Co., for example, produced the world's first tanks in 1917.

It was a supposed shortage of shells which led to the war's first political crisis and a reshuffle which saw Lloyd George moved to run munitions production and the Conservatives brought into government. Eighteen months later, Asquith found himself ousted as Prime Minister and Lloyd George installed in his place, although reliant on the backing of the Tories.

The calls made on the public finances by Prime Minister Lloyd George would have been unimaginable to the pre-war Chancellor Lloyd George. In 1913/14, total government expenditure (even after the dreadnought arms race and the expansion of social insurance which had caused such a fiscal stink) stood at £197 million. Taxes, which he had had to fight so hard to increase, were bringing in £198 million. By 1917/18 spending had risen to £2,696 million, more than 13 times the pre-war level. Taxes had also soared, increasing by three times to £707 million. That, though, still left a gap of around £2 billion – some 47 per cent of total national income – in that financial year alone.

The so-called McKenna doctrine, actually drawn up by Lloyd George, argued that Britain should seek to raise taxes by enough to pay for post-war spending and to cover the interest bills on any borrowing taken out by the end of the war; everything else could be borrowed. While some in Treasury argued for more expansive tax increases, that was seen as politically impossible. While income taxes and excise duties did rise, around one quarter of the increased tax burden took the form of an excess profits tax first introduced in 1915 and charged on firms involved in war work. By 1917 firms were charged an 80 per cent rate on any profit beyond an amount 1.2 times their pre-war profit level. Again, this kind of tax rate would have been unthinkable pre-war. But even with such hefty tax rises the McKenna principles failed to be carried out in full, and debt service costs would be a major problem of the 1920s.

Heavy government borrowing and the demand placed on the economy from hugely increased government spending saw the general price level double over the course of the war. The price of a pint of beer rose from threepence in 1914 to sixpence by 1918, while the price of a rail ticket from London to Brighton more than trebled. This, though, was quietly welcomed by policy-makers as a way of holding back consumption. The essential economic challenge for Britain's war leaders was to direct as much of national output towards war-fighting as possible and that meant suppressing demand for consumer goods. Britain needed more guns and less butter. Tax rises were one way of pushing down consumer spending but a politically fraught tool to use; inflation did the job just as well. Despite national income per head growing by 10 per cent over the four years of the conflict, the volume of consumer spending fell by around a quarter.

Britain's deficit levels were not radically dissimilar from those of Germany over the course of the war; neither country could raise the taxes to meet their war bills. But Britain, unlike its opponent, generally managed to fill the gap between spending and taxes with borrowing rather than relying on money printing.

The war opened with a financial crisis that was amongst the most severe that modern capitalism has ever faced, and yet tends to get buried under everything else that was happening at the time. Stock markets had taken the assassination of Franz Ferdinand in Sarajevo in their stride with barely a wobble; the markets had seen plenty of Balkan crises over the past few years and did not expect this one to be any different. But the Austrian ultimatum to Serbia four weeks later got their attention. In the last week of July 1914 there was an international scramble for liquid assets, a dumping of stocks and a calling in of loans. London, as the leading financial centre, was particularly exposed. So much of the business of London brokers and banks was overseas that it was entirely unclear who would be able to call in what if war did occur and who would be left insolvent. The great merchant banks of the day, firms such as Barings, Kleinworts and Grenfell, had extended millions of pounds' worth of loans to German clients. The discount houses that financed international trade had accumulated claims on the German manufacturers whose products had caused such outrage by filling British stores before the war. In such circumstances the rational thing to do was to cut back on any risky holdings and retreat to the safety of assets such as gold. Of course the rush of everyone to sell the same kind of thing whacked the price of risky assets even harder and put a greater premium on anything seen as safe. These were the dynamics that played out in the subprime crisis of 2007/08 but compacted into a couple of weeks. By the end of July there were queues outside the Bank of England as depositors rushed to transform their cash into gold. The crowds soon overflowed from the Bank's courtyard and out onto Cheapside. To try to stem the flow the Bank began hiking interest rates to encourage depositors to keep their gold in its vaults. After each hike the news was conveyed to the crowd by messengers. When interest rates hit 4 per cent the *Daily Mirror* reported that 'hired runners on the outskirts of the crowd darted away shouting "Four" at the top of their voices as if they had gone quite mad'. Rates rose from 3 per cent to 10 per cent in a matter of days.

The crisis was dealt with quickly, with a young Maynard Keynes acting as an unofficial advisor to the Chancellor throughout. The stock market was closed from the beginning of the war until January 1915. An extended bank holiday in the first days of August, as Britain declared war, allowed the Treasury the time to take action to stem a developing run. One bank boss complained it involved a lot of 'bank' and not much 'holiday' for him. A three-pronged strategy saw the Bank Act (which forced the Bank of England to honour a pledge to hand over gold in return for notes) suspended and new paper notes (called Bradburys after the Treasury permanent secretary whose signature they carried) issued to stop the outflow of gold from the Bank. The authorities also stepped into the market and pledged to buy up pre-war bills at decent prices to restore some calm to the money markets. Meanwhile a moratorium was put in place suspending payments on many commercial contracts until market conditions calmed. In September public money was used to recapitalise some smaller banks in danger of failure. Taken together this was robust intervention in financial markets to restore a sense of orderliness.

The City was back on its feet by September 1914 and, the government hoped, ready to begin doing its national duty in financing the war effort. Despite all the talk of national duty and patriotism, though, investors were still offered a very decent return on their war bonds. The first issue was priced to give a yield of 4.1 per cent, well above the 2.5 per cent available on existing government debt. Crucially for the 1920s it was also structured very differently. The usual Victorian, and indeed pre-Victorian, form of government borrowing had been through consols. Consols had no fixed redemption date but could be redeemed by the government in certain circumstances; the war loans by contrast mainly took the form of ten-year bonds. That is to say, the government agreed to pay the annual coupon (so called as it used to be a literal coupon that was cut off the side of the certificate and redeemed each year) each year for a decade and then to repay the capital amount. A holder of a £100 War Bond issued in 1914 could expect £4 2s each year until 1924 and then their £100 back, whereas the holder of a £100 consol would simply expect £2 10s a year for as long as they lived.

Recent work by investigative financial historians has demonstrated that war financing was not as smooth as once thought. The first bond issue received far less demand than hoped for and the Bank of England's ledgers reveal it engaged in a cover-up to hide this information from the markets and general public.

The enormous volume of government issuance over the course of the war was funded by continually offering chunky interest rates to entice savers to part with their cash (over 5 per cent by 1917) and increasingly by restricting other financial activity. By January 1915 private companies were not allowed to raise capital without ministers' permission and the general public were banned from buying most new stock-market issues. The Treasury essentially funded itself in part by giving savers no other options.

The real constraint from 1914 to 1918 on British armaments production was not the ability of government to finance it but the supply capacity of private industry to deliver the goods. The shipbuilding industry struggled to meet both rising demand for new ships and the need to replace sunk merchant vessels, while the metals industries saw an exponential increase in demand. Chemicals, necessary for explosives, were in acute shortage due to a pre-war reliance on German imports.

The core problem, though, was one of labour. The early surge in Army enlistments led to the loss of around 25 per cent of the industrial and mining workforce by 1915, a figure that rose to 45 per cent by 1918 after conscription was introduced. Already by 1915 the War Office was forced to release skilled workers from their service and men in essential industries were issued with special badges to wear to save them from the social stigma of being seen as military shirkers. Engineering workers, coal miners and locomotive drivers were among the first taken out of uniform. Some 2.5 million new workers moved into industry over the course of the war, around one third of them women, but mostly men from non-industrial occupations. This proved to be a bone of contention for the union movement until the negotiation of the Treasury Agreement, which saw union leaders agreeing to suspend strikes for the duration of the conflict in return for heavier taxes on producers to prevent profiteering.

Lloyd George's new Ministry of Munitions was packed full of experienced businesspeople who took a hand in reordering production and imposing systems of government control. Typical of them was William Weir: a Glasgow pump manufacturer before the war, he found himself appointed to the new post of Director of Munitions (Scotland) in 1915. Although the job was officially unpaid, he did receive a knighthood later that year and a peerage before the end of the war. Some of the new commercial recruits to government, such as arms manufacturer Percy Girouard, lasted only a few weeks or months before deciding they could not work for a politician; others took to the task of organising production at a national level. The state began to build its own factories in 1915 to supplement those of private industry. Control was taken of the railways, shipping and collieries in 1916. The output of whole industries, particularly in chemicals, was requisitioned by the state. Food supply too gradually came under state control, although rationing was not introduced until 1918. The Ministry of Food was responsible for about 85 per cent of purchasing by 1918. If Treasury financial control was an early casualty of the war, the doctrine of laissez-faire did not last much longer. Pubs too felt the long arm of the growing state with opening hours restricted to help boost munitions output by ensuring that the workers were not too tipsy when their shifts began. Although why anyone ever wanted to have a pint or two before handling explosives is an unanswered question.

By 1918 Britain was not quite a command economy but it was getting there. Output and direction, and even where people worked, were controlled to a greater or lesser extent from Whitehall. Private enterprise found itself even taking direct orders from the ministries or at least being firmly nudged in one direction or another. As previous sacred cow after sacred cow was slain, free trade was not spared. The McKenna Duties of 1915 imposed tariffs on luxury imports such as cars and watches to dampen down imports and clamp down on consumer spending. A small measure perhaps but a significant one – most significant, as this breach of seven decades of British trade policy was passed with barely a muttering of dissent.

The war not only rewrote the economic borders of the state and market domestically, it also transformed Britain's place in the global economy. The headline figures, surprisingly enough, do not give the impression that a great deal was going on, but a closer look at the detail tells a more accurate story. The trade balance in goods deteriorated sharply over the course of the war. The demand from the British government sucked up capacity at manufacturers that might otherwise have been used to produce exports, while imports rose sharply, especially from 1916 onwards. The modest trade deficit of £170 million in 1914 hit a record high of £784 million by 1918. But Britain's traditional strength in 'invisible exports' – insurance, shipping and the like – continued to perform well. The surplus there rose from £395 million in 1914 to £5,802 million by 1918, offsetting some of the goods balance. Indeed until 1917 the booming invisibles helped keep the current account in rough balance despite surging imports.

The real action, though, was happening on the capital side of the balance of payments, the new factor at play being that Britain was advancing huge loans and subsidies to its continental allies. The problem, as it would be again in the Second World War, was dollars. Britain and its allies needed them to finance purchases in the United States, and Britain, as the allied nation with the strongest credit rating, took over all dollar financing for both France and Russia. Dollar-based securities held by British residents, such as shares in American companies, were requisitioned by the government and either sold to raise cash or used as collateral for loans. Some gold was shipped across the Atlantic to raise more. Most of the dollar needs, however, were met through the British government's agent in New York, J. P. Morgan raising large dollar-based loans for the government. In 1916 Keynes warned the government that of the £5 million that was required daily to finance the war, £2 million had to be dollars and most of that was borrowed. If the US government ever moved to restrict British borrowing on its money markets, the allied war effort would be fatally undermined. In November 1916 exactly that happened, when the US Federal Reserve warned US investors to be careful of further exposure to the already potentially overstretched UK government. By March 1917, the UK's stock of dollars was down to around one month's worth of US purchases. Only US entry into the war in April 1917 prevented an acute crisis, as the US then took over dollar financing for the allied nations. It was, though, a close-run thing. Britain's overall financial standing in the world was fundamentally changed by its new indebtedness in America and the running down of pre-war overseas assets to finance its campaigns. Decades of Victorian overseas accumulation were substantially reversed over the course of just four years. Just like the debts taken on domestically, this would have large and negative consequences throughout the 1920s.

The economic costs incurred in victory were high – perhaps around 15 per cent of national wealth was lost in four years according to one modern estimate. But victory was finally achieved and one reason for that success was the structure of Britain's pre-war economy. While the overall size of Britain's and Germany's economies were roughly similar going into the war, Britain had a smaller population and a higher GDP per head. This turned out to be a significant advantage. Higher income per head allowed for each British person to in essence sacrifice more of their income towards the war effort than was the case in Germany. The reallocation of resources towards the needs of total war significantly reduced the amount of effort placed into meeting the wants of consumers. But for Britain, with national income per head almost 70 per cent higher than in Germany, even a large percentage drop in consumption would not force people back to subsistence living. Britain, as a whole, found it easier to shift economic production towards the war effort. Equally, Britain's dependence on food imports and lack of a large agricultural sector was advantageous. The mobilisation of large armies pulled men away from industry, but policy-makers, business leaders and trade unions found a way to manage that shift and still increase production.

Germany's larger farming sector meant that mass mobilisation drew workers away from food production and risked serious shortages. The collapse of German food production, with imports hampered by a British blockade, would have serious consequences for its war effort.

For all the talk of the need for national food security in a war, the lesson of the Great War was the opposite. Britain could feed itself through importing foods from neutral countries and devote more of its economic resources towards munitions production, while Germany struggled to keep up. Beef still came from the River Plate and bacon from Denmark throughout the conflict. Of course, that ability to import relied on the Royal Navy holding up the sea lanes. Germany's move to unrestricted submarine warfare looked at times to come close to damaging that ability, but Britain's adoption of the convoy system eventually drove losses down to acceptable levels. The ultimate result of Germany's submarine tactics was not British exit from the war but America's entry. One irony of the naval campaign is that the dreadnoughts that had so dominated pre-war planning and budgetary politics mostly stayed in port. After the indecisive battle of Jutland the German High Seas Fleet remained in harbour and the real work of the naval campaigns was done not by hugely expensive battleships but by cheaper cruisers, commerce raiders and submarines.

Britain emerged from the Great War militarily and politically victorious. The taking of 'mandates' to run ex-German colonies in Africa and Ottoman provinces in the Middle East left its Empire larger than ever. Britain was one of the Big Three at the Paris peace conference and a major player on the global scene. Yet its economy was in a bad place. Its international position as a creditor nation had been transformed. Decades of Victorian fiscal conservatism had reduced government debt to GDP to about 25 per cent by 1913 but in 1919 it was back up to 135 per cent. British industries had been twisted out of shape by the war with a renewed emphasis on heavy manufacturing and armaments for which there was considerably less demand in the post-war world. Export markets had been lost to competitors as British firms had withdrawn to focus on meeting government demand. But, for a generation of economic policy-makers, the larger concern was that the rules of the 'knave-proof' system had been torn asunder. The state had intervened left, right and centre across the economy, it was indeed running entire industries. The notion of a balanced budget had vanished. Even the gold standard had been suspended. The Rubicon had been crossed on free trade and laissez-faire looked to be dead. What is more, the small increases in social spending contentiously fought through by the Liberals before the war paled in comparison to Lloyd George's post-war promises to the veterans of the Western Front of a land fit for heroes.

The 1920s, and much of the 1930s, would be a difficult time for the British economy. Much of that was the direct result of both the costs incurred directly during the war and the forlorn attempts of post-war policy-makers to put the pieces of the pre-war Humpty Dumpty back together again. Britain's economic model was transformed by the Great War; the state took a large step forward and never went all the way back. But it took decades for the policy elite to accept this. That made for turbulent politics and grim economics in the inter-war period.

9

The Not So Roaring Twenties

Few things annoy economic historians of Britain as much as the phrase 'the roaring twenties'. Certainly, in the United States the 1920s were a time of post-war release and a stock market boom, a good decade followed by the misery of the Great Depression. But Britain's 1920s were rather different. In terms of political economy, the decade was more akin to the 1970s: marked by a soggy economy and tumultuous and unstable politics.

The decade opened with a recession that would not be equalled until the COVID-19 crash of 2020. The economy slumped as the war ended, managed to stage a brief recovery measured in months rather than quarters and then fell again into a deep recession in 1920. The best modern estimates point to an economy which failed to return to 1913 levels of output until around 1925. GDP per head was below 1913 levels as late as 1927. A decade and a half of growth was lost to a combination of post-war adjustment, terrible macroeconomic policy choices and disease.

Modern estimates of the post-war performance of the economy are complicated by the changing shape of the United

Kingdom itself. The Irish War of Independence, which resulted in a British withdrawal from most of the island of Ireland by the early 1920s, altered the composition of the United Kingdom that had been created by the Act of Union with Ireland. While there is a strong tendency to emphasise the continuity of British history, at least compared to its European neighbours, in terms of constitutional evolution rather than revolution, it should not be forgotten that a large chunk of the supposedly stable United Kingdom fought and won a war of independence in the aftermath of the Great War. But although Irish independence was a major political event, it mattered less economically. Irish GDP per head at the time of the Anglo-Irish Treaty was still materially below mainland levels and what little industry the island contained was concentrated in the north.

The immediate problem in 1919 was the immediate problem usually faced after a major war: demobilisation. Just as at the end of the Napoleonic Wars, a century before, the sudden cessation of hostilities resulted in a slump. This slump, though, was accompanied by a pandemic.

The Spanish Flu of 1918 to 1919 killed around 50 million people globally and more than 200,000 in Britain. Unlike most pandemics the deaths were highly concentrated among prime working-age people in their twenties to fifties. The outbreak seemed, until 2020 revived interest in pandemics, to be for ever in the historical shadows cast by the First World War and the general turmoil of the collapse of the Russian, Austro-Hungarian, Ottoman and German empires. But timing alone is not the only reason for its absence from many histories. Most contemporary political memoirs of the time also fail to dwell on it – fail in a way one cannot imagine the memoirs of 2020's political leaders will fail to engage with COVID-19. That reflects the lack of tools that policy-makers had at their disposal in 1918 and 1919; there were no effective treatments available and the need to win the war would have ruled out any form of social distancing, even if the science had suggested it would be useful. Such social distancing as the pandemic did see came mainly post-war and was limited in scope. The disease spread like wildfire in crowded troop transports and munitions factories. The very notion that the state was somehow responsible for managing a medical emergency would have seemed questionable to contemporaries. Health spending in 1920 was less than 3 per cent of all public sector expenditure, which gives some indication of the state's relative priorities. There were no enforced shutdowns of the British economy in 1919 or 1920 although some theatres and cinemas did close on a voluntary basis.

Around one in five British workers experienced bouts of sickness in 1919 or 1920, which, alongside the high death toll, further hampered economic performance. Still, it is hard to separate out the direct impact of the pandemic from the wider post-war fallout. A government which had been spending around £1.8 billion on goods and services in 1918 was spending less than £500 million by 1920, a drastic fall in any circumstances. Just as the fiscal squeeze took hold, though, the export-dependent British economy found itself afloat in more perilous economic seas. The option of simply picking back up from where things had been left in July 1914 was not available. Export markets had been lost during the war and financial leadership had crossed the Atlantic. The old industrial staples of the regions and the service-based economy of London both found themselves adjusting to new, and unpleasant, circumstances. Few parts of the economy were functioning well enough to absorb a coming rush of labour.

As the size of the armed forces was reduced from almost four and a half million in 1918 to under 800,000 by 1920, unemployment rose sharply. By 1921 2.2 million were out of work, an unemployment rate of over 11 per cent – the highest in decades and some three to four times the level in the years leading up to the war. Lloyd George's 'land fit for heroes' did not last long. Unemployment would still be above 7 per cent as late as 1929, at the time of the Wall Street crash. The British economy that entered the global depression of the 1930s was one that had still not fully recovered from the disruption of 1914–1918.

It is hard to view the economic history of Britain's 1920s as anything other than a series of colossal policy failures. The reasons for those failures may be understandable but the results were the same.

Both major tools of macroeconomic policy – fiscal policy and monetary policy – played a disastrous part in the grim decade that played out, and both were driven by political reasoning. While most of Britain's peers joined it in an immediate post-war slump, few managed to prolong the pain all the way until 1929.

The lost markets and disjointed economy that resulted from the Great War would always have made for a grim post-war adjustment, but the problems were compounded by another consequence of the war: Britain's high level of debt. Or rather, by the way the government sought to manage it.

By comparison with the 210 per cent of GDP that debt had stood at after the battle of Waterloo in 1815, the circa 140 per cent of GDP in 1918 seems on the face of it manageable. But the comparison is misleading. Firstly because the Britain of 1815 was a country in the process of experiencing economic take-off. While Victorian fiscal prudence had helped slowly pay the debt down, the real work of reducing the debt to GDP ratio had been done by rapid economic growth. Secondly, the nature of the debt was rather different. The Napoleonic Wars had been funded, as we have seen, by extremely long-term securities with generally low interest rates; the debt incurred in 1914 to 1918 was relatively short term and at a higher rate of interest. All of those ten-year bonds issued while the fighting was continuing would have to be either paid off or, more likely, refinanced (that is to say, a new loan taken out to pay off the old one) in the mid-1920s.

The sudden jump in interest costs threw pre-war financial planning out of the window. Whereas debt interest payments had amounted to around £40 million a year in the decade before the Great War, they came to closer to £350 million a year in the decade afterwards. The tax system of 1920 was almost unrecognisable from that of 1913: a much heavier burden on the economy than that proposed by Lloyd George in his People's Budget. But whereas the mere proposal of that budget had provoked a constitutional crisis, the tax rises of the war had been mostly waved through. As a share of national income, the tax take had risen from under 10 per cent in 1913 to over 20 per cent by 1920 – still very low by modern standards but without precedent in British history until that point. Just over a million households paid income tax in 1913 compared to approaching four million in 1920, and the highest marginal rate had soared from 8.3 per cent to 52.5 per cent.

Although the end of the direct costs of fighting the war allowed state spending to fall drastically, the need to service the debts taken on over the course of the conflict kept it much higher, as a share of GDP, than in the Edwardian era. Public spending amounted to about 20 per cent of GDP in 1920, compared to 12 per cent in 1913. But most of those eight additional percentage points of expenditure took the form of additional debt interest costs. In effect, the taxpayer of 1920 was being asked to find around twice as much as the taxpayer of 1913, and the money was being used to pay for war debts rather than enhanced government services. Even at the best of times, taxpayers were unlikely to be especially pleased with these circumstances and the 1920s were not the best of times.

The result was a great deal of anger from the kind of middle-class workers who increasingly found themselves liable for income tax bills, which had previously been confined to higher earners, without seeing many of the benefits. Not only did many in the middle classes feel themselves hammered by higher taxation, they also fretted at the supposed power of the more unionised and increasingly demanding working class. The early 1920s saw the first major wave of what became a regular feature of modern British politics: a newspaper-led campaign against government waste. While Lloyd George continued to lead a 'coalition government' (in reality an almost entirely Conservative government headed by a former Liberal), the Conservative newspaperman Lord Rothermere threw the backing of both the *Daily Mail* and the *Daily Mirror* behind a new party, the catchily titled Anti-Waste League.

The League put the government under pressure, performing well in by-elections and attracting the support of many former Conservative (and indeed Liberal) voters. Lloyd George, the former radical proposer of the People's Budget, found himself asking Sir Eric Geddes, a Tory businessman, to chair a committee looking for public sector savings to appease the middle-class revolt. The Geddes Committee, as the Committee on National Expenditure quickly became known, reported back to the Cabinet in January 1922 that it had identified around £85 million of potential spending cuts of which the government carried out over £50 million in the following financial year. Large cuts in defence spending were coupled with a sharp squeeze on the building of social housing and education spending. The cuts became known as the Geddes Axe. In other words, the price of appeasing the middle-class ratepayers who made up the core of the government's political coalition was a contractionary tightening in fiscal policy which sucked more demand out of an already demand-deficient economy.

One reason for that shortage of demand, even before the public sector squeeze, was the changing nature of the international economy. As we have seen, late Victorian and Edwardian Britain was a uniquely open trading economy. But the Great War ended the first modern era of globalisation. Cross-border trade fell away as nations turned inward, and Britain never regained many of the export markets taken by American and Japanese firms during the war. Before the war Blackburn had been a booming cotton town, with most of its produce going to India. Exports had ceased during the war to free up shipping capacity and, in the interim, India had developed its own domestic supplies. Simply carrying on in 1919 as if it were still 1914 was not an option; around a third of the mills had closed by 1923 and half by 1930. Exports as a whole were running at around three quarters of their pre-war levels throughout the 1920s.

The supply side of the economy too was changing. The growth of trade unions and trade union power that had been occurring in the two decades before 1914 was accelerated by the conflict. Whereas 20 per cent of those in employment had been trade union members before 1914, it was above 30 per cent throughout the 1920s. A post-war wave of strikes to maintain wage rates helped workers to protect their living standards but also clearly demonstrated that the ultra-flexible economy of the pre-war days was a thing of the past. Indeed, according to one modern school of thought it was increased trade union power and a less flexible labour market which pushed unemployment higher in the 1920s. By this way of thinking, the ability of trade unions to hold wages higher than they otherwise would have been meant that some people who would have been in work in, say, the early 1900s or 1890s (at much lower wages) found themselves unable to work as unions prevented such jobs being created. Coal mining, as was to be the case throughout much of the twentieth century, was a particular flashpoint for poor industrial relations. Wages rose by around 50 per cent over the course of the war and the unions resisted any cuts in 1919. Even if returning servicemen were prepared to work for the old going rate of six shillings a day, such jobs were no longer available. No doubt the less flexible labour market of the 1920s did contribute to higher unemployment but it is hard to conclude that anything other than a major shortage of demand was the primary cause.

If 1920s British fiscal policy was bad, it nevertheless looks positively excellent compared to the monetary policy that accompanied it. The key macroeconomic policy decision of the 1920s was actually taken in 1919: Britain, it was decided, would return to the gold standard.

Understanding what the gold standard was, and why it was a reasonably workable system for monetary policy in the decades before 1914 but a calamitous one in the 1920s, means delving a little into international macroeconomics and, in particular, understanding the so-called trilemma. The trilemma, or impossible trinity, was not to be formally theorised by economists until the 1960s but it is a useful framework for understanding monetary policy regimes across history. Simply put it is a statement of fact: an economy can only ever have two out of the following three features: a fixed exchange rate, an open capital market and domestic control of interest rates. Implicitly or explicitly (and since the 1970s such choices have usually been explicit) policy-makers have to choose one of these three economic attributes to forgo. If for example a country (such as Britain today) wants to have an open capital market (meaning money can freely flow into or out of the country) and domestic control of interest rates (so that the Bank of England can lower or raise them in response to domestic economic conditions), then the country must accept that the value of its currency, relative to its peers, will fluctuate on a daily basis. If the Bank perceives that the economy is doing well and increases interest rates then sterling will become more attractive to foreigners (as the rate of interest available on sterling assets increases), who will want to buy some more of it, pushing up its price. Sterling will strengthen, to the delight of British tourists looking to buy euros and dollars who will experience a cheaper holiday, and to the grimaces of manufacturers who will find their goods cost more on international markets. Conversely if the Bank cuts rates, the lower returns available on sterling could cause money to leave the UK seeking a better rate of return elsewhere and pushing down the value of the pound. In either case, domestic control of interest rates coupled with an open capital market means that a fixed exchange rate is impossible to maintain.

But Britain has not always chosen to be at this point of the impossible trinity. From the end of the Second World War until the 1970s, for example, Britain chose to have fixed exchange rates and domestic control of interest rates whilst giving up on open capital markets. Money could only enter or leave the economy subject to government's dictate, with even tourists being limited in how much cash they could take abroad with them. A British saver could, in general, invest only in British concerns, and firms needed government permission to buy assets overseas, just as foreigners needed to seek official permission to move money into Britain. In theory at least, interest rates could be set at whatever level the Bank of England desired even whilst maintaining the pound–dollar or pound–franc exchange rates at their pegged and predetermined levels. In reality, of course, money finds a way to flow, and the system of pegged exchange rates would come with its own dramas, but that is a post-Second World War rather than a post-First World War story.

The gold standard represents the third potential choice from the trilemma: enjoying a fixed exchange rate and an open capital market but giving up control over interest rates. Prior to 1914 the value of sterling was pegged to the price of gold, as were most major world currencies, at least from the 1870s onwards. Since each currency was pegged to the value of gold at a set rate, currencies were effectively pegged to each other, so the sterling–dollar exchange rate, for example, was $4.86 to the pound. The job of the Bank of England was, when it came to monetary policy, simply to set interest rates to maintain that value. Britain's capital markets were not just open but extraordinarily open – as we have seen. British investors gladly funded infrastructure projects across the globe and received a steady stream of payments in return.

Free trade, the gold standard and the balanced budget were the building blocks of the pre-war knave-proof system. Politicians could not attempt to game the economy for political advantage but nor could they seek to manage it. That system worked well enough in a generally benign international economic environment, especially one Britain sat at the centre of, but was a recipe for disaster in the more challenging circumstances of the 1920s.

In theory – a theory dating back to at least the 1700s – the gold standard was supposed to be a self-correcting mechanism for running the global economy and maintaining some sort of balance. If a country were running a trade deficit (buying more from abroad than it sold overseas) then those imports would have to ultimately be paid for in gold and thus decrease its stocks of the precious metal. A lower balance of gold would decrease the amount of money in circulation, eventually pulling down prices until the country became competitive enough to sell goods overseas and eliminate its trade deficit. A country running a persistent surplus would accumulate gold until its price level rose enough to erode its competitive edge. The theory was elegant, but the reality rarely matched it. Especially in the 1920s. The theory for example assumed flexible prices that adjusted to maintain the balance of payments; but prices have a tendency to become sticky – especially the price of labour. Pushing down wages to restore competitiveness was, fairly obviously, much harder to do in the more unionised environment of the 1920s.

The gold standard had been suspended on the outbreak of war as hostilities caused international payment systems to break down. The Cunliffe Committee (early twentieth-century governments were very fond of committees), chaired by the then Governor of the Bank of England, had recommended in 1919 (with the one dissenting voice being Maynard Keynes) that the pre-war standard should be re-established as soon as possible. In the end it took until 1925.

The problem with the return to gold was twofold. Firstly, giving up control of interest rates – especially at a time when fiscal policy was unnecessarily tight – meant giving up the chance to stimulate growth and put un- and under-employed resources to work by loosening policy. Secondly, and more seriously, the very process of returning to gold meant actively tightening monetary policy. Returning to gold was bad enough but the problem was exacerbated by policy-makers' fixation on not only repegging sterling but repegging it at the pre-war rate. Across most of officialdom there was an inability – or at the very least an unwillingness – to recognise that Britain's place in the world, and the nature of its economy, had been fundamentally shifted by the events of 1914 to 1918.

The problem was divergent inflation. The overall level of prices had increased by 2.5 times between 1913 and 1920. This was a new phenomenon for Britain. The overall price level in 1913 was broadly similar to that found in the 1690s. For more than two hundred years there had been occasional bouts of inflation and frequent episodes of deflation but the broad picture was one of essentially unchanged prices overall (price rises in some goods having been offset by falls in others). Total war had changed that. In the United States, by contrast, inflation had also been unprecedentedly high but the price level had 'merely' doubled. The post-war recession there, often forgotten from the popular roaring twenties narrative, helped reduce the price level further. Whichever way one cut it, prices had risen considerably more in Britain, and so if the pre-war sterling–dollar exchange rate of $4.86 was to be returned to, then the price level in Britain would have to be pushed back down to restore competitiveness.

This is the context for the Geddes Axe. Reducing public spending not only helped appease revolting middle-class voters, it functioned as part of a package of policies designed to push down prices and wages across the economy to pave the way for a return to the pre-war gold standard. The costs were paid in high unemployment and real wages, which fell around 5 per cent in the first half of the 1920s.

Pushing down prices meant keeping interest rates high in the post-war period even as the economy struggled. Real interest rates (after accounting for inflation) averaged around 7 per cent per year in the 1920s, their highest sustained level until the 1970s and some three times as high as pre-1914. Such high borrowing costs might have helped drive down prices but also made the burden of the vast government debts that had to be refinanced in the decade materially higher. Indeed despite the taxpayer funding large primary surpluses (that is to say budget surpluses excluding interest costs), the overall level of debt to GDP actually rose from 140 per cent in 1920 to almost 170 per cent by 1929. The painful tax rises and spending cuts were simply outweighed by weak growth and high debt service costs.

The striking thing when looking back on the period is the broad political and economic consensus behind the return to gold. Churchill, Chancellor when the standard was finally restored, was not exaggerating too much when he claimed that 'no political party, no previous holder of the Office of Chancellor of the Exchequer has challenged, or so far as I am aware is now challenging, the principle of a reversion to the gold standard'. Keynes foresaw the disaster but also noted that Churchill 'was deafened by the clamorous voices of conventional finance; and, most of all, because he was gravely misled by his experts'.

Spending cuts and high interest rates helped to drive down the overall consumer price level by around a quarter between 1920 and 1925, but even that was not enough to restore competitiveness once $4.86 had been accepted. To this day economists disagree on quite how overvalued sterling was after the return to gold, although a figure in the region of 10 per cent seems about right. Overcostly sterling made already struggling British exporters less competitive in the latter half of the decade.

One consequence was the general strike of 1926. Coal had long been a British staple but, like many others, it was badly impacted by the war. Heavy domestic use had both depleted the richer seams (annual output per worker had fallen by a fifth compared to the pre-war norm) and resulted in lost export markets as foreign producers had stepped in to fill the gaps left by smaller British exports. Miners' pay had already fallen by around 40 per cent in the seven years before 1926, and an attempt to reduce it further – whilst lengthening hours – was met with a predictable response. Less predictable was the fact that the TUC, initially at least, backed the coal miners. On 4 May 1926 1.2 million striking miners were joined by 1.7 million workers in transport and heavy industry in an effort to force the pit owners and government to reverse course. The strike was generally peaceful – with only sporadic and limited examples of violence – but unsuccessful. By 12 May the TUC had called it off, although the miners, bitter at the rest of the labour movement's supposed betrayal, stayed out for another few months before poverty forced them back to work. The TUC's leadership, on the whole fairly moderate, were always nervous that prolonged conflict would embolden more radical unionists to take leadership positions and, after a high court ruling that the strike was 'political' rather than 'industrial' and so not covered by the provisions of the 1906 Trade Disputes Act, they increasingly feared the legal and financial consequences. Union laws were moderately tightened in 1927 – with sympathy strikes being banned – but the long-term impact on the labour movement was negligible. The weak jobs market of the inter-war period was a bigger problem for unions than any legislative change. Unions always struggle to hold on to members and push for higher wages when unemployment is high.

Still, even if the general strike was unsuccessful, it demonstrated the fundamental problem with the return to gold. The knave-proof system of a self-adjusting mechanism to manage the economy was reliant on a flexible and freely adjusting system of prices and wages which simply no longer existed. The working classes had grown not only in numbers but in industrial organisation too. Crucially, they now held more political power. The Representation of the People Act in 1918 had given all men aged 21 or over and all women aged 30 or over (the gender gap would not be equalised until 1928) the vote. In an era when unions were more common and working people had the vote, a system which ultimately relied on the ability to cut wages in a downturn would have a limited shelf life.

Like the Edwardian period before and the 1970s and the 2010s afterwards, the 1920s saw a troubled economy giving rise to volatile politics. General elections were held in 1918, 1922, 1923, 1924 and, after five years of the British people not being bothered for their opinion, in 1929. Lloyd George was eventually ditched by the Conservatives in late 1922; their new leader was first Andrew Bonar Law and then Stanley Baldwin, both former bosses in the iron and steel industry. This was a far cry from the old pre-war leadership of aristocrats and their hangers-on. The journey begun under Disraeli and Salisbury was completed in the 1920s with the party that had once been the political wing of the landed interest reinventing itself as the voice of the middle class, of property owners, and of a patriotic working class that wanted to 'get on' in life.

On a first glance the broad story of 1920s politics looks to be the decline of the Liberals and their supplanting by Labour. By the 1922 general election Labour had pole-vaulted the Liberals into second place and formed the official opposition. By the end of the decade the Liberals (who spent many of the intervening years split between factions led by Asquith and Lloyd George respectively, before reuniting after Asquith's death in 1928) had been firmly reduced to the status of third party. Keynes, an instinctive Liberal if ever there was one, pondered whether the function of the party was now to simply provide Labour governments with ideas and Conservative ones with ministers.

The expansion of the franchise and the realignment of politics around, broadly, working-class versus middle-class interests that occurred in the first decades of the twentieth century were always going to be tricky for the Liberals. The vicious infighting between the Lloyd George and Asquith factions hardly helped. But there is too much of a tendency among modern observers to look at the changing headline numbers, of seats and vote share, over the 1920s and assume that Labour's replacement of the Liberals as the major non-Tory party was a smooth process and somehow represented a different wing of a supposed 'Progressive Alliance' taking the lead. Certainly that was the tone adopted by Tony Blair seven decades later. The reality was more complicated – it was not simply a case of many former Liberal voters deciding to plump for Labour. Many former Liberals threatened by the rise of Labour actually began voting Conservative. Similarly, Labour was able to appeal to some working-class Conservative voters in a way the Liberals had never achieved. There was a great deal of churn over the decade as Labour won some seats directly off the Conservatives and some formerly Liberal seats elected Tories.

The messy election of 1923, in which the Conservatives won the most seats but were well short of a majority and had clearly 'lost', brought the first Labour government. Reliant on Liberal votes to pass legislation it lasted only nine months. Ramsay MacDonald, the illegitimate son of a farm labourer, may have spent much of his career in Labour politics but his instincts were more in keeping with the Edwardian New Liberalism of the pre-Great War period. Lacking a majority, his government achieved little on the economic front except a modest rise in unemployment benefits. If MacDonald was vaguely Asquithian in his inclinations, his Chancellor, Philip Snowden, was positively Gladstonian. A rigorous supporter of free trade and balanced budgets, he even managed to repli-cate the Grand Old Man of Victorian politics' dour sense of Christian morals. The inequities of capitalism horrified him, but so did the notion of an unbalanced budget. The party itself was becoming more radical and more explicitly socialist. The new party constitution of 1918, drawn up by the Fabian Webbs, contained the now-famous Clause IV – committing the party to the 'common ownership of the means of production, distribution and exchange'. MacDonald and Snowden lacked the majority to attempt much in the way of socialising the economy in 1924 – though even if such a power had been in their grasp it is hard to imagine either being especially keen on the notion.

The real story of the 1920s was not the rise of Labour or the decline of the Liberals but the domination of government by the Conservatives for most of the decade. After losing power in 1923, after fighting an election on the issue of protectionism, Stanley Baldwin was quick to realise something had to change. Although he once declared to a rally that 'I am not a clever man, I know nothing of political tactics,' Baldwin had an instinctive feel for what worked. He was quick to grasp the possibility of the radio for political communications and accepted that the British public were not yet ready to really reopen the question of free trade versus tariffs. Baldwin's 'New Conservativism' involved pitching his party as the only viable non-Labour government, to woo away concerned middle-class Liberals, whilst offering a positive programme of social reform, within reason, combined with a traditional, patriotic appeal to working-class voters in the spirit of Salisbury and Disraeli. The government of 1924 to 1929 is nowadays most associated with the return to gold and the General Strike, and yet it was energetic, for its time, in social reform. Neville Chamberlain, Joseph's son, served as Minister for Health (a much broader remit in those days, covering much of local government under the heading of 'public health'), overseeing a reform of the benefits system, an expansion of old age pensions and the building of social housing.

But for all Baldwin's political skill and Chamberlain's

reforming zeal, the 1929 general election would see the Conservatives booted out of office. It would also be the first general election campaign fought on the kind of macroeconomic issues that would dominate British politics for most of the twentieth century's remaining campaigns.

10

A Kind of Depression

The 1929 General Election was the first to be fought on universal suffrage. The addition of young women, aged 21–29, to the electoral roll led to contemporaries dubbing it the flapper election. For the first time Britain's politicians fought a truly democratic election and, for the first time macroeconomics dominated the campaign. Of course economic issues had mattered in elections before – but usually they had taken the form of questions about free trade versus tariffs as in 1923 or 1906, or the level of taxation as in 1910. In 1929 the core macro issues of unemployment and wider fiscal policy came to centre stage, a place they were to retain for much of the next ninety years.

Four years after the return to the gold standard, Britain faced a grim catalogue of economic woe: unemployment remained high and wage growth tepid, public debt was still rising and the traditional staple export industries of coal, metals and textiles remained in the doldrums. Lloyd George, once again leading a reunited Liberal Party, offered the boldest prospectus. Advised by Keynes, the Liberal manifesto claimed that 'We can conquer unemployment' and offered a bold and at the time novel case, that by borrowing to invest in public works programmes the country would not only gain new and useful infrastructure but would save money by comparison with continuing to pay the unemployed their dole. Such ideas were not especially welcome in the Treasury. Indeed, one civil servant scrawled the words 'extravagance', 'inflation' and 'bankruptcy' on the Treasury copy of the document in block capitals.

Baldwin responded in typically Baldwinian terms with the slogan 'Safety first' heading a campaign that warned against the dangers of Lloyd George's bold experimentation. For Baldwin, and many others at the time, the problems facing the British were not 'macroeconomic issues' such as an absence of demand that could be alleviated by government spending, but more microeconomic troubles – for him the core problem was that British industry was not competitive internationally, and prosperity would not return until that was resolved. Uninspiring as 'Safety first' might sound as a rallying call and, despite the mixed record of the last five years in government, the Conservatives secured some 38 per cent of the popular vote against just 23 per cent for Lloyd George's Liberals. The quirks of the first-past-the-post system gave Labour, who had sneaked through the middle with a rather insipid manifesto, 287 seats to the Tories' 260 despite them receiving the backing of just 37 per cent of the electorate. MacDonald and Snowden were back in power, although once again heading up a minority government.

Snowden, good Gladstonian that he was, would of course never support an unbalanced budget. The Labour manifesto pledged action on unemployment but offered little in the way of detail. More precise was a pledge to rebalance taxation away from the poor and towards the rich as well as a promise to nationalise the troubled coal mining industry. Oswald Mosley, an ex-Tory turned independent turned Labour MP, was one prominent voice calling for deficit spending on public works to revive the economy – but then for Mosley doing something bold often seemed a worthwhile end in and of itself.

If the new administration's ambitions were limited, even so it got little time to act on them. The troubled economic backdrop which had brought Labour to power once again was about to get an awful lot worse. Five months after MacDonald and Snowden re-entered Downing Street, the Wall Street Crash of October 1929 brought about what we now typically call the Great Depression but which British observers at the time dubbed simply 'the slump'.

Slump is, to be fair, probably a better description of Britain's economic woes in the 1930s than 'depression'. Much as with the notion of a 'roaring twenties', the popular image is more coloured by the American than the British experience. Peak to trough, while the United States economy contracted by around a quarter in the early 1930s, Britain's fell by more like 7 per cent. A major event in any case, but a world away from the pain experienced across the Atlantic.

The crash wiped out many a fortune, whacked business confidence and caused both consumer spending and business investment to nosedive. It was only after 1929 that the biggest problem with the reconstructed international gold standard came to light. The fixing of international exchange rates, the inability of monetary policy to respond to shocks and the open capital markets across the globe together acted as a shock transmitter. Overtly tight monetary policy in the United States, now the centre of the global financial system, had to be matched by other central banks to maintain their gold pegs. Interest rates rose even as the economy began to contract.

A wave of bank failures in America and central Europe, added to the tight monetary conditions, caused the global supply of money to shrink. Trade tensions became more acute as the process of deglobalisation which had begun after the First World War accelerated. Countries increasingly turned their backs on global markets in an effort to look after their own people. For an open, exporting economy such as Britain this was a disaster. Exports fell by around 50 per cent in the two years to 1931 with a devastating impact on the still employment-intensive sectors that produced them. Whereas British shipbuilders had laid down work on some 362,000 tonnes of new ships in the first quarter of 1929, in the first quarter of 1931 the figure was just 33,000 tonnes. The United States was experiencing an economic crisis that followed the giddy years of growth and booming asset prices; Britain was caught up in the collapse but had not enjoyed the run-up either.

A call by Mosley for deficit-financed public works, on a similar basis to the pre-election Lloyd George plan, was rejected, leading to his resignation from the government and in time to the formation of his New Party, which enjoyed modest support before eventually transforming into the reactionary British Union of Fascists. Instead of following the advice of the so-called Mosley Memorandum, the government instead turned to the tried and tested approach of inter-war British government: it formed a committee. The MacMillan Committee, chaired by a Scottish jurist, included among others a former Liberal Chancellor, a former permanent secretary of the Treasury, trade union leader Ernie Bevin and Maynard Keynes. While the proceedings of the committee make for a fascinating window into the developing theories of Keynes – which would be codified later in the decade – by the time it reported in 1931 events had overtaken it. The lasting significance of its work was perhaps that by putting Keynes and Bevin, a hugely influential figure in the wider Labour movement, together it established lines of communication between the great economist and the Labour Party that were to prove important later. Much of the report stayed clear of wider macroeconomic issues and concentrated on the structure of British banking, which was seen as less able to support domestic firms than its rivals overseas. The so-called 'MacMillan Gap', the idea that British banks were serving small to medium businesses poorly, was a theme that would crop up again throughout subsequent British economic history. Notably the committee did not question the commitment to gold.

By the summer of 1931 the minority MacDonald government faced an acute crisis. Not much of the blame could be directly laid at their feet; they had simply had the misfortune to be elected at the worst possible time. Trade and industrial production had slumped on their watch. The Labour Party had pledged to tackle unemployment and yet it had risen from around 10 per cent at the time of their election to above 20 per cent by May 1931. The supposed timidity of this government in the face of economic crisis has led to frequent condemnations from the left. But few governments proved up to the task or were willing to adopt untried methods to combat the downturn. The Labour government in Australia in the same period was just as bound to the prevailing orthodoxy. Franklin D. Roosevelt's New Deal, the economic impact of which is debatable anyway, would emerge only after the crucial events of 1931. Opponents of MacDonald's approach would have struggled at the time to point to any examples of what the government could be doing instead.

The toxic combination of an exceptionally weak economy, high interest rates, falling tax revenues and increased demands on the Exchequer risked wrecking the public finances. Austerity and deflation in the 1920s had failed to contain the debt to GDP ratio and by mid-1931 it had leapt to 180 per cent. Interest payments were now swallowing around one quarter of tax revenues even as the debt total rose further – an unsustainable position.

Under pressure not only from the Conservatives but also from the Liberal Party, whose votes the government relied upon, MacDonald formed yet another committee in February 1931 to examine the government's finances. Sir George May, a former government financial advisor and insurance company boss, reported back in July 1931. By now sterling was under serious pressure with gold leaving the Bank of England at a rapid clip, pushing the Bank to raise rates from 3 per cent to 6 per cent to try to stem the flow. Rising rates of course put further pressure on the government's finances. While the two Labour appointees to the committee dissented, the Liberal and Tory members and the conventional experts who made up the bulk of the May Committee dusted down the spirit of Eric Geddes from a decade before. They recommended tax increases worth some £24 million on the wealthy, coupled with £96 million of cuts in public spending. Unemployment benefit was to be slashed by 20 per cent, public housing spending cut back, and the salaries of police officers, soldiers and local government workers were to be lowered.

Throughout August the Cabinet debated its response to the calls for austerity. Snowden, backed by MacDonald, argued for a compromise position of cutting benefits by 10 per cent together with pay cuts across the public sector. The Cabinet, though, was having none of it and would rather resign than sign up. MacDonald tendered his resignation and that of his government to the King at the end of the month. But then an odd thing happened.

Implored by the King to stay on as head of a new 'National Government' to see out the immediate crisis, MacDonald agreed, earning himself the lasting enmity of the Labour Party. The original intention had been to form a 'ministry of all the talents' drawing on the best MPs from across the parties. The resulting administration was a reincarnation of Baldwin's government with a thin veneer of ex-Labour MPs such as MacDonald and Snowden (both of whom were expelled from the Labour Party) and a couple of dozen Liberals tacked on.

The new National Government may have been headed by MacDonald but it was really led by Baldwin. Within days of taking office it had passed the May package of cuts through Parliament. That, though, was not to be the end of the crisis. The news of benefit and salary cuts went down very badly indeed with those affected. Indeed, it went down so badly with the armed forces that, in an event which shocked the British establishment, it provoked a naval mutiny.

Around one thousand sailors greeted the news that they faced pay cuts of between 10 per cent and 25 per cent by refusing to follow orders and effectively going on strike at Invergordon in Scotland. The mutineers, as they became known, initially met on a football pitch and, after voting to cease work, sang 'The Red Flag'. On the morning of 15 September the sailors of HMS *Hood* and HMS *Nelson* refused to put to sea, while the crews of HMS *Valiant* and HMS *Rodney* refused to perform anything but essential duty. The Royal Marines, expected to enforce military discipline, joined in the protest. Only by the government agreeing to a maximum pay cut of 10 per cent was discipline restored.

While the breakdown in naval discipline was quickly mended, the damage to financial confidence appeared irreparable. Investors and overseas holders of sterling took fright at the news, causing a crash on the stock market and a step up in the daily gold outflow from the Bank of England.

With its reserves crucially depleted the Bank took a step that had appeared, until that point, unthinkable: it unilaterally withdrew from the gold standard. As one well-informed

Labour ex-minister was to put it, 'no one told us we could do that'. The pain of the deflation that had prepared Britain for its return to gold and the crisis of its time back on the peg all proved to be for nothing. Britain was embarking on a new economic experiment, one which only the most radical of economic thinkers had argued for in the past: a freely floating currency. So much for 'Safety first.'

Ditching gold was a turning point for Britain's slump. In effect the country had shifted its position on the impossible trinity and retaken domestic control of interest rates by accepting a non-fixed exchange rate. The relief was almost immediate.

Leaving gold had two distinct effects. Firstly there was an immediate drop in the value of sterling by around 25 per cent, which provided some support for exporters whose goods were now materially less costly on world markets. Occasionally modern observers of the period point to the devaluation of the pound as a driver of recovery. That, though, is the wrong lesson. Britain's recovery from the slump was not based on exports. And the advantage of a cheaper currency proved fleeting in any case as other countries slowly followed Britain's lead and dropped their gold pegs, allowing their own currencies to fall in value. The United States left the standard in 1933. Far more important was the new-found freedom of the Bank of England to set interest rates at a level more appropriate to Britain's dire domestic circumstances. Rates fell to 2 per cent by 1932 and remained there for the rest of the decade. Cheaper borrowing costs not only helped stimulate business investment and house building but took some of the pressure off the government's finances.

The National Government, a supposed innovation for the crisis, took on a permanent feel after winning a landslide majority in 1931 and large one in 1935. Its character became distinctly more Conservative as time went on, especially after Baldwin formally assumed the Prime Ministership in 1935.

The nadir of Britain's slump had been passed by the end of 1931 but the recovery that followed was a deeply uneven one. Still it is important to recognise that the economy did recover. The folk memory of the 'hungry thirties', coloured partly by the American experience and partly by the cross-party political rhetoric of 'no return to the pre-war world' that lasted through-out the 1940s to the 1970s, has sometimes obscured that reality.

The 1930s was a decade of sharp contrasts for Britain's economy. Official unemployment passed two million for the first time on record but so too did car ownership. While the old export-associated staples that had powered nineteenth-century growth, such as coal mining, textiles and shipbuilding, suffered amid a global depression, the new lighter industries – car manufacturing, electrical engineering and the nascent aerospace sector – began to pick up, as did services. This all resulted in a strange regional patchwork of different economic outcomes. By 1935 overall unemployment had come down to 15.5 per cent – still extremely high by any objective measure but a world away from the 22 per cent peak. But that national rate hides a more nuanced regional picture. In the southeast of England unemployment was down to close to 8 per cent by the mid-1930s, a touch worse than the pre-1931 level but lower than in much of the 1920s. By contrast unemployment in the industrial northeast was at 21 per cent; south Wales, central Scotland and the northern reaches of England continued to experience depression-like outcomes even while towns in the south of England and increasingly across the midlands pros-pered. The mid-1930s almost certainly witnessed the largest regional gaps in GDP per head Britain has experienced since the industrial revolution. While output per head in London and the wider southeast was some 140 per cent of the national average, that of the north of England was just 63 per cent of the national median and that of Wales 68 per cent.

A look at the results of the 1935 election gives a decent approximation of how the economy was performing across Britain. Labour's 102 seats were concentrated in the high unemployment areas associated with the old staples. The post-1931 recovery was real enough, even if it was slower than it could have been and even if it failed to lift all boats equally. In terms of political economy it succeeded in creating enough winners, concentrated in enough seats, to deliver a very healthy majority for the government. Just as in the 1980s, a Conservative government demonstrated that high unemployment is not necessarily a bar to re-election as long as enough areas continue to perform well.

Jarrow, near Newcastle, was not an area performing well. Employment had been reliant on the local shipbuilding industry, which had sunk with the drying up of its global trade. With the yards running at around 50 per cent of their capacity, local unemployment was well over 30 per cent for most of the decade. The Jarrow March, or Jarrow Crusade, of 1936 is one of the decade's most iconic images. Two hundred ex-shipyard workers walked the 300-odd miles to London over the course of three weeks in October to present a petition to Parliament asking for the re-establishment of their industry. The last legs of their long march took them through booming towns such as Luton, Bedford and St Albans.

The Special Areas Act, designed to help the hardest-hit regions, had actually been passed two years before in 1934. The locales covered – Tyneside, south Wales, west Cumberland and Scotland – were targeted for extra government investment. Like so many subsequent attempts at regional support the amounts of cash involved were small and government failed to stick to a long-term plan.

Outside of the attempts to directly help the worst-affected regions the government's wider industrial strategy was often called 'rationalisation'. In sharp contrast to the traditional Smithian emphasis on the virtues of competition, inter-war governments often lamented the fractious and disjointed structures of many of Britain's industries. There was a hope that one way to restore competitiveness in overseas trade would be to encourage mergers into larger firms that could, hopefully, reap economies of scale and perform better on international markets. Imperial Chemical Industries (ICI), created by a four-way merger in 1926, was typical – it was believed by many that only a British national (or Imperial) champion could compete with the American chemicals giant DuPont or the German IG Farben. The Railways Act of 1921 reorganised some 60 companies into four. Coal mining was similarly reorganised in the late 1930s, and much, ultimately unsuccessful, effort was put into attempting to create a new metals company.

Alongside the new industries the major component of the recovery of the 1930s came from house building. Indeed the 1930s saw a house building boom. Interest rates pegged at 2 per cent promoted a revival in consumer confidence – at least in the better performing areas of the country – and so a huge upswing in demand for homes. The much less restrictive planning laws of the time allowed builders to respond quickly. House building hit 350,000 units a year by the middle of the decade – leaving its footprint all over Britain in the form of the three- and four-bedroom semi-detached houses that still make up a large chunk of the housing stock in the suburbs where land had been cheapest.

Home ownership rose from about 10 per cent of the population on the eve of the Great War to closer to 30 per cent by the end of the 1930s. These new homeowners were exactly the kind of reasonably well off, middle-class and, occasionally, working-class voters that Baldwin and his Chancellor (and successor as Prime Minister) Neville Chamberlain regarded as the bedrock of their political coalition.

Still, even after a large expansion of ownership, most Britons rented their accommodation. Council housing had expanded after the First World War (although few of the new homes were genuinely fit for heroes) and received a second boost under the MacDonald governments, but for most people renting meant renting from private landlords. In the poorer parts of Britain, such landlords were often not especially well-to-do themselves. As George Orwell was to write: 'ideally, the worst type of slum landlord is a fat wicked man, preferably a bishop, who is drawing an immense income from extortionate rents. Actually, it is a poor old woman who has invested her life's savings in three slum houses, inhabits one of them and tries to live on the rent of the other two – never, in consequence, having any money for repairs.'

Baldwin was the real architect of the National Government but Chamberlain was the dominant figure in 1930s politics and economic policy-making, Chancellor from 1931 to 1937 and then Prime Minister until 1940. Forever now associated with appeasement, his contemporary stock ran much higher – at least until the end. A sharp political operator who took great delight in hammering Labour (it is hard to imagine him being able to preside over the kind of wartime cabinets that Winston Churchill was to assemble), he was, in the context of his time and conventional economic thinking, a successful Chancellor. In 1932 he persuaded, with the moral screws firmly turned on, holders of the 5 per cent 1917 war bond to agree to a voluntary reduction in the interest rate attached to it from 5 per cent to 3.5 per cent. In 1932 Britain defaulted on its war debts to the United States amid a general series of inter-Allied debt write-offs. Those steps coupled with lower interest rates in general and a healthier economy overall allowed Britain to stabilise its precarious debt situation, which had spilled over into political crisis in 1931. After peaking at 190 per cent of GDP in 1933, the debt ratio was back down to 150 per cent by 1939.

A former Mayor of Birmingham like his father, Chamberlain was an acknowledged expert in local government. But a background in municipal government was not the only legacy Joseph left. In the 1930s Neville oversaw the realisation of the three-decade Chamberlain family project: protectionism.

The tariff question had kept the Conservatives out of office before the Great War and lost them the 1923 election afterwards. And yet, with barely a whimper, free trade – part of the bedrock of British economic thinking for almost a century – was dropped not long after the gold standard was laid to rest. Import tariffs were put in place in 1932, and the Ottawa agreements of that same year allowed preferential access to the British market for the goods of the rest of the Empire. Imperial Preference had been established.

After the contentious debates of the previous decades it all happened rather quickly. What had changed since the 1920s or the 1900s? The answer is twofold, part domestic and part international. Domestically, the Conservative-dominated National Government was triumphant in politics. The election of 1931 had left it holding 554 of the House of Commons' 615 seats. Philip Snowden, Gladstonian to the end, had stuck with MacDonald over austerity and benefit cuts but finally resigned over free trade. Few others batted an eyelid.

Internationally, Imperial Preference seemed more in keeping with the world of the 1930s. The United States had embarked on its damaging path towards even higher levels of tariffs in 1930. Across continental Europe and its empires tariff walls were rising. The globalisation of the 1870s to 1910s had been halted by the First World War, gone into reverse in the

1920s and crashed throughout the 1930s. Whereas around 15 per cent of global goods had crossed borders in 1913, only 5 per cent did in 1938.

The results of Britain's protectionist turn were distinctly mixed. Imperial Preference 'worked' to the extent that it encouraged Britons to purchase from the Empire rather than foreign countries. The imperial share of imports rose from around 30 per cent in 1932 to 40 per cent by 1935. The change was especially marked in food. Shops now advertised 'delicious EMPIRE butter' imported from New Zealand, in contrast to the Danish butter that had been a British staple since the nineteenth century. Spanish oranges were replaced with those of Australia, Rhodesia and South Africa. But it failed to do much on the export side of the ledger. Neither Australia nor Canada, the two largest imperial markets, materially increased the share of British goods in their imports. For India the situation was little changed. In the medium term the whole agenda – especially when coupled with the cartelisation and mergers that constituted the 'rationalisation' industrial policy – was damaging to British productivity. Freed from much international competition, and with domestic competition more constrained, much of industry ossified. But then, in reality, Imperial Preference was always more of a political project – aimed at binding the Empire closer together – than an economic one.

Yet while the old orthodoxies on free trade and gold had been broken in the 1930s, the conventional wisdom on the need for a balanced budget remained – at least until rearmament got seriously under way towards the end of the decade. But then war – and the preparation for war – had always been seen as the one time when borrowing was sensible.

Of course, there were some voices calling for borrowing for economic reasons – to give people employment via public works spending. Lloyd George had based his pitch in 1929 around the notion and it had formed the basis for Mosley's rejected memorandum to MacDonald. The 'Treasury view', as the prevailing logic became known, was that a government could not spend its way to prosperity. The economic reasoning behind this argument appeared sound enough to many: if the Treasury was borrowing to spend then that money would not be available to the private sector. Under the so-called loanable funds doctrine the pool of savings was limited to whatever the private sector wanted to save. Only a finite pool of investment was available. If the Treasury chose to use those funds on public works there would less available for businesses looking to expand. The public sector would 'crowd out' the private by taking up resources.

Keynes, by now Britain's most high-profile economist and something of a public intellectual, was the sternest and most vocal critic of this view. His theories, naturally, developed over time, but the great drawing-together came in *The General Theory of Employment, Interest and Money*, published in 1936, a book which has strong claim to being the most influential economic publication of the twentieth century.

The Keynesian revolution would sweep the economics profession over the next decade, replacing much of the old classical view of Smith, Ricardo and Marx, but the take-up by policy-makers and officials was slower.

The General Theory is both infuriating and brilliant at the same time. Beautiful flourishes of prose sit amongst dry academic passages, while the organisation of the theoretical section is haphazard to say the least. There is so much in it that, as with the Bible, readers can draw their own conclusions and choose to emphasise different aspects of the teachings of Keynes. Paul Krugman, a prominent modern-day follower of Keynes, argues that there are two types of Keynesian today: 'Chapter 12ers' who preach the idea that Keynes' belief in the problems of making investment decisions when the future is subject to radical uncertainty means that capitalism will also be unstable and 'Part 1ers' who instead emphasise the possibility of a general shortfall of demand in the economy and the means through which a government can stabilise it. Of course, the great bulk of Keynesians over the years have been neither Chapter 12ers nor Part 1ers: most have simply never read *The General Theory*.

The real genius of the work is not its challenge to conventional theory in economics but that it essentially invented a whole new field: macroeconomics – the study of the economy as a whole. Much of the terminology and framework for how modern macroeconomists think can be traced back to Keynes. Milton Friedman is popularly viewed as the great challenger to Keynes, and the man whose ideas overturned his influence on economic policy-making in the 1970s and 1980s. But Friedman was working in a Keynesian framework of macroeconomics, even if his own ideas led to different recommendations.

The fundamental point of Keynes' work was the rejection of Say's Law. Jean-Baptiste Say, a French economist, had argued in the early 1800s that the very act of producing output creates demand for goods. In effect demand is determined by the state of supply. The central insight of Keynes is that there can be situations in which the overall health of the economy is harmed by a general lack of demand – that supply does not create its own demand and that governments have a duty to stabilise the economy by creating more demand when it is weak. Capitalism, according to Keynes, could produce great prosperity but it was also unstable. It had to be carefully managed.

The General Theory brought together two Keynesian concepts to provide the intellectual framework for challenging the 'Treasury view'. Firstly, the paradox of thrift. This is the idea that while saving may indeed be a virtuous activity which provides the resources for later investment, it is possible to have too much of a good thing. One person's spending is another person's income. If, for whatever reason, a great many firms and households choose to increase their saving at the same time, then spending can begin to dry up and the income of most businesses and workers can fall. The end result, hence the paradox, is that if everyone tries to increase their saving at the same time overall savings will actually fall as incomes wither.

Allied to this is the notion of the multiplier, the idea that any spending (although it is most associated with government spending) can have an outsized impact on the economy, above and beyond the initial outlays. Say the government in 1935 had chosen to spend £250 million on public works: while some of that £250 million would have gone abroad to pay for imports most of it would have ended up in the hands of British workers and firms. Those workers and firms might have saved some of their payments but would likely spend much of their windfall on new purchases, kick-starting another rod of the multiplier.

Taken together these ideas represented a rejection of the notion that the available pool of investment was finite and also of the Treasury view. If there were idle resources available – the unemployed – then paying to put them to work would add to overall economic activity rather than simply cannibalise funds from the private sector. Keynes had provided a framework for reimagining how economic policy worked – and indeed what the very objectives of policy should be.

While government borrowing did begin to rise after 1936 as rearmament began – providing a much-needed boost to employment in heavy industry – it would be perverse to credit Keynes for this. The case for radar, Spitfires and new bombers did not rely on his General Theory.

Britain's inter-war period was a miserable one. Unemployment was high for two decades and wage growth was weak. Monetary policy was inappropriately tight until 1931, while fiscal policy remained equally unhelpful until the late 1930s. Victorian statesmen who had feared mass democracy would have perhaps been surprised that the mass electorate of the time did not support radicalism and a levelling-down agenda but instead repeatedly elected Conservative governments, often with very large majorities. But the Tory party of Baldwin and Chamberlain was a very different beast from its mid-Victorian ancestors, much more in the spirit of Disraeli and Salisbury in terms of its carefully presented mass appeal.

The 1930s had seen a multi-generation consensus on dropping both the gold standard and free trade. The 1940s would see an even greater change in the role of government in the economy. But first Britain would have to fight another total war.

11

All Change

The Britain that fought the Second World War had one crucial advantage over the Britain that had fought the First World War – it had done it before. Unlike in 1914 there was no messing around with 'business as usual' volunteerism or a laissez-faire approach to managing the war effort. The generation of policy-makers that commanded the war effort knew, or at least thought they knew, exactly what to expect. And while the Great War seemed to emerge from the Balkans as some sort of bolt from the blue, the Second World War was more predictable. British governments had been preparing for it from the mid-1930s onwards.

Drawing on experience of the earlier conflict, economic considerations were crucial to how Britain approached the war that came in 1939. The lesson of the Great War seemed clear: industrial and financial capacity were crucial to waging total war. Indeed by the 1930s politicians were explicit in regarding the strength of the economy as the 'fourth arm of defence'. There is sometimes a tendency to suppose that Britain was unprepared for war in 1939, a view influenced both by the scale of the allied defeat in France in May and June 1940 and by the first draft of history penned by Churchill after the conflict. While no country was totally prepared for what followed in 1939–1945, and while the policy of appeasement was ultimately a geopolitical failure, the case for an under-prepared Britain is usually overstated. From the mid-1930s onwards Britain had been rearming in a serious fashion, even if were not as fast as Churchill (then a backbench critic of Chamberlain) would have liked.

Defence expenditure, as a share of GDP, had been around 4.6 per cent in 1920 and was hit heavily by the Geddes Axe. The government's planning assumption throughout the 1920s (an assumption first suggested by one Winston Churchill in 1919) was that Britain would face no major war in the next decade; this 'ten year rule', which was rolled forward each year before being dropped in the mid-1930s, was used to justify keeping the annual defence estimates low. In the early 1930s the defence budget was taking up around 2.8 per cent of national income.

But by the mid-1930s Britain faced a very different global environment. Nazi Germany was clearly arming for war, Fascist Italy was becoming a serious rival in the Mediterranean and an authoritarian Japan (formally a British ally) a threat to the Empire in the east. Not only was Chamberlain prepared to increase the defence budget but he was prepared to borrow to do so. Defence spending was above 4 per cent of GDP in the 1936/37 financial year, 5.5 per cent the next year and 7.7 per cent of national income in the last financial year before war. These were serious amounts of money – well above any-thing Britain had spent in peacetime in the preceding 150 years. The 'shadow factories' established in the mid-1930s – privately owned but government-supported manufacturing centres – would prove crucial in ramping up aircraft produc-tion when the war came. Military aircraft production rose from close to 600 in 1933 to almost 8,000 in 1939. In 1940 some 15,000 planes left the factories – outproducing Germany by 50 per cent.

Churchill was not alone in calling for an even faster pace of preparation, but a shortage of skilled labour created a bottleneck in production, at least until the eve of the war. Moreover, just as important as industrial capacity was the Treasury's view on the nature of a coming conflict. British officials were, rightly, confident of their ability to win a long war in which economic factors would be crucial. Britain was after all a richer country than Germany with a higher income per head. There was fear that rearming too quickly would put Britain's financial and industrial strength at risk – trying to build up weapons too fast could both undermine Britain's finances and push up prices in key industries. The balancing act was to rearm enough to prevent being quickly defeated in a short war whilst retaining the economic strength to fight and win a long one. The Treasury did not get many things right in the 1930s, but on this it judged its hand well.

It was during the Second World War that Keynes and his macroeconomic theories not only gained official acceptance but became central to the conduct of economic management. Indeed much of the statistical basis of how economics is nowadays understood dates back to the conflict. The point of measuring total economic output was partly to deploy it in defeating the enemy. In *How to Pay for the War*, originally published as a series of articles in *The Times* and in 1940 as a book, Keynes put the theoretical framework of the General Theory into practice. Keynes himself – the starkest critic of pre-war economic policy – found himself becoming the government's key economic advisor during the war, a director of the Bank of England, and ultimately ennobled as Baron Keynes.

In contrast to 1914 the authorities quickly moved to

take more control of both production and finance. Market mechanisms were suspended, many goods rationed and manufacturing directed. Initially the Treasury estimated that around 50 per cent of national income would have to be devoted to the war effort and set aside some industrial capacity to maintain export markets and help cover the import bill. The planning assumption was for a three-year war. Only after the fall of France did the government throw caution to the winds and subordinate all other considerations to winning the war. Unlike in the First World War, when inflation had been allowed to play the role of suppressing consumption, the Treasury relied more on taxation in the Second. An excess profits tax of 60 per cent coupled with much higher rates of direct personal taxation (the standard rate of income tax rose from 25 per cent to 50 per cent) and higher duties on luxuries did much of the heavy lifting. One lasting innovation of the war was the introduction of Pay As You Earn (PAYE) income tax – directly, as today, deducting tax liabilities from wage payments. PAYE allowed income tax to be extended further down the income spectrum, not only raising funds for the government but, crucially, further crimping back consumption. Household spending, which had been around 80 per cent of national income before the war, was squeezed down to 50 per cent by 1944. Prices more than doubled between 1914 and 1918 but rose by 'just' 50 per cent during the second conflict.

The fall of France did not cause a reassessment of economic war planning but did instigate the formation of a true National Government under Churchill, with Labour entering government for the first time since 1931. The formation of that government allowed one of the key domestic appointments of the war to be made: Ernie Bevin became Minister of Labour with unprecedented powers. Bevin, a tough-talking autodidact trade union leader, was not even an MP when appointed to the

Cabinet. A by-election to bring him into the Commons had to be quickly arranged. The 1939 Emergency Powers Act gave him almost complete control over the labour force and he set about using it, not just to win the war, but to strengthen the hand of organised workers. Industrial relations were generally much smoother in the second war than the first, with around half as many days being lost due to strikes as in 1914–1918. In part the lack of militancy was down to a lesser reliance on inflation as a restrictor of consumption – the contained rises in the cost of living dampened the need to push for higher wages.

The war saw the sweeping growth of a Whitehall-led military-industrial complex that planned production, modernised shipyards, directed labour and set production targets. The state moved to take powers sooner than in 1914 and used those powers in a wide-ranging manner to steer the economy towards munitions production. The Royal Air Force ended the Battle of Britain with more fighters than it began it, despite heavy losses over the summer of 1940. Germany could simply not keep up. The output of machine tools, crucial to expanding munitions production, rose from less than 20,000 annually before the war to over 100,000 by 1942. Taken together, munitions output rose by about six and half times between 1939 and 1944.

Britain's wartime economic effort, despite the pre-war years of Imperial Preference and the deglobalisation of the inter-war period, was a global one. Hitler may have conquered much of Europe in 1940 but he was, to an extent, trapped in the continent while Britain retained access to the industrial might of the United States and the resources of Africa, much of Asia, Australasia and Latin America. The greatest myth of Britain's war is the notion that she ever truly stood alone. Even after Dunkirk and the fall of France, Churchill was leading not a national but an imperial war effort and wartime economy.

And the Empire was backed by the governments in exile of much of Europe together with, in most cases, their fleets, merchant marines and colonies.

Take food as an example. Despite all the posters, not that many Britons were actually digging for victory. Employment in agriculture rose from around 800,000 before the war to one million during it and productivity was boosted by increased mechanisation, but food still came, in the main, from abroad. Food imports, as measured by tonnage, were indeed reduced, but that raw number overstates the change. Imports of beef fell from 0.6 million tons in 1938 to 0.35 million in 1944, but imports of tinned meat rose from 0.07 million tons to 0.21 million. The association of Spam with the war is a fair one. Corned beef, which had previously been sold in various grades of quality, now came in just one grade, the lowest. What was really going on was a substitution away from bulky items. The total amount, by weight, of food for human consumption imported during the war fell by 25 per cent but calories per tonne rose by 25 per cent. Fruit and vegetable shipments fell while frozen meat imports rose. As in the previous war, Britain's reliance on the resources of the world to feed its people allowed a greater share of the country's population to be directly employed in the war effort or supporting it.

Germany too had learned the lessons of the past conflict and devoted more effort to sinking British merchant shipping than in 1914–18; unrestricted submarine warfare was the norm from the start of the war and the merchant fleet suffered higher proportional casualties than any of the three uniformed services. The convoy system and the code crackers at Bletchley Park though meant that losses, as a percentage of shipping, actually fell throughout the war – from 1 ship in 181 crossing the key Atlantic route in 1941, to 1 in 344 by 1943, and just 1 in 1,000 by 1945.

Of course this colossal war effort, and the imports it relied upon, all had to be paid for. The extensive increases in taxation took government revenues up from under £700 million in 1938 to over £2.9 billion in 1944, but spending rose over the same period from just under £800 million to £5.7 billion. In other words, the annual deficit was about four times as large as the pre-war tax base. Expressed as a share of GDP, government borrowing peaked at almost 27 per cent in 1941/42. That all meant a great deal of borrowing. Domestic finances were handled much better than during the Great War: unlike in 1914 there was no attempt to maintain even an illusion of business as usual in the City of London, nor was the government keen to repeat the errors of the last conflict and lure in investors with chunky yields, saddling itself with crippling debt-service bills further down the road. The intention was to fight a '3 per cent war' and preferably less. There would be no repeat of the 5 per cent war loan which had caused such troubles in the 1920s. Moral suasion played a role, with the City and its institutions being leant upon to lend freely, but as in the last war a Capital Issues Committee kept a tight lid on other sorts of capital-raising to prevent competition for funds. In effect the financial system was being channelled into supporting the war effort by either directly lending to the government or the war industries. A further innovation came in the form of the Treasury Deposit Receipt, which allowed the government to borrow directly from high street banks on six-month terms at a rate of just over 1 per cent.

External finance was also managed better than in the previous war – when much of it had been outsourced to J. P. Morgan in New York. Still, this was Britain's area of most acute economic vulnerability. Especially as the experience of the first total war had left US policy-makers wary of becoming too economically entangled in any European conflicts. The US

Johnson Act of 1934 prevented US citizens from lending to any country which had defaulted on its previous war debts, closing that market for British borrowing. The US neutrality acts, which would have prevented Britain not only from borrowing in the United States but from purchasing any war materials there, were relaxed on the outbreak of the conflict. But all such purchases had to be carried out on what was rather quaintly called a 'cash and carry' basis.

The fall of France and the loss of much army equipment after Dunkirk forced Britain to ramp up its procurement of war materials in the United States, with the UK stepping in to take over purchases originally ordered by the French government, paid for by running down gold and dollar reserves or with the scant earnings from exports. Dollar resources were exhausted within months, especially as the sector of British industry previously devoted to maintaining some export market share was switched to direct military production.

The Lend-Lease arrangement of March 1941 was a turning point. Under this deal America agreed to supply food, oil and war materials effectively for free. The US would not directly enter the war until December that year, but North American finance and production were now a vital part of the British war effort. Two thirds of the $50 billion of US support extended by the scheme went to Britain. By 1944 Lend-Lease aid was responsible for about 15 per cent of Britain's economic war effort. That US aid was crucial to sustaining Britain's war effort, although it did not come entirely free of strings. Article VII of the agreement required Britain to end discrimination against US goods after the war (essentially reversing Imperial Preference and tearing up the 1932 Ottawa agreement) but that was a problem for after the fighting ended.

But Lend-Lease alone was not enough to cover Britain's external payments between 1940 and 1945. A vital role was played by the arcane-sounding 'sterling balances'. Global financial leadership may have passed from London to New York in the years after the Great War but the City remained a major financial sector. The pound sterling was no longer the anchor of the global payments system but it too retained an important role. As the gold standard fell apart in the 1930s a sterling bloc developed, of countries which conducted most of their trade in pounds and generally carried out any required payments in London. Whereas Canada was essentially in a US-led dollar bloc, the other Dominions and the rest of the Empire were still on a sterling standard. As were important British trading partners such as Argentina.

During the war these countries continued to supply Britain as before, and the goods were paid for in sterling with an acceptance that these payments would be held in London. As the cash would remain in London this was effectively buying goods on credit. Most participants had little choice: either they were in essence ruled from Whitehall or they had few economic alternatives. Take Argentina for example: its meat industry was reliant on sales to Britain, especially with most other European markets now closed. Better to continue shipping frozen beef from the River Plate to Liverpool in return for the promise of payments later than see the farms mothballed. About two thirds of Britain's external deficit was covered by Lend-Lease and the rest by the sterling balances, with India, Egypt and Australia among the major creditors.

By 1944 the Western allies can almost be regarded as a single economic unit – and one that utilised the comparative economic advantages of its components. The United States, where manufacturing productivity was higher, produced a greater share of the munitions, whilst Britain mobilised a larger proportion of its population. By the time of D-Day in June 1944, some 55 per cent of the British workforce was either in the armed forces or in war-related work, compared to 40 per cent in the United States. Indeed Britain's armed forces were much larger than the country's capacity to equip them, hence the reliance on the factories of North America.

The Great War had seen the use of a British blockade, to striking effect, but the second total war saw a more direct form of economic warfare: bombing. Inter-war politicians had a fascination with the new world that bombers had brought about. 'The bomber will always get through' was taken as a truism, and it was widely believed by many that any war would be relatively quick as the two sides' aerial fleets rained down destruction on each other. In reality, hype had run ahead of technology.

Britain's cities, industries and population were subjected to the Blitz throughout 1940 and 1941 but the economic impact was relatively minor. The planes of the era simply did not have either the ability to target industry effectively or large enough bomb loads to do lasting economic damage. Some 60,000 people were killed by German bombing over the course of the war, two million homes damaged or destroyed and railway lines occasionally cut, but production was never seriously imperilled. The later Anglo-American bombing of occupied Europe and Germany was on an entirely different scale. Around 50,000 tonnes of bombs (including the V-rockets in the later years) were dropped on Britain during the war, compared to 2.7 million tonnes on mainland Europe. The sheer scale of the strategic air campaign is staggering. Laid end to end in an eleven-yard-wide road, the runways constructed in the early to mid-1940s in Britain would stretch for almost ten thousand miles, more than twice the length of its modern motorway network. The impact of the air war is still debated. It failed to break German morale but by 1944 put a great deal of pressure on the ability of Germany to wage total war. Far more Axis equipment was destroyed by air warfare than in land fighting.

Churchill had prioritised victory at all costs in the Second World War and the victory that came was certainly costly. Economic losses – the factories and houses destroyed by bombing, the shipping sent to the bottom of the sea and the overseas assets sold off to pay for imports – amounted to around 19 per cent of their pre-war total compared to a 15 per cent reduction in the Great War. The ratio of government debt to GDP soared to 260 per cent, almost twice as high as in 1918 and higher even than the 215 per cent seen after Waterloo in 1815. As in the First World War, financial resources had been exhausted, assets sold off, export markets lost, and industry repurposed for war. But the aftermath of this total war would be vastly different from the previous one.

Lloyd George may have promised a land fit for heroes after the Great War but his plans remained sketchy and under-developed; the same could not be said about the post-war planning with which the wartime government of 1940 to 1945 busied itself. William Beveridge, a Liberal civil servant turned academic, was tasked by government – under pressure from its Labour ministers – with compiling a report on post-war social provision. The white paper he presented to the Cabinet in late 1942 was rather more sweeping than many of them had expected. The Chancellor, the Tory Sir Kingsley Wood, regarded it as representing an impracticable financial commitment and many of his party colleagues agreed. The Labour ministers, though, whose handling of the labour movement had proved essential to the war effort, were insistent and, with a feeling that mid-war public morale needed a boost, the government agreed to publish the report in full that December. It was a surprise best-seller and even sold 50,000 copies in America. The Ministry of Information's intelligence-gathering apparatus reckoned it was received with almost universal acclaim.

The Beveridge Report is the founding document of the modern British welfare state. Victorian politicians, of both major parties, had introduced some social reforms. Edwardian New Liberalism had created an unemployment insurance system and old age pensions. Inter-war governments had reformed poor relief, expanded council housing and improved public health provision but all against a backdrop of budgetary cuts. Beveridge proposed to sweep away this patchwork system and replace it with a cohesive system of social insurance building on the work of the Asquith government. The 'five giants' of want, disease, ignorance, squalor and idleness were to be abolished by formal government action.

Beveridge's blueprints set out a basic system of universal benefits to prevent any family falling below a certain minimum, coupled with a contributory system of pensions and unemployment insurance, all underpinned by free at the point of use healthcare and, crucially, by a government commitment to make full employment a goal of policy. All of which was very much in the spirit of the New Liberalism of his youth. Beveridge was by no means a socialist, and the left would later attack his report for failing to abolish poverty and for failing to do more to encourage equality. Feminists would note that his concept of full employment in reality meant full male employment, with women's benefits linked to their husband's earnings. For the right, there was plenty to object to. The nature of universal benefits struck some as perverse. As Sir Kingsley Wood was to put it, 'the weekly progress of the millionaire to the post office for his old age pension would have an element of farce for the fact that the pension is provided in large measure by the general taxpayer'. The Treasury did what the Treasury has always done and fretted about how this would all be paid for.

While the government did commit itself, eventually, to

implementing the report, the more enthusiastic backing it received from the Labour Party was one factor in Labour's (surprising to many of the political elites) victory in the 1945 election – fought after the defeat of Germany but while war still raged in Asia.

That election victory brought in Britain's first government not dominated by the Conservatives since 1931. And the first with an effective parliamentary majority since 1915. It was led by Clement Attlee, 'a modest man with much to be modest about' as one contemporary quipped. Born in 1883, Attlee was only nine years younger than his predecessor but came from a vastly different generation and background. The son of a solicitor, he had a public-school and Oxford education, but Churchill was the grandson of a duke. Churchill may have been only 25 when Queen Victoria died but he was fundamentally a Victorian, an army officer who had fought on the edges of Empire. Attlee on the other hand was an Edwardian. He had come of age during the high noon of Edwardian progressivism and joined the young Labour Party while working with the urban poor in London's East End before fighting as an officer in the Great War. He was elected to Parliament in 1922 after some time in local government and became leader of the Labour Party in 1935 almost by accident. The 1931 landslide defeat meant that there were few other serious candidates to succeed the ineffectual George Lansbury in 1935. He would remain leader for twenty years and prove to be, in economic terms, one of the two most important Prime Ministers of the twentieth century.

The Attlee government would last only six years; elected in 1945 with a majority of 70, it would scrape through a tight election in 1950 only to be narrowly defeated (in fact it won the popular vote) in 1951. But in those six years it was to change the nature of Britain's political economy and put in place a system which dominated policy-making until the 1980s. Others of its transformations and reforms remain in place today.

The Attlee era is rarely judged, as it should be, as a post-total-war government. The two great conflicts that Britain fought in the first half of the twentieth century placed its economy under enormous strain, and the challenge of demobilisation – and the reconstruction of some form of normality – was immense. Whatever criticisms one might have of the 1945 government, it is hard to argue how it could have performed the task of demobilising better. In 1946 unemployment was 1.9 per cent. That reflected the combined effects of a much more benign international economic environment, the learning of lessons from 1918 and a whole different set of policy aims. In 1918 the aim of policy-makers was to return – as quickly as possible – to the knave-proof world of the gold standard, balanced budgets and free trade. In 1945 the aim was to build the 'new Jerusalem'. The last thing Attlee and his ministers wanted was a return to the old world of the 1920s and 1930s or even the older world of the 1910s. In 1945 Gladstone, at least for a time, was ejected from the Treasury.

The Labour Party of 1945 was committed to the idea of economic planning; it just wasn't quite sure exactly what that meant. A commitment to the abstract notion of a planned rather than free market economy was not especially radical by 1945. Talk of planning was very much in vogue in the 1930s across all the major parties. The seeming economic success of authoritarian planners – whether Stalin's USSR or Hitler's Germany – had attracted the intellectuals of the left and the right. America's New Deal had piqued some interest and, of course, the successful experience of a planned wartime economy offered a contemporary British example. The Labour Party itself had done a great deal of economic thinking in the 1930s, during the long decade of opposition, drawing lessons from the failure of the MacDonald government in the face of economic crisis. Across the party as a whole the commitment to some form of planning was almost total, but the young Keynes-influenced economists such as Harold Wilson, Hugh Gaitskell and Douglas Jay saw planning very differently from the more explicitly Marxist thinkers of the party's left.

What was beyond doubt was the government's commitment to the idea of full employment and that this should be the central aim of macroeconomic policy. Under the wartime coalition government a 1944 white paper, heavily influenced by both Keynes and Beveridge, had made this target explicit, and much of Labour's political agenda was essentially 'no return to the 1930s'. But if the ends were clear the means were up for debate. The more left-leaning economists in government circles became known as the Gosplanners (named for the Gosplan, the Soviet Union's national economic planning regime). While not in favour of Soviet-type repression, they essentially advocated a wartime-style planned economy with production targets, labour allocation and quotas: a British command economy. Opposing them were the so-called Thermostaters, the disciples of Keynes. To them the inter-war unemployment problem was fundamentally a question of insufficient demand in the economy. A government committed to full employment could achieve that end through stimulatory fiscal policy to boost spending power when it was needed. The annual budget would cease to be simply a case of deciding spending priorities, raising the taxes required and allocating the cash between departments, and instead would represent an active tool of *macroeconomic* policy. If things were running too cold, more demand could be pumped in via tax cuts or spending increases, and if the economy was running too hot and inflation picking up, the government could run a budget surplus to trim back demand. Policy would be adjusted to change the economic temperature – hence the name Thermostaters.

In the end the Thermostaters won out, backed by the Trades Union Congress. The trade union movement was fully committed to the doctrine of full employment – nothing strengthens a union's hand more in wage bargaining than a healthy jobs market after all – but equally committed to the notion of firm-level collective bargaining. The unions, under sufferance, would put up with active government allocation of labour during a war but would not wear it in peacetime. Workers had to be free to work where they wanted to work and at a wage bargained for collectively by their union. Whatever the ideological appeal of a more 'socialist' Soviet-style planned economy, it was incompatible with the British tradition of trade unionism that had originally created the Labour Party as its political arm.

Of course demand management, which became the lodestar of British macroeconomic policy from 1945 onwards, could have utilised fiscal policy or monetary policy. Expansionary monetary policy had already been demonstrated to be effective after the abandonment of gold in 1931. But, in those first years after the war, it was fiscal policy that was dominant. Fiscal policy was the go-to tool of the Attlee government (and their Conservative successors of the 1950s) for two primary reasons: firstly it could be more targeted in its approach – whereas a cut in interest rates is a fairly blunt tool, running a larger budget deficit allows policy-makers to make a range of choices about the exact balance between taxes to cut and spending areas to increase. More importantly, though, monetary policy had a very different job for the 1945–51 government: keeping interest rates low to help contain the costs of government debt. For decades the Bank of England's macro policy function had been to maintain the gold standard, but from the 1940s onwards it was tasked instead with helping contain the debt ratio by keeping interest rates low. The Bank itself, a core national institution, was nationalised in 1946, but that was really the extent of the Attlee government's shake-up of the City of London. Attlee had once noted that 'the City in the middle of a socialist state is as anomalous as the Pope in Moscow', but it seems the Pontiff could be safely left to wander the corridors of the Kremlin. The failure of Britain's first majority Labour government to seriously reform the City looks a little strange by contrast with their sweeping reforms in industry and social security and is often taken as a sign of small-c conservatism. The reality was that the City remained a crucial earner of foreign exchange for Britain, even if it was somewhat diminished, and the government was not about to risk messing that up at a time when dollars were precious.

Radicalism was certainly in evidence when it came to social policy. Cradle-to-grave social security was implemented in a series of acts. In some areas, such as health policy, the government went beyond Beveridge – creating the National Health Service rather than relying on local-authority-provided health services as recommended in the 1942 report. In others the reforms fell short of Beveridge's hopes. The Beveridge principle of universalism as opposed to means-tested help was never applied, well, universally, and means-testing remained an important part of much welfare policy. Still, even with those constraints, benefits spending amounted to around 4.4 per cent of GDP by 1950, more than double its proportional level in 1938. Public spending on health rose from around 1.5 per cent of GDP before the war to 2.5 per cent by 1950 – universal healthcare was surprisingly cheap but reflected the state of medical knowledge and the younger demographics of post-war Britain compared to recent decades. The education budget rose from 3.5 per cent of GDP to almost 4.5 per cent with the school leaving age raised from 14 to 15. This was a large expansion of state public service provision, as was obvious from the number of public sector workers. Central government employment rose from 2.6 per cent of workers in 1938 to 4.8 per cent in 1951 (excluding the armed services and the newly nationalised industries) while that of local government increased from 6.2 per cent to 11.5 per cent. Adding in the military and the nationalised sectors, total public sector employment was around one in four workers at the beginning of the 1950s. The state's footprint in the jobs market had grown fourfold since 1913. Still, the creation of the modern welfare state should not disguise the fact that Attlee's Britain remained a warfare state too. It was under Attlee that Britain developed its own atomic weapons, maintained a large foreign military presence and helped found NATO. Charges for NHS prescriptions and opticians were introduced, in part, to free resources for the Korean War. In every year of the Attlee government more was spent on defence than on health.

If the new macroeconomic framework which sought to maintain high employment was guided by Keynes (who died at the age of just 62 in 1946), then the social security owed much to his Liberal compatriot Beveridge; but the key industrial policy was distinctly Labour: nationalisation.

The party had been committed to public ownership since the end of the First World War but had never had the majority to put its plans into effect. In the years between 1945 and the mid-1990s many of Britain's industries would find themselves on something of a see-saw between private and public ownership. The country's first-past-the-post electoral system, coupled with a two-party system cleaved along class lines, would cause more regular changes in the economic borders of the state and market sectors than in most of western Europe. That pendulum began swinging in 1945.

The Attlee government nationalised – with compensation for shareholders – the rail, coal, gas, electricity, iron and steel industries together with some road haulage and, oddly enough, Thomas Cook the travel agent. What became British Airways had already been nationalised during the war and what became British Telecom grew out of the state-owned General Post Office. Nationalisations were generally of two types: either natural monopolies such as energy where competition was considered impossible, or 'strategic industries' (such as steel) where the state wanted to keep a firm hand on the tiller. The model of nationalisation was very much one pioneered by Labour Minister Herbert Morrison, who had run London local government in the 1930s: the public corporation. Little attempt was made to introduce any form of industrial democracy or worker involvement in management; the state simply replaced private shareholders as the ultimate owner and relied on, often, the same managers who had run the industries previously to continue day to day operations.

In theory, of course, such industries could now be run for the public good with no need to make a profit. But, sheltered from competition, inefficiencies began to build. More seriously, the nationalised industries suffered from a problem that was to plague the economy in the Attlee era: a lack of investment.

If the first macroeconomic priority of the Attlee government was maintaining full employment, then the second was returning the economy to some sort of balance – especially when it came to its international position. The pressing fear in 1945 had been of a repeat of 1919, a collapse in post-war demand leading to an immediate slump and rising unemployment, but by the late 1940s macroeconomic worries were more focused on the balance of payments – concerns which would bedevil British governments for the next four decades. Indeed the thermostat of fiscal policy was trying to cool the economy after 1947, and a budget surplus was run to try to reduce consumption and allow more resources to flow towards exports. Exports were down 70 per cent on their pre-war levels in 1945 and the loss of shipping resources together with the liquidation of overseas assets (and the loss of their payment flows) had lowered capital income. Invisible earnings too were down as much as visible ones.

The ending of Lend-Lease in 1945, sooner than the government had hoped, was an immediate problem. The Anglo-American loan of 1946 (negotiated by Keynes in one of his last public acts) that tided Britain over was less generous than had been hoped for. The US loaned $3.75 billion, and Canada chipped in with an additional $1.2 billion, at 2 per cent payable over 50 years. The sting came with the conditions attached. Sterling was to be made convertible into dollars within a year of the deal being signed. British policy-makers nervously eyed up the large sterling balances accumulated over the course of the fighting and wondered how they could go about meeting those obligations if Britain's creditors asked for payment in dollars.

The global shortage of dollars was the pressing international economic issue of the mid-1940s. There was much pent-up demand for goods, after six years of global war, and only US industry was in a realistic position to meet this. But other countries, Britain included, found it difficult to either find the domestic resources to export to the US or to compete with US producers in that market. The post-war Ealing comedies did well at the British box office, but that was partly because the government refused to allow precious dollars to be used on frivolities such as importing American films. The US domestic audience meanwhile preferred to stick with Hollywood. The dollar shortage would eventually be solved by the Marshall Plan of 1948, the huge programme of US economic aid to western Europe which provided the dollars to balance international flows. But that came too late to prevent a huge outflow of dollars and gold from Britain once sterling was made convertible, in line with the deal struck by Keynes in 1947. Convertibility had to be suspended within weeks of being introduced. It was the need for dollars that sat behind much of the colonial policy of the Attlee government. Whilst pursuing progressive social reform in Britain, extremely harsh methods were used to reimpose control over Malaysia – rubber exports were a very useful source of dollar earnings on international markets.

The expansion of the state and the simultaneous attempt to bring international payments back into balance meant a tough squeeze on consumption: taxes remained high while rationing and controls remained in place. The British people might be enjoying higher employment and more generous public services, but they were not free to rush out and spend – and especially not on imported goods. Such policies did much to undermine the popularity of the Attlee government among its electorate. Especially as there were no serious calls from the opposition Conservatives to roll back the new larger state. Sterling was devalued by 30 per cent in 1949 in order to ease the balance of payments problems, by pushing up the cost of imports and easing the situation for exporters. Rough external balance had been achieved by 1950 but at a cost not only of delayed consumption but also of relatively weak investment.

The most accurate critiques of the economic record of the Attlee government lie not with its overall macro management of the British economy but in the field of microeconomics. Little was done to tackle the underlying problems afflicting British business, from poor management to low investment rates. British shipbuilding, for example, once a world-beating industry, now found itself struggling to compete with overseas rivals, whose newer yards were much more capital intensive and automated. While British yards still relied on flexible, craft-based skilled workers, the newer Swedish, German and American yards employed larger-scale mass-production techniques that took account of the rapid changes in welding and fabrication technology. Their productivity was some 30 to 40 per cent higher by the late 1940s and the gap was growing. In the nationalised industries directly under public control, the previous management were generally left in place and investment trimmed back to allow more resources for exports. The balance that was achieved by 1950 came at the cost of future growth. The planning reforms of the period, which sought to rebalance the economy among the regions, hamstrung London and Birmingham without achieving much uplift elsewhere.

The 1940s were a period of huge change for the British economy and for Britain's political economy. The Keynesian theoretical revolution of the 1930s became a reality. In the language of political science, Britain experienced a paradigm shift. That is to say that not only did the tools of economic policy change but the targets of policy moved too. Britain emerged from the war with the explicit goal of maintaining full employment. And that goal required a much larger and more active state. In contrast to the 1920s there was no attempt to shrink the role of government back to the pre-war norm. Government spending and government tax receipts (both around 20 per cent of GDP in the 1930s) stabilised at around 40 per cent. The state was raking in twice as large a share of output in the form of tax, and spending it.

The 1940s can be seen as a time of shift in another important regard too. Britain had been the leading globaliser of the pre-1914 world, a uniquely open economy from which goods, money and people flowed freely. The deglobalisation of the inter-war period and the Imperial Preference of the 1930s had pushed that into reverse, but the process would not be completed until the 1940s. Immigration picked up sharply in the mid-1940s as the Windrush generation and other imperial and Commonwealth citizens (not to mention another wave of Irish immigrants) helped post-war Britain rebuild. But the Labour government of that time thought in implicitly national protectionist terms. The target after all was full *British* employment, not a prosperous open economy.

Still, for all the change of the 1940s, and those changes were of an order of magnitude not seen again until the 1980s, some things remained. While the doubling of the size of the state, the increases in taxation, the nationalisation of whole sectors and the adoption of active fiscal management of the economy all point to a more collectivist Britain, important aspects of the nineteenth-century liberal regime remained: competition between firms based on market mechanisms, free collective bargaining at the firm level, a national training system based around individuals acquiring general rather than specific skills, and a relatively unreformed City of London and banking system. Mr Attlee's revolution was less complete than it often appears.

12

Never Had It So Good

Given the lasting impact of the Attlee government, the fact that it lasted only six years is somewhat perplexing. By 1951, though, the government was already looking tired. The key ministers had been in office not since 1945 but since 1940. Waging a total war and then fundamentally reshaping Britain's political economy over the course of a decade was presumably rather taxing work. The introduction of some NHS charging provoked Cabinet resignations (including that of Nye Bevan, the minister who had presided over the NHS's birth) and left the government looking not just listless but also divided. In the long run the expansion of welfare payments, the provision of free healthcare, the material increase in education funding and the commitment to full employment would offer a great deal to many British voters, but in the short term life under the latter half of the Attlee government did not necessarily appear great.

The devaluation of 1949 was not only a blow to prestige but materially raised the cost of imported goods. Cigarette prices rose by 14 per cent, which is the kind of thing a nation of smokers tends to notice. That, combined with continued rationing and restrictions, not to mention a higher tax burden, left workers feeling somewhat squeezed. The prioritising of exports and public services over investment not only crimped business investment but also house building. Offered a choice between the larger state of the Attlee government and a return to the pre-war norm, it is almost certain that the British people would have stuck with Labour in the 1950s. But that was not the choice that was before them. The Conservative Party that was re-elected in 1951 had once again re-invented itself. Churchill might still be leader, but his domestic agenda was more in keeping with the New Liberal reformist spirit of his youth than his spell as a tight-money Chancellor overseeing the return to gold in the 1920s. Fundamentally the Conservative electoral proposition in 1951 amounted to 'You can keep all the stuff you like, but we'll also roll back restrictions on personal spending and build more houses.' That proved a popular offer, one that would keep the Conservatives in power until the mid-1960s. Such was the perceived continuity with Labour, in terms of the overall economic approach, that the term 'Butskellism' (named for Labour's last Chancellor, Hugh Gaitskell, and his Tory successor Rab Butler) has come to be used to describe the broad macro policies of 1945 to 1979. Butskellism was never as coherent or as unchallenged as is sometimes believed. But there was certainly a great deal of economic continuity over the three or so decades following the Second World War.

In 1957, Harold Macmillan, the Conservative Prime Minister, proclaimed in Bedford: 'Go around the country, go to the industrial towns, go to the farms and you will see a state of prosperity such as we have never seen in my lifetime.' As he famously put it, 'most of our people have never had it so good'. What makes the Macmillan speech striking is that, not only was it true, but he was speaking to a country only twelve years on from a total war. The economic costs of the two wars were, as we have seen, comparable, and Britain fought the second without having truly dealt with the lasting impact of the first. And yet the post-war trajectories were radically different. Both wars saw huge rises in the ratio of government debt to GDP, to 125 per cent in 1918 and over 240 per cent in 1945. But while debt rose from 125 per cent in 1918 to just over 150 per cent in the twenty years to 1938, during the twenty years after the second war the debt ratio fell from its record high to 84 per cent by 1965. That large fall in debt was accompanied by a much weightier state and far better economic outcomes. There was no return to mass unemployment and, as Macmillan noted, prosperity spread widely among the populace.

The seeming success of the post-war years, in contrast to the miserable inter-war period, was based on two major differences: a vastly different approach to macroeconomic policy and, crucially, an equally different global economic environment.

The global economy of the inter-war years was not a happy one. Bitter battles over war reparations and international debts stifled economic diplomacy while rising tariff levels and the legacy of total war put globalisation firmly into reverse. The reconstructed gold standard not only hampered responses to the Great Depression that began in the United States but transmitted the shock globally. The 1950s and 1960s could not have been more different. In Germany they are known as the *Wirtschaftswunder* (or economic miracle) while in France the three decades from 1945 to 1975 are, economically speaking, *Les Trente Glorieuses*. Some have gone as far as to christen the period 'the golden age of capitalism', a time of high employment, fast growth, strong rises in real wages and a period of relative financial calm.

The bustling growth of the global economy in part was reflecting the pent-up demand released after six years of warfare, but post-war booms are not inevitable, indeed post-war busts have been just as common. More important was the industrialisation of Europe on a scale not before seen. Take France as an example: at the beginning of the Second World War some 35 per cent of the workforce was still employed in agriculture. By 1960 that was down to 20 per cent, and, as in Britain a century earlier, the movement of workers from low-productivity rural jobs to higher-output-per-hour roles in the growing towns and cities pushed overall growth higher.

The messy international monetary politics of the 1920s was avoided by a new framework for global monetary co-operation which became known as the Bretton Woods system, named for the New Hampshire town where the details were hammered out towards the end of the war.

The logic of Bretton Woods, at which Keynes (who else could it be?) had headed the British delegation, appeared sound. The old gold standard had not only propagated a global shock in the 1920s, it had led to vastly inappropriate domestic policies too. Added to this was a sense that international movements had increased economic fragilities. In 1914 Keynes's tea-sipping Englishman had enjoyed the chance to venture his capital freely in any market of the world. But in the 1930s that same but now more wizened tea-drinker had found Britain vulnerable to sudden capital outflows.

There was also a worry that allowing currencies to float freely could result in a rapid race to the bottom as nations sought to gain a competitive advantage against each other by devaluing their own currencies in order to make their products cheaper and grab global market share.

The solution appeared to be to move to another point on the global monetary trinity. The gold standard had embraced fixed exchange rates and free-flowing capital markets but at the cost of domestic control of monetary policy. Under the Bretton Woods system it was open capital markets that were closed. Currencies would be pegged to the dollar (although the value of the pegs was to be adjustable), which was itself tied to gold, and the movement of money across borders was to be regulated. Individuals and firms needed permission to move large values of cash internationally. The limited, but not entirely constrained, movement of capital brought central banks more power to set interest rates that were appropriate to domestic conditions without worrying so much as to the value of their currency. Even if, for example, British investors wished to move their money out of sterling to take advantage of higher returns available in, say, dollar markets, they would be constrained from doing so, hence putting less pressure on the value of the pound.

The Bretton Woods system was to last for three decades, from which global financial and banking crises were to be mostly absent. But the seeds of its failure were present from its creation. For a start, the capital controls were always porous: firms found ways to avoid them and move money, and those holes became larger over time. The City of London was to play a large role in driving them wider in the 1960s. Balance of payments problems, as Britain would discover over the 1950s, 1960s and 1970s, still had the capacity to derail domestic policy.

More seriously, though, while Bretton Woods was designed to help balance the global monetary and economic systems and created the so-called Bretton Woods Institutions (the International Monetary Fund and what became the World Bank) to do just that, there was no mechanism to force a country running a substantial surplus to pare it back; instead the burden lay with deficit countries to cut back their imports. If a country ran a persistent deficit then pressure would mount against its currency, eventually forcing a change in policy. Whereas a country running a persistent surplus could merrily continue to do so. At the conference itself Keynes had argued for a symmetrical approach, and indeed for the system to be anchored not on the US dollar but on a new global reserve currency. But elegant arguments could not outweigh the then existing balance of economic power. The United States would rather have a system based on its own currency and, being the largest surplus country in the world, preferred one where adjustment was handled by other people.

If any British observers did not fully grasp where global financial and economic power, and with it global leadership, now resided they got a rude awakening in 1956. The Suez Crisis occupies a strange place in post-war British history; it is still the touchstone the commentariat reach for when looking to express the gravity of a crisis. 'The worst debacle since Suez' was an analogy drawn both in the immediate aftermath of the Argentinian seizure of the Falklands in 1982 and again after the Brexit vote of 2016. It is somewhat telling of the charmed nature of Britain's later twentieth century that the great disaster used to benchmark subsequent crises was, for all its drama, not a military occupation or defeat but the failure to impose the nation's imperial will on Egypt. Suez was ultimately not a military defeat but a financial one.

Egypt's nationalisation of the Suez Canal in July 1956 was seen as a dire threat to British interests by the country's military-political elite and it was just the kind of thing that that elite would have been able to stop in the 1920s or 1930s. But the 1950s were different. Under a secret agreement with France and Israel, a plan was hatched to regain control of the canal and also to depose Egypt's military leader Colonel Nasser; Israel would go to war with Egypt and British and French troops would seize the canal in order to safeguard it. Militarily the plan went as smoothly as these things ever do; financially it was a disaster.

The British current account was in surplus in 1956 but

speculative pressure began to build on the pound regardless. Investors began to bet that the pound's value of $2.80, established in 1949, would have to be lowered as the crisis dragged on. Such a devaluation would not only increase the price of imports and drive up inflation but further undermine the integrity of the sterling bloc and the pound's role as a reserve currency. To Harold Macmillan, the Chancellor when the crisis arose, such a development was not unexpected. But he assumed that the US would offer support, either by offering direct bilateral support in the form of US loans or by allowing Britain to tap the still-new International Monetary Fund (IMF) for access to short-term funds to tide sterling over. Such US support did not arrive. Instead the US, outraged at a European-led imperial adventure that risked pushing Egypt towards Soviet support, stepped up the pressure – threatening that unless Britain agreed to a ceasefire and the withdrawal of its forces, then the US would itself start selling down its own holdings of sterling. Under pressure the Cabinet was forced to accept a UN-brokered ceasefire and begin withdrawing troops. The IMF, having got the nod from the US administration, then announced a $1.3 billion package of support for sterling, ending the immediate financial pressure. That came too late for Anthony Eden, who was soon ousted as Prime Minister and replaced by his Chancellor Macmillan.

Suez demonstrated that Britain might still have the means to deploy serious military assets in the Middle East, but now lacked the financial clout to act against US interests. The old Empire was dismantled over the course of the 1940s to 1960s. Indian independence in 1947 removed the crown jewel and was followed by a wave of imperial retreat out of Africa in the 1950s. And yet, the old territories were never more important to Britain's economy than in the post-war decades. As western Europe moved towards customs unions and increased economic integration, Britain found itself more reliant than in the past on what had been imperial markets. This all came against a backdrop of diminished trade in general. The share of GDP of imports and exports combined had usually been over 50 per cent in the pre-Great War days and occasionally as high as 70 per cent in the late Victorian period. But the Britain of the 1950s was a much less open economy. The combined trade share of GDP was more like 40–45 per cent most years, and under 40 per cent by the 1960s. International supply chains were cut back. More food was produced domestically. The traditional English breakfast became more English, with domestic bacon replacing Danish imports. Cars were increasingly British made and the declining shipbuilding industry produced fewer vessels for export. Britain was not an outlier here: the 1950s and 1960s saw a more constrained globalisation than earlier years. But the changes were perhaps most felt in the United Kingdom, a country which had defined itself by its economic openness since the 1840s.

Bretton Woods was not a perfect regime for managing international monetary and financial flows. Countries, as Britain discovered in both 1949 and 1956, were still vulnerable to global investor opinion. But, outside of acute moments of crisis, capital flows were notably lower and domestic policy was, in the main, insulated most of the time from the need to strive for external balance. That would be hugely important in the (often under-remarked) great economic success story of post-war Britain: the management of government debt.

Post-war policy-makers had many things to worry about, from the fear of a return to mass unemployment to the need to balance international payments, but, especially compared to the 1920s, the burden of debt was not one of them. That is particularly surprising when one remembers that the bill incurred in 1939–1945 was so much higher.

By 1970, the government debt to GDP ratio in Britain had been reduced from almost 260 per cent to just 55 per cent. Not only a sharp contrast with the failed debt management of the 1920s and 1930s but a more impressive performance than in the austere days of Victorian Chancellors. This was achieved despite a much larger state and, most perplexingly to many non-economists, without running a persistent budget surplus. Indeed, while the debt ratio fell in every fiscal year from 1945/46 until 1970/71, Britain ran, over the course of those 25 years, 8 surplus budgets and 17 deficits.

Government debt dynamics can seem a touch bewildering at first glance and much of that confusion arises from homely metaphors comparing the finances of a government to those of a household. States, though, are not like families. For a start they, in theory at least, live for ever. In the main, government debt is never actually 'paid off', it is simply refinanced by borrowing again. The actual level, in cash terms, of Britain's national debt grew from around £25 billion in 1945 to around £35 billion in 1970 but the economy grew by a great deal more. The size of the debt in absolute terms increased but the burden of managing it fell substantially. The key to understanding government debt over the medium term is to grasp that if GDP is growing at a more rapid clip than the real interest rate (the interest rate after taking account of inflation) on that debt, then the burden of the debt will fall over time. If interest rates are low or growth rapid, then a high level of debt can be managed downwards.

Both sides of the growth/interest rates equation worked in favour of the British government in the 1950s compared to the 1920s. Growth was higher and real interest rates much lower, although it was the rates side which did the real heavy lifting. For most of the 1950s and 1960s the real return on government debt was negative – which is to say that after taking into account inflation, holders of government debt made a loss. An investor buying a ten-year UK government bond, known as a gilt, in 1950 would receive an annual interest payment equivalent to around 2.6 per cent of the amount invested until 1960, when they would get the principal back. Over the course of that decade, though, inflation varied from an annual low of 3.2 per cent to a high of 4.8 per cent. In other words, the real interest rate would vary from a 'high' of −0.8 per cent to a low of −2.2 per cent. Over the decade as a whole prices rose by almost 50 per cent. The principal they received back in 1960 would have lost much of its purchasing power. Buying a gilt in 1950 was obviously a poor investment and the question becomes, why did anyone do it? The answer is straightforward: mostly they had no choice.

The policy of the time is now usually called 'financial repression'. This can best be understood as regulations designed to ensure that interest rates remain below the level of inflation. To work, it required the capital controls of the Bretton Woods era, creating a pool of domestic savings that could not simply seek higher returns abroad but were essentially trapped in Britain. Insurance companies, pension funds, banks and other pools of assets could then be compelled to hold a large percentage of their balance sheets in the form of government debt. The government essentially forced the private sector to pay for its debt reduction through a stealth inflation tax. The Bank of England had set interest rates to maintain the value of sterling against gold in the world before the Second World War. Interest rate policy then was, to a large extent, all about managing the value of the currency. For much of the immediate post-war decades monetary policy played a different macroeconomic role: helping to manage down the level of government debt. Nowadays such policies have a bad reputation. 'Financial repression' does not exactly have the ring of something that states wish to emulate. There is of course the argument that an equally valid name would be 'successful debt management policies'. Savers did lose out from negative real interest rates but, on the other hand, it allowed the government to adopt a far more expansionary policy than the debt repayment prioritisation of the inter-war years. Lower returns for investors seem a fair trade-off for avoiding a stagnant economy and mass unemployment.

Of course macroeconomics very rarely, if ever, serves up a truly free lunch. For financial repression to work, real interest rates had to be either extremely low or negative, and for that to happen, inflation had to be higher than in the past. Whereas policy-makers had reacted to the jump in price level after the First World War with horror and tried to push it down again, the reaction after 1945 was different. A bit of inflation now seemed to be a useful tool. It helped governments to pay down their debts and seemed to lubricate the economy more widely, helping growth along. It was, after all, very hard to cut wages in cash terms during a downturn, but, when the need came along, they could perhaps be held constant even as prices rose, thus achieving cuts in real terms without creating as much labour unrest. By the late 1960s it seemed British governments had become a bit too relaxed about inflation, and that, while it brought some benefits to economic management, stoked up troubles too.

That this was the case was already apparent by the late 1950s. Macmillan's Bedford speech is still mostly known for the 'we've never had it so good' part and not the following section, in which the Prime Minister wondered if the good times could really continue. 'What we need is restraint and common sense – restraint in the demands we make and common sense on how we spend our income.' By 1957 many were already beginning to worry that inflation was becoming a real problem, hampering investment and impacting international competitiveness. The point of the Bedford speech was not just to celebrate Britain's late-1950s prosperity but to warn that it was at risk.

Butskellism became the default policy setting of both major parties but the 'post-war consensus' was never quite as all-embracing as it sometimes appears in hindsight. Gladstone had now been entirely ousted from the Treasury. In 1952 the highest levels of British economic policy-making drew up plans called Operation ROBOT. The name came from the drafters involved – Sir Leslie ROwan, Sir George BOlton and OTto Clarke: the two top civil servants at the Treasury and the Governor of the Bank of England – and, on paper at least, the plan was presented as a way to achieve external balance. The pound's Bretton Woods system peg to the dollar would be allowed to float until it found a level supported by the markets. The economy would then adjust to the new rate. In effect the authors argued for more use of market forces to dictate economic outcomes and a step back from the notion of Keynesian demand management. The price would likely, as they acknowledged, be somewhat higher employment. The name then referred not just to the authors' names but to the supposedly automatic way the economy would adjust to the new foreign exchange price. In some ways the 'robot' was just a 1950s techno-inspired update to Adam Smith's invisible hand. The Cabinet, though, was having none of it. Robot remained a memo rather than a policy.

But as the decade wore on officials received a more sympathetic ear from their political masters. In 1958 Macmillan's successor as Chancellor, Peter Thorneycroft, resigned from government (together with two of his junior ministers, one of whom was Enoch Powell) over the rising level of government expenditure. Macmillan, always quick with a homely phrase, dismissed this as 'just a little local difficulty'. But the resignation of a Chancellor over the direction of economic policy is not something that can simply be dismissed. The Tory governments of the 1950s had denationalised (privatised was not yet a word) the steel industry and they had rolled back some restrictions and rationing, but much of the economic legacy of Attlee remained in place. The borders of the state had advanced in the 1940s and remained broadly in place until the 1980s. That essential continuity of policy was central to the Conservatives' electoral offer to the mass working-class electorate but it slowly built up problems with other parts of the core Conservative electoral coalition. High taxes and seemingly ever-present inflation were causing mounting resentment among business people, savers and the middle class in 1958; it would be a decade and a half, however, before those tensions rose to breaking point. As Thorneycroft was to put it, with almost Macmillanesque levels of understatement, 'perhaps we went a little too early'.

If one lasting legacy of the two total wars of the twentieth century was a larger British state, then the other was a much lower level of inequality. The two wars both ran down levels of assets and were both accompanied by much higher tax rates, especially on top earners. Both also saw unionisation increasing, boosting the bargaining power of organised labour. In 1913 the top 0.1 per cent of British earners had taken home 11.6 per cent of national income. About one in ten pounds earned in Britain went to just one in one thousand people. But by the 1950s the top 0.1 per cent's share of national income had fallen to more like 2.5 per cent. The top 1 per cent's share of total wealth (as opposed to income) fell from around 70 per cent to just under 50 per cent over the same period. Britain was far from an equal country but certainly a much more equitable place than it had been in Victorian and Edwardian times.

Economically the 1950s were a strange decade for Britain.

The Prime Minister could openly, and rightly, talk of people never having had it so good. The number of cars on British roads doubled from under five million in 1950 to more than ten million by 1960. The black and white television was a rarity at the time of the Queen's coronation in 1953, so that people crowded into the houses that had them, but 80 per cent of households owned one by 1960. Unemployment was low and real wage growth decent, especially compared to the 1930s or 1920s. The state offered people more – whether in the form of welfare payments, education or health – than it ever had before. But rising inflation was already leading to some discontent and, as people increasingly became aware, the golden age of capitalism seemed to be somehow less golden in Britain than elsewhere in western Europe. By the 1960s it seemed something had to change.

13

Strife. Britain in the 1960s

The Beatles got a surprising amount of official attention for a pop group. In 1965 the fab four received MBEs for services to popular culture. Critics argued, with more than a whiff of truth, that this was simply cynical politics from Harold Wilson, the Labour Prime Minister. But a strong case can be made that they deserved the awards for services to the balance of payments. Between 1964 and 1966 the group's US tours earned record amounts. The contemporary press reckoned they earned (in modern terms) about $650 a second playing to sold-out concert halls. At a time when Britain was short of dollars this was a meaningful prop to the capital account. Americans paying to see the Beatles was a dollar-earning export that helped contain the trade deficit. Tours in Japan and Germany provided mark and yen earnings too. The traditional 'invisible' service exports of shipping, financial services and the like were receiving an important helping hand from the four Liverpudlians. Sadly for Britain's balance of payments, as well as for fans of live music, the group ceased performing live after 1966. Nowadays it seems odd that a major advanced economy could be, even to a small extent, supported by the overseas earnings of a music group. But, at least economically speaking, 1960s Britain was not in a good place.

By any objective absolute measure, British growth in the 1950s and 1960s was strong. GDP growth averaged an annual rate of 3.2 per cent in the 1950s and 3.4 per cent in 1960s. That was not only a huge improvement on the 1920s or 1930s but compares well to more recent outcomes. Between 1993 and 2007, for example, a time usually lauded as 'the good years' before the 2008 crash, growth averaged just 3.0 per cent. But many Britons were not judging growth on an absolute standard, they were measuring it on a relative basis – and much of Europe was growing faster. It was in these years that Britain lost the decisive lead over the rest of the continent that had been established in the late 1700s and early 1800s. Take France, as Britain's nearest peer both geographically and in terms of population size. British GDP per head was some 30 per cent higher than the French equivalent in the late 1940s. But by the mid-1960s the gap had vanished and by the late 1960s France had pulled slightly ahead. Adjusted for purchasing power, France's GDP per head was above that of Britain by 1968. A similar story could be told about West Germany, the Low Countries or Italy.

The decline of the post-war years needs to be put into a longer-term perspective. Yes, British GDP per head slipped against western Europe but against the global economic leader, the United States, the picture is more nuanced. Indeed, leaving aside the US crash in the Great Depression and the impact of 1939–1945, British GDP per head had consistently been around 70 per cent of US GDP per head ever since 1918. What really changed in the 1950s and 1960s was that much of western Europe caught up to British levels. That was, over the longer run, almost certainly inevitable. It is hard to argue that British GDP per head could ever have been consistently higher than that of countries with similar economic and social systems and access to broadly the same technology. The remarkable thing is that Britain's post-industrial revolution lead lasted a century and half rather than the fact it eventually eroded.

But the end of the lead attracted a great deal of declinist commentary both at the time and since. One reason for that was that the statistics were now more widely available. The modern framework of national accounting used to measure economic growth began to be more widely used to publish quarterly updates in the 1950s. Britons began to get near enough real-time updates on the relative state of their economy just at the point when that relative performance looked to be at its worst. The right could of course blame the post-war settlement and the policy choices adopted by Attlee between 1945 and 1951; the left could always say the real problems came in the 'thirteen wasted years' of Conservative rule between 1951 and 1964. Both sides tended to underplay the extent to which what was happening was a European catch-up rather than a British decline.

But a story of European catch-up does not capture everything that was happening; it cannot for example explain the fact that western European GDP per head began to pull ahead of British in the mid- to late 1960s. Declinist accounts are usually overplayed, but the anti-declinist argument sometimes runs too far. With the benefit of hindsight it is clear that Britain faced two real and distinct sets of economic problems – on the supply side and the demand side – from the 1950s until the 1970s, which became very apparent in the 60s.

On the supply side of the economy, productivity growth was hampered by what became known as the 'British disease'. The nature of the disease varied depending on the diagnoser, but it was some mixture of poor, unproductive company management, and difficult labour relations that tended to inflate wages and make change harder. The fundamental problem was that British productivity was now materially lower than that of some industrial rivals and seemed to be growing at a slower clip too. The gap was widening. Management seemed less entrepreneurial in Britain than in western Europe or North America, strikes were more common and training systems less advanced. The *Sunday Times* caught the national mood in 1964 with an article asking, 'Is Britain a Half-time Country getting Half-pay for Half-work under Half-management?'

These supply-side problems reflected a lack of competition in the economy. The competitive structure of the British economy by the 1960s looked very different from what had come before the Second World War. The utilities, and several other sectors, were now nationalised and insulated as monopolies. The economy had become less integrated with the rest of the world, lowering competition from imports and reducing the need for firms to remain highly competitive against their foreign peers to secure export markets. The Mini was the iconic British car of the decade but it failed to sell well outside of the UK. In Germany it was priced at almost DM 5,000 against DM 4,500 for the comparable, and equally iconic, VW Beetle. The Beetle was cheaper to manufacture and more reliable overall. Where consumers had a choice between the two, they usually opted for the Volkswagen. But most domestic consumers were not offered that choice. The 'rationalisation' of the 1920s and 1930s had continued into the 1940s and 1950s, with the trend being towards mergers and cartels rather than domestic competition within industries. Whether the root of the problem was indeed incompetent management, over-mighty unions, a lack of investment or some combination of all of these, the situation was allowed to fester due to a lack of competitive dynamism to drive change.

Alongside these supply-side problems, the demand side

of the economy too was troubled. The notion that the government should be actively managing demand to ensure full employment was the guiding light of economic policy throughout the first three post-war decades, but while this was a relatively straightforward idea in theory, it was rather harder to put into practice outside of a textbook. For a start, the fears of pre-war vintage Gladstonian Treasury officials that handing democratic politicians the tools to actively manage the economy would lead to political, rather than economic, considerations driving decisions turned out to be not always too wide of the mark. Chancellors tended to be more generous with their spending decisions and keener on cutting taxes as elections approached, and then to be forced into making up the ground after the results. The balance of payments, and the need to maintain sterling's value against the dollar, acted as further constraints on effective demand management. As 1956 had demonstrated, the pound remained vulnerable to swings in global confidence. Since monetary policy primarily concerned itself with keeping rates low to help manage down the real burden of government debt, it was fiscal policy (taxes and spending) that had to do all the heavy economic lifting.

The result was what became known as 'stop-go': a rather juddering approach to economic management, whereby the Chancellor would cut taxes or increase spending as an election neared to create an economic feel-good factor, only to be forced to slam on the brakes when confident consumers stepped up their purchases of imported goods and put pressure on the trade balance. Long-term planning became difficult for firms, hampering their investment decisions.

Governments of the 1960s were not totally blind to these issues. They could read the economic statistics as well as anyone else. The answer they reached for was what is now sometimes called 'Keynesianism Plus' – keeping Keynes's emphasis on the aggregate management of demand but coupling with it a more ambitious agenda of supply-side reform. In effect this was reaching back to the 1940s language of planning. And just as in the 1940s the nature of planning remained disputed.

The turn to planning began towards the end of the Conservatives' thirteen-year spell in office. Macmillan, who had himself been a keen planner in the 1930s, had often spoken of a 'middle way' between capitalism and socialism in the form of a more ordered approach to economic management. He was no ideologue and had been impressed by the French experience of planning in the 1950s and early 1960s. He had warned in 1957 that the good times were at risk unless accompanied by a strong dose of moderation. By the early 1960s, with inflation still ticking upwards and the balance of payments threatening to put pressure on the pound, it was clear that calls for moderation had not been heeded.

Hence the Prime Minister's 'New Agenda' of the 1960s, which consisted of two key plans: to join the European Economic Community (EEC) that had developed on the continent, and to set up some form of British economic planning. Sadly for Macmillan his attempt at joining the nascent European Community was vetoed by French President de Gaulle and he himself was forced out of office by illness in 1963 before any of his planning initiatives bore fruit. Still, it is important to remember that the 1960s turn towards greater planning began under a Conservative government rather than with its Labour successor.

The National Economic Development Council (invariably known as Neddy) was established in 1962 and modelled on French lines. A tripartite committee (in the language of the time), it brought together government ministers, industrialists and trade union leaders to discuss wages, inflation, investment and productivity, and to attempt to steer the economy over the medium term. Industry-specific Economic Development Committees (the Little Neddys) sat below it, feeding through ideas and discussions. Neddy would be an important forum for economic policy-making throughout the 1960s and 1970s before falling into disuse in the 1980s and finally being abolished in 1992. Neddy began by producing economic forecasts and identifying barriers to growth – whether that was a lack of investment, a failure of training or a need to change working practices. The hope was that unions and business could be brought together, with government acting as an honest broker, to find mutually beneficial ways to boost growth. But the Neddys quickly degenerated into fruitless talking shops more often marked by loud disagreement than by quiet consensus. This was a British attempt at the corporatism (or the involvement of unions and private sector leaders) which worked, with varying degrees of success, across post-war Europe.

If the Conservatives had begun to dabble in Keynesianism Plus and planning in the early 1960s, the Labour government that took power in 1964 positively embraced it. Labour had had a difficult 1950s: losing elections in 1951, 1955 and 1959. The party spent much of the decade doing what it enjoys most and fighting a vicious civil war. Hugh Gaitskell, leader from 1955 until his early death in 1963, was what would in the 1980s or 1990s be called a moderniser, who sought to make the party relevant to the newly prosperous electorate by broadening its appeal. The great thinker of the Labour right was Tony Crosland, whose 1956 book *The Future of Socialism* sought to make a distinction between the 'means' and 'ends' of socialism. For Crosland and Gaitskell the ends were a broadly social democratic country with higher levels of equality and social mobility. The 'means' did not have to involve nationalisation and public ownership. Crosland went as far as to question whether the Britain of the 1950s with its larger state, welfare system and stronger unions, was even 'capitalist' any more. Certainly he believed it was not the world that Marx and Engels had catalogued in the 1840s. Gaitskell went as far as attempting to change the Labour Party's Clause IV and drop the commitment to public ownership, but the party would not wear it. This, to them, was a betrayal of what the party stood for.

Gaitskell's successor was Harold Wilson. Wilson was the first economist to become Prime Minister: a grammar school boy who studied under Beveridge at Oxford, he became a lecturer in economic history before the war and then a civil service economist during it. Elected to Parliament in 1945, he was in the Cabinet as the President of the Board of Trade by 1947. Yet in 1951 he resigned from government over the issue of NHS charging, alongside Nye Bevan. Throughout the 1950s he was closely associated with the Labour left and a critic of Gaitskell, Crosland and the revisionists. Once elected, though, he was quick to move towards their position. A consummate politician with a flair for self-promotion, he was to lead the party for over a decade and serve as Prime Minister twice. Still, Britain's first economist Prime Minister is rarely lauded for his economic management. The 1964–1970 government was a great reforming one – under it the death penalty was abolished, homosexuality decriminalised, and abortion legalised. But the Home Office had a better late 1960s than the Treasury.

Wilson embraced the language of modernisation and reform; he wanted to unleash the 'white heat' of a technological and scientific revolution to power Britain's economy forward. While productivity growth is rarely the kind of thing politicians make speeches about, Wilson wanted to talk of little else. Grand plans were hatched and grand projects set in motion. A new Ministry of Technology was established to co-ordinate research and spearhead the rapid roll-out of new breakthroughs, backed by government infrastructure. A serious attempt was made to challenge the power of the Treasury by setting up a new Department of Economic Affairs (DEA). The feeling was that while the Treasury had gradually evolved into the role of the leading *economic* ministry it was a still a *financial* ministry at heart. In the end it was still, critics not unfairly argued, a department which thought about the budget as something to balance rather than one that saw its role as boosting economic growth. The Treasury was a place where civil servants rose to prominence through their ability to say no to spending and safeguard the public purse. The DEA would be a place that said yes.

Much faith was placed in indicative planning, the notion that government, business and unions between them would draw up a set of national targets and then work through how to deliver them. Specific investments and training requirements were itemised and, in theory, progress could be monitored against a checklist. The DEA's National Plan, produced in 1965, aimed for growth of 3.8 per cent throughout the latter half of the 1960s. Growth would in the event be closer to half that.

Reshuffling Whitehall and making impassioned speeches is a far more straightforward task than reforming an economy. Wilson's plans came to little, partly due to a poor choice of minister. George Brown, the first Secretary of State for Economic Affairs, was rather too fond of a drink and not fond enough of serious work. But the institutional arrangements had deeper problems than a few people being in the wrong seat. British attempts at corporatism suffered from the more decentralised nature of Britain's trade unions and firms compared to their continental peers. The General Secretary of the TUC could, in theory, agree to something, but the dozens of unions that made up the organisation might not play ball. And even if their leaderships did, their branches might not. The business organisations could speak for what business desired but they could not bind their members into carrying out their will. The whole framework was rickety from the start.

A deeper problem, though, came from the balance of accounts. There is, it always bears repeating, nothing especially wrong with running a trade deficit and nothing virtuous about running a trade surplus. Trade, conducted on fair terms, enriches both sides – consumers and firms get access to the products they desire. But a persistent imbalance in the current account, the fact that a country is consistently either borrowing from the rest of the world or lending to it, suggests something is out of whack. In the era of Bretton Woods, when the maintenance of a currency peg was a target of policy, it was even more troublesome. Britain had bound herself, since the 1949 devaluation, to a sterling–dollar exchange rate of $2.80 to the pound. That rate was simply higher than the British economic fundamentals could support: it priced many imports at a level that British producers could not compete with and made British exports uncompetitive in many markets. Shipbuilding is a classic example. Whereas in the 1930s and 1940s almost 100 per cent of newly launched British-flagged vessels had been constructed in British yards, by the mid-1960s 75 per cent were made overseas. Poor productivity and an overvalued exchange rate simply made buying from the West Germans or the Swedes much cheaper.

At the time the Wilson government took office the current account deficit was already a higher than expected £800 million, the largest since the Second World War and some 1.4 per cent of GDP. Over the next year the touring of the Beatles would provide some respite but the fab foursome could only do so much.

Of course a core tenet of Bretton Woods was that currencies

were fixed but adjustable. Britain had already reset the value of sterling once before. But just because something was adjustable in theory did not mean changing it was easy in practice. Wilson worried that devaluation would undermine Britain's place in the global economy further: a second devaluation just a decade and a half after the last one would raise question marks over the future value of sterling in the long run, making it less attractive to foreigners. It would raise the costs of Britain's still extensive overseas military deployment – even after the Suez debacle Britain maintained a large military presence in the Middle East and Asia. Wilson kept Britain out of the Vietnam War, but British soldiers fought an undeclared war with Indonesia in Malaysia in the 1960s and took part in counterinsurgency in the Aden emergency. A devaluation it was feared would put these deployments at risk, undermining Britain's position as a great power, and it would inflict a loss on the holders of sterling balances – a pretty poor thing to do to those who had funded Britain during the war. It would also cause inflation to rise further as the cost of imports increased, which would spur trade unions to push for higher wage settlements in compensation, further squeezing British industry. An immediate devaluation in 1964 could have, perhaps, been blamed on the outgoing Conservative government, but once that chance was missed the political costs of devaluation weighed heavily on Wilson and his Cabinet's minds. They feared, coming after 1949, that Labour would be labelled as the party of devaluation in the minds of the public.

Crimped by too high an exchange rate, growth disappointed the National Plan in 1965 and 1966 and pressure on sterling continued to build. In July 1966, the government adopted the July Measures – a programme of public spending cuts designed to cool demand, lower inflation and cut back imports in order to achieve some sort of external economic balance. This was a damning indictment of the Wilson government's approach – a government determined to end 'stop-go' was engaging in classic stop-go behaviour and, when push came to shove, the need to forlornly attempt to prop up the value of the pound trumped the ambitions of the National Plan drafted the year before. Power, despite the machinery of government musical chairs, still lay with the purse strings, and the Treasury remained the economic ministry rather than the new DEA, which itself would only last until 1969.

The July Measures bought the government time but alienated much of the Labour Party. In 1967 a dock strike, which disrupted trade, and the higher oil price after the Six Days War in the Middle East together caused the pressure on sterling to build once more, and the current account deficit reached a previously unimaginable 2.5 per cent. Inflation rose to over 4 per cent. With the Bank of England running, once again, low on reserves defending the exchange rate, the inevitable decision was taken in November 1967. The pound was devalued by 14 per cent to $2.40, interest rates increased and hire purchase restrictions tightened to dampen down consumer spending. Painful though these measures were in terms of the implicit dropping of the National Plan and the hoped-for rapid growth, they did at least bring the current account back into rough balance by the end of 1968. It was in the aftermath of the devaluation that defence secretary Denis Healey announced the decision to withdraw military assets from the Middle East and Asia (with the exception of the still British governed Hong Kong), partially to help shore up the balance of payments.

One sector of the British economy was turning a positive corner in the 1960s, although it was not one which received much attention in the National Plan: the City of London. The City's role as the pre-eminent financial sector had been lost in the Great War and diminished further in the 1920s and 1930s. The low interest rates and financial repression of the 1940s and 1950s hardly made for a great time for bankers. But beginning in the 1950s the City began to carve itself out a new global niche, one that was to become much less niche as the years wore on. This was the Eurodollar market, which confusingly has precisely nothing to do with the European Union's common currency. A Eurodollar, simply put, is any dollar held outside of the United States. Dollars held overseas either in the subsidiaries of US banks or by foreign banks were not subject to Federal deposit insurance but also escaped the regulation of the Federal Reserve. They tended to attract higher interest rates. Over the course of the late 1950s London's banks became the centre of the global Eurodollar market, a relatively unregulated, free-flowing global market at a time of tight capital controls. Higher oil prices in the 1960s led to rising Eurodollar balances as the newly enriched oil states of the Middle East decided they would rather hold their new-found wealth outside of the United States in order to escape US regulation and to gain higher returns. This left predominantly London-based banks holding dollars which could be loaned out. The global market for eurocurrencies (all deposits held outside of their home jurisdiction) was around $9 billion in 1964 but had leapt to $57 billion by 1970. Whereas most European states acted to prevent their financial centres handling such business, the Treasury and the Bank of England were at least content to tolerate it. If nothing else it helped Britain earn precious foreign currency. By 1970, the City had re-established itself as a financial centre of some global importance. Now, though, it was handling international business in dollars, and was stuffed full with branches of overseas banks, rather than managing the flow of capital out of Britain as it had in the era when sterling was the prime global currency.

But while the City of London was beginning a resurgence the wider Metropolitan area was not. London's population, which had peaked at 8.6 million in 1939, declined throughout the 1940s to 1960s. It was down to 7.5 million by 1970, despite the overall national population having grown from 50 million to more than 56 million over the same period. Those raw population numbers help tell a wider story about regional growth in the post-war years.

The 1950s and 1960s were, by some measures, the peak of Britain's industrialisation, a long process that had been building for more than a century and a half. Manufacturing's total share of economic output rose to around one third, up from a quarter in the early twentieth century, whereas the contribution of services marginally declined. Manufacturing employment peaked in 1966 at over 9 million workers. Although London and the wider southeast retained their economic lead over the rest of the country, those gaps narrowed in the 1950s and 1960s as manufacturing grew in importance. Powered by the car industry, the west midlands briefly enjoyed higher output per head than the southeast in the 1950s, at just about the time that Birmingham displaced Manchester as England's second largest city by size.

Regional growth received a boost from discretionary government spending targeted at areas outside the southeast, spending which grew through the 1960s and peaked in 1976. Firms opening factories in the 'right' locations, such as the northeast of England or south Wales, could expect their construction costs to be co-funded by the government. Manufacturing firms required permits to expand production, allowing the government to shift activity to where it felt it was required. The peak of refusals came in 1966, when 30 per cent of applications in the southeast and midlands were declined. Equally important in the late 1960s was a tax system designed to encourage firms to boost employment around the UK's old periphery. Between 1966 and 1970 Selective Employment Tax was charged on all employees but with exporters then receiving their cash back plus a bounty. In effect the tax system was forcing non-exporters to subside exporters to help the balance of payments. But while the target was external balance, the fact that manufacturers were more likely to be exporters, and so pay less tax than service-sector firms, meant it had a large regional footprint.

For all the experiments with Keynesian Plus, indicative planning and clever tax wheezes, the economic policy-making of the 1960s suffered from a belief in what can be termed 'hydraulic economics': a belief that the essential nature of dynamic capitalism had been tamed and that policy-making had been reduced to pulling on levers which had a measurable effect. That notion sat behind the way fiscal policy was run in the era of Butskellism and, whilst it drew on essential Keynesian insights about the importance of aggregate demand and the role of policy, it also ignored Keynes's own wider beliefs on the inherent uncertainty that affects all economies.

In 1958 the New Zealand born but British based economist Edward Phillips wrote a highly influential paper on the relationship between wages and unemployment over the preceding century. By the 1960s belief in the 'Phillips Curve' was widespread amongst policy-makers and economists. Rationally, and it seemed empirically too, there was an inverse relationship between the level of unemployment and the rate of inflation. If unemployment was low, then wage growth would quicken as firms competed for workers, and this faster growth would push up prices. If unemployment was high, then wage growth would be slower and so prices would rise less rapidly. There is no doubt a relationship between prices and unemployment but, despite the relatively widespread beliefs of the 1960s, it is not a stable one. Phillips-curve-type thinking encouraged policy-makers in their hydraulic beliefs, an ultimately self-defeating view that they had a good handle on the various economic factors and the relationship between them, that pulling lever X would always achieve result Y.

By the late 1960s something was clearly going wrong. Unemployment, after the July Measures of 1966 and the tightening monetary policy of 1967, drifted higher. The joblessness rate had been held at under 2.5 per cent for more than two decades but was 3.5 per cent by 1968 and approaching 4 per cent by 1970. And yet rising unemployment was not matched by falling inflation, quite the opposite. Annual inflation was running at over 4 per cent by the mid-1960s and at 6.5 per cent by 1970. Unemployment and inflation were rising together. The roots of the crisis of the 1970s were already apparent in the decade before.

The textbook solution to rising inflation in the 1950s and 1960s was to call for wage restraint, perhaps through the tripartite bodies that had been established at the tail end of the Tory governments. The 'two sides of industry' could come together and, prodded on by the government, find an acceptable solution.

The problem was this rarely worked in practice. Trade unions, by the 1960s, were in a much stronger position than they had ever achieved before, outside of periods of total war. Membership passed ten million for the first time in 1962, with around 40 per cent of workers unionised by the late 1960s. Union leaders sat down with industrialists and ministers to help establish indicative economic plans. High employment in the manufacturing industry meant large workplaces that could be organised: this was fertile territory for unions.

Just as in the 1920s, however, a strong Labour movement

led to growing middle-class concern over the power of the unions. Trade union power, as an economic factor, was never higher in peacetime than in the late 1960s, but the size of the potential backlash was growing too. Faced with a Labour government that had pledged an end to stop-go and faster growth, only to deliver setbacks and restraints, strikes and disputes rose to their highest levels since the 1920s. The dock strike of 1967 was an immediate catalyst of devaluation, just as the seamen's strike in 1966 had contributed to the run on the pound that drove the introduction of the July Measures. In both cases wage disputes spiralled into strike action that disrupted trade and put the balance of payments under pressure. Devaluation pushed up prices further, leading to more demands for higher wages.

In 1969 the government published a white paper on trade union reform. The blueprint came from Barbara Castle, the Secretary of State for Employment, and was entitled *In Place of Strife*, with a conciseness echoing 'In Place of Fear', as the Beveridge proposals had been dubbed. The government proposed a new trade union regime which would require ballots before strikes and establish compulsory arbitration in some disputes by an industrial panel. The unions reacted with fury that the party established to be the voice of organised labour should seek to increase regulation. Ambitious members of the Cabinet, who could see which way the wind was blowing and wished to enjoy union support within the party, joined them, and the proposals were quickly dropped. This was, although it was not obvious at the time, a major turning point in post-war British economic history.

Compared to the restrictions on trade unions introduced in the early 1970s and the 1980s by Conservative governments, *In Place of Strife* is mild in its proposals. With the benefit of hindsight, many union leaders would later admit that it was a lost chance to accept a new framework drawn up by allies rather than having one imposed.

The broad sweep of British economic history from 1945 until 1970 had been a story of an increasingly organised working class extracting more of the value from the economy. Even though the party of organised labour was in power for less than half of that quarter-century the outcome was high wages, higher employment, falling inequality and a larger state providing more services. Indeed, the state performing roles that would have been unimaginable in the 1930s. But the system had problems: inflation had helped to reduce the burden of government debt but now seemed to be spiralling upwards, unemployment was edging up, Britain risked falling behind its European peers. The rejection of *In Place of Strife* ultimately set the scene for a decade of clashes between the union movement and the government. The unions would win the first round but be heavily defeated in the rematch.

14

1976 and All That

The 2011 movie version of John Le Carré's 1970s espionage thriller *Tinker, Tailor, Soldier, Spy* is a solid piece of cinema but most fans would agree it fails to reach the heights set by the 1979 BBC television version starring Alec Guinness. Watching the two back to back is an interesting exercise in how the 1970s were perceived three decades later. Gary Oldman's Smiley character lives in a world of tones of grey. Everything is drab and dour and it always seems to be raining. This is the view of 1970s Britain as told by most historical fiction. By contrast, the 1979 version was not historical fiction, it was contemporary drama. The odd flash of colour appears on screen and occasionally it is even sunny.

The 1970s is, alongside the 1930s, a key decade in the development of Britain's political economy. It serves the role of cautionary tale, something to be avoided at all costs, just as the 1930s served for the 1940s and onwards. No return to the mass unemployment of the 1930s was a powerful political rallying call for the four decades afterwards, just as no return to the high inflation of the 1970s has been ever since. And just as the 1930s were not quite the total economic disaster zone they were sometimes characterised to be, neither were the 1970s.

The decade's grim reputation is understandable. Annual inflation averaged over 12 per cent during the decade, a pace Britain had never experienced outside of wartime and resulting in the price level almost trebling between 1970 and 1979. A pint of lager that had cost 17p in 1973 was going for 40p by 1979. A first-class postage stamp, 3p in 1971, was priced at 10p by the end of 1979. By the late 70s the unemployment rate had risen to over 5.5 per cent, a low enough number by comparison with what would follow but then the highest level in four decades. This blend of high unemployment and rising inflation caused economists to coin the now dreaded word 'stagflation' to describe this previously unimaginable combination. But it is not the just the raw numbers that define the economic history of the 1970s, or at least not in later political rhetoric about the decade. In 1976 the UK would go 'cap in hand' (to use some favoured journalese) to the IMF for a loan, while in the 'winter of discontent' labour unrest would see (switching back into tabloid journalese) the 'dead going unburied' and 'rubbish piling up in the streets'. Weak governments, strong unions and mounting violence in Northern Ireland all led to speculation that Britain was ungovernable. By the middle of the decade officer cadets at Sandhurst, the military academy, were not only conducting exercises in how to respond to potential civil war but allowing the BBC *Panorama* programme to film their training. Britain certainly seemed to be in a mess.

The usual history of the 1970s misses some important elements, however. Women received the right to equal pay, there was important legislation on racial equality, regional gaps in Britain narrowed and, in the mid-1970s, overall economic inequality hit its lowest levels on record. Even taking account of the often sky-high inflation, real wages (earnings after adjustment for price rises) rose by 2.9 per cent on average each year over the course of the 1970s – a much stronger result than in the 1990s or 2000s. Those rising wages could be seen in continuing mass prosperity: car ownership rose from around 45 per cent in 1970 to 70 per cent of households in 1980.

But while workers continued to make gains, the overall economy had a tougher ride. The 1974 recession was the deepest Britain had experienced since the 1920s, and the average annual GDP growth over the 1970s was around 2.5 per cent, a big step down from the rates seen in the 1950s and 1960s. As in the 1920s, a tougher economic backdrop drove more volatile politics. From 1959 until 1979 no government managed to serve two full consecutive terms. The 1970s were a decade of four general elections and bouts of minority government and informal coalition. The two-party system appeared to be breaking down, just as it had briefly fallen apart in the 1920s, with the combined vote shares of the Conservative and Labour parties dropping from close to 95 per cent of votes cast in 1959 to closer to 75 per cent in the mid-1970s. Scottish and Welsh nationalism appeared on the parliamentary scene and the Liberal Party began a slow recovery.

Edward Heath, who became the Conservative Prime Minister in 1970 (after a surprise general election win), saw himself as a new kind of Tory leader. Like his predecessor (and successor) as Prime Minister Harold Wilson he was an Oxford educated grammar school boy and, like him, he sought a form of economic modernisation of Britain. But whereas for Wilson that had meant doubling down on the existing broadly social democratic model of post-war government with indicative planning, new ministries and national targets, for Heath reform meant more radical change. Indeed the manifesto on which Heath fought the 1970 election is best thought of as a form of proto-Thatcherism. Growth and dynamism were to be boosted through some selling off of state-controlled firms, sectors would be deregulated, taxes would be cut and trade unions restricted. The country would pull back on direct subsidies and grants to firms while opening up by joining the European Community to expose its tired firms to greater foreign competition. Of course very little of this agenda would actually be followed through on, hence it nowadays being named Thatcherism rather than Heathism. Even before Thatcher's leadership, there was little talk of Heathism. The agenda instead became characterised as 'Selsdonism' after a meeting of the Conservative shadow cabinet and their policy advisors at the Selsdon Park Hotel in the run-up to the 1970 election where it was unveiled. Britain it seemed was set to dial back the role of the state in the economy and turn back towards the market mechanisms of the pre-1945 world.

Heath did make a start with his agenda; the 1971 Industrial Relations Act outraged unions by banning some wildcat (that is to say unballoted) strikes and establishing an Industrial Relations Court which could outlaw some strikes and settle disputes. More charges were introduced for things such as dentistry, school meals and medical prescriptions. Education Secretary Margaret Thatcher got branded a 'milk snatcher' for ending the provision of free school milk to 8- to 11-year-olds (a charge not levelled at the Wilson era ministers who had removed it for 12- to 15-year-olds). The tax system was reformed, with purchase taxes mostly eliminated and replaced by the new Value Added Tax at a rate of 10 per cent, and with income taxes simplified. The Wilson government's Selective Employment Tax was abolished and the tax bill for corporations was effectively cut by dropping the rate at which distributed profits were taxed. Banking was liberalised by a series of measures designed to free up lending by removing the old ceilings on loans enforced by the Bank of England.

Joining the European Community proved to be Heath's lasting change, although the impact of that would not be fully felt until the 1980s.

But Heath's Selsdon programme of deregulation rapidly ran out of steam. A deteriorating global economy saw unemployment begin to tick upwards whilst the unions began to push back against the new industrial relations legislation. A nine-week strike by the National Union of Mineworkers (the NUM) in 1972 forced the government to settle for a pay increase of 27 per cent in the nationalised mining industry after shortages of fuel led to rolling blackouts. Days lost to strike action per worker per week hit 0.14 in 1972, the highest level since the 1920s.

When unemployment rose above one million for the first time since 1940, the Heath government made its now famous U-turn. In much the same way that MacDonald's acceptance of public spending cuts in 1931 forever sealed his reputation with much of the Labour Party, Heath's dropping of liberalisation in the face of unemployment and union pressure sealed his reputation with much of the Tory right. When the crisis came, he buckled. Subsidies to struggling firms began to grow once again and government once more turned to attempts at tripartite bargaining to put a lid on wage gains. This time, though, the atmosphere was especially poisonous.

What followed was a form of 1950s or 1960s stop-go policy-making on speed. Heath's initial choice as Chancellor, Iain Macleod, had died just weeks after the election and was replaced by Anthony Barber. Barber in his 1972 and 1973 budgets attempted what he called a 'dash for growth' with more generous spending rises and tax cuts (the new VAT was dropped from 10 per cent to 8 per cent one year after its introduction) coupled with further relaxation of controls on banking. It has since become known as the Barber Boom.

The government had actually been running a small surplus in 1970, but by 1974 the deficit stood at over 4 per cent of GDP. The current account, which had also been in surplus in 1971, stood at −4.1 per cent by mid-1974, far higher than the levels which had forced the devaluation of 1967. This was a classic case of boom and bust. And the bust was a painful one. A situation not helped by the generally chaotic backdrop of the global economy.

In the late 1960s and early 1970s the Bretton Woods system collapsed. The capital controls that were at the heart of the arrangement had always been porous, and the gaps had widened substantially throughout the 1960s as the Eurodollar market boomed in London. More significant, though, was waning US enthusiasm for the system. The Belgian-American economist Robert Triffin diagnosed the fundamental problem as early as 1960, setting out what became known as the Triffin Dilemma. While the system was technically built upon the principle of every country pegging its currency to the dollar, which in turn was pegged to gold, in practice most states and private-sector actors chose to hold dollars in preference to gold. It was constant deficit in the US balance of payments that kept the system liquid by supplying the global economy with a steady flow of dollars out of the US. But those very same US deficits raised longer-term question marks over the value of the dollar. Hence the Dilemma: for the system to work the US needed to run deficits to provide dollars, but those very same deficits made the dollar less attractive in the long run. Increasingly those deficits caused a domestic push-back in America itself. Britain's devaluation of 1967 allowed sterling-based exporters to grab some market share but put more pressure on American manufacturers. From 1968 onwards the US dropped its own peg of $35 to an ounce of gold and allowed the gold–dollar rate to float with demand. International monetary authorities, over the course of a series of multilateral crisis summits, attempted to manage the outflow of gold from the US and keep some form of stability in international exchange rates. But in 1971, in the so-called Nixon shock, the US president cancelled the direct convertibility of the dollar into gold. Within months other countries dropped their commitments to pegged exchange rates and allowed their currencies to float. Bretton Woods was effectively dead although the last rites would not be officially read until a summit in Jamaica in 1976. With foreign travel, although increasing, still a comparative rarity the direct effects of freely moving exchange rates were not at first visible to consumers; they felt it more keenly once the price of imported goods began to move in line with the pound. For firms reliant on cross-border trade, however, the removal of the certainty offered by fixed exchange rates was a more obvious concern. Planning for the future suddenly became an awful lot trickier.

This brave new world of managed and then freely floating exchange rates was not a happy one for the pound. Although sterling initially strengthened from its post-devaluation rate of $2.40 to around $2.50 in 1971, by 1974 it was down to $2.34. The real action, though, happened against other currencies. The effective exchange rate fell by 11 per cent in the three years to 1974 when measured against a broad basket of other currencies.

The timing of the end of the Bretton Woods system was unfortunate for Britain. In 1973 the Yom Kippur War broke out in the Middle East and was accompanied by an oil embargo. By 1974 the price of a barrel of oil had rapidly quadrupled from under $3 to over $12.

The Heath government faced a combination of soaring energy prices, a declining currency, a deregulated banking system where lending was rising quickly, and emboldened unions demanding pay rises. All at a time when macroeconomic policy was set firmly to easy mode to support the dash for growth. The result was inflation. Consumer prices rose by more than 9 per cent in 1973 and by almost 16 per cent in 1974. The unions pushed for yet larger wage increases to protect their workers. Profits were squeezed. Unemployment ticked higher again.

All around the developed world the sudden ending of Bretton Woods, combined with the oil embargo, provoked crises. But in Britain the impact was especially acute. The golden age that was ending had simply been less shiny in the first place. The Heath government was by the beginning of 1974 clearly floundering. A botched attempt at liberalisation followed by a rapid U-turn and then the easing of macroeconomic policy in the face of rising inflation had left the country in a mess. In December 1973 a three-day week was imposed across much of industry to reduce energy usage. In January 1974 the NUM once more went on strike after rejecting a proposed 16 per cent pay rise.

In the first quarter of 1974 GDP fell by 2.7 per cent: a larger drop in one quarter than the total depth of any previous post-war recession, indeed the largest drop in a single three-month period the economy would experience before the COVID-19 shutdown of 2020. At this point the response of the Heath government was almost irrelevant to the situation; they had lost control.

Heath felt he needed a fresh mandate to allow him to impose the government's will on the unions and went to the country in February 1974 with a snap general election campaign under the slogan 'Who governs?' Of course the fact he had to ask the question suggested the answer was 'Probably not you.' The actual answer the British people gave was 'We're not sure.' The election resulted in a hung Parliament with Labour the largest party but short of an overall majority. Almost 20 per cent of the electorate went for the Liberals, their best performance since the 1920s although they only won 14 seats. Still, Harold Wilson was back in power although more by default than by design.

The Heath government of 1970–1974 had a torrid time in office, but the Labour governments of 1974–1979 (at first under Wilson and, after 1976, under James Callaghan) had a worse one. Britain itself was still changing, in a way which fundamentally undermined the old governing ethos of the Labour Party but which much of the party's leadership did not yet recognise.

Housing is perhaps the most dramatic example. For most of its post-industrial revolution history Britain had remained a nation of renters. House prices, in real terms, fell reasonably consistently for the seventy or so years after the 1840s. That mainly reflected the same factors that drove the globalisation of the late nineteenth century: the growth of new transport technologies and the annihilation of distance. The railway had many effects on Britain, but one of the most dramatic was on housing markets. The ability to travel quickly, and in reasonable comfort, at an affordable cost meant that people could live further from their place of work. Commuting ten miles a day would have been unthinkable in the mid-nineteenth century but was common by the early twentieth. Whereas a worker in 1850 would want to, ideally, be within easy walking distance of their place of employment, by the early 1900s they could happily live many miles away. Transport expanded the effective supply of housing available to workers and helped push down prices.

Nonetheless, since a house cost, on average, around four times the average wage in 1918, financing a purchase was not an option easily available for most Britons and they still rented. Only around one in five British households owned their property in 1918 but, with low interest rates and the house building boom in the 1930s, that gradually rose to around one third by 1939. After 1945 the pace of change accelerated. An expansion of council housing ate into the private rental sector but the more dramatic shift came in ownership. Just like their predecessors in the National Governments of the 1930s, the Tory governments of the 1950s were keen to encourage home ownership. Popular attitude to mortgages changed, and rather than being a burden to be repaid they were seen as the key to buying a stake in one's future, preferably a stake with three bedrooms and a garden. The low interest rates and higher inflation of the 1950s and 1960s played an important role: financial repression was designed to help the government manage its own debt burden, but it also made household mortgages more attractive too.

By 1961 owner occupation, usually with a mortgage, had hit around 40 per cent and in 1971 it moved to 51 per cent. This was a landmark moment in British economic history that helped drive a major change in political economy over the coming two decades. The politics of a nation of homeowners differs from that of a nation of renters in a myriad of ways – on the most basic level, rising house prices suddenly become the one type of inflation that the public seem content with. Since 1850 British house prices had declined for seventy years and, apart from a brief early 1950s episode, were then broadly stable for fifty years. But once the home ownership rate passed 50 per cent, they began to climb. Taking a wider view, a nation of mortgage payers is a nation much more concerned with the level of interest rates. Rate changes in the 1950s and 1960s had been something which most concerned business leaders planning investment or those working in the financial sector, but by the 1990s and 2000s they were the kind of thing politicians put on posters. What should be a tool of macroeconomic policy aimed at ensuring decent employment and stable inflation became an end in and of itself; low interest rates were now a thing to boast about.

The Heath government's deregulation of lending resulted in a boom in mortgage lending during the early 1970s. The volume of credit extended rose by 50 per cent year on year in 1972 during the Barber Boom and house prices jumped from just over four times the average income to over six times. Of course, for more than half of households, this was now something to be welcomed.

The old, collectivist spirit of the Labour Party sat uneasily with a new nation of asset owners. But housing tenure was not the only thing changing. Looking back on the decade, the Marxist historian Eric Hobsbawm would catalogue the reasons that 'the forward march of labour' had been, as he termed it, 'halted'. The share of the workforce involved in manual work had, by Hobsbawm's reckoning, fallen from 75 per cent in 1911 to 64 per cent by 1961 to just over half by the mid-1970s. Home-owning, white collar workers were certainly not the basis of a mass party of the working class in a traditional Marxist sense. The role of women too was changing. As Hobsbawm noted, in the days of Engels the organised working class had been almost exclusively male and women workers were mostly in domestic service. By the 1970s around half of married women were in work.

Of course the working class had never uniformly voted Labour. From Disraeli and Salisbury onwards Tory leaders such as Baldwin and Macmillan (and indeed Heath) had been able to capture a large share of what Labour regarded as its own core vote. Now, with that core vote so diminished as a share of the overall electorate, the Labour Party began to find itself in a new and more challenging environment.

Macroeconomics and political economy are often about

trade-offs, about achieving one end at the cost of another. Such trade-offs are always harder when the wider economy is in a tough position. It is, after all, easier to talk about the division of the spoils of growth than about allocating the costs of recession. The Labour governments of 1974–1979 found themselves in an almost impossible position: beset by high inflation, rising unemployment and balance of payments issues that threatened to spiral out of control. The economic inheritance from Heath was disastrous and any course they tried to steer risked offending one part or another of their fragile political coalition.

Amid the economic turbulence of the 1960s and, still more, the 1970s, macroeconomics – as a discipline – did not stand still. Keynes had seemed to offer the promise of stabilising capitalism but, his critics alleged, his latter disciples were now overseeing a period of rising unemployment and simultaneously high inflation that their basic models said were essentially impossible. Two distinct but related schools of thought, schools of thought that would be increasingly influential in 1980s and 1990s Britain, had developed by the mid-1970s.

If Keynes was the twentieth century's most influential economist, then Milton Friedman probably deserves the silver medal. Like Keynes he had wide-ranging interests and like Keynes he was an excellent communicator and populariser of his notions. He received the Nobel prize in economics in 1976, just as his ideas were beginning to gain more official acceptance in Britain. Much of the output of the so-called 'Chicago school of economics' (named for the university where Friedman and many of his followers were based) was not especially new, it was restatement of older ideas. Classically liberal in its emphasis on the benefits of trade, free exchange and market functions, it would have come as no surprise to nineteenth-century readers of Smith or Mill. Still, in a era when the state had never been larger, such ideas seemed more radical. Keynes had in his time revolutionised the teaching of economics, but his insights had been macroeconomic in nature, indeed he had essentially invented the very concept. Microeconomics – the study of individual markets – remained much as it had been in the 1920s. Looking back at the late 1960s, one academic has argued it was always a little strange to teach undergraduates about the efficiency of market mechanisms and the role of the invisible hand in one class and then to argue for the vital role of the state in steering the overall economy in the next. Friedman's genius was to find a way to square the belief in free markets and classical liberal ideas with the disaster that had been the 1930s. Monetarism argued that supply was a key driver of macroeconomic performance. If the money supply was allowed to fall (as it had in 1930s America as banks failed) then the result would be deflation and depression, but if it was allowed to rise too quickly then the result would be inflation. Friedman rejected the gold standard and instead argued that the appropriate role of macroeconomic policy-makers was to keep money growth relatively stable. Government deficits, which could push up the money supply, were something to be avoided. In the international economy, countries should keep capital markets open and allow savings to flow to where they offered the best returns and the most efficient outcomes. Currencies could adjust to find their appropriate value, guided by market forces, rather than being pegged by government fiat.

Targeting money supply, as policy-makers would discover in the 1980s, was never straightforward nor entirely successful. But in the 1970s that lay in the future – what mattered then was that Friedman was a renowned economist who appeared to offer a viable theory to explain the misery of stagflation.

Robert Lucas, a Friedman follower with a lower public profile but an equally important theoretical contribution, helped to round out what was to become known as the New Classical

Economics. In the 1970s Lucas argued that the expectations of economic actors – such as households and firms – were rational. That might sound obvious but it has important theoretical consequences. Take the Phillips Curve as an example. Some policy-makers looked at Phillips's work on the historical relationship between inflation and unemployment and saw it as almost a menu of options from which they could choose: 'if we want unemployment to be 2 per cent then inflation will be 4 per cent'. But rational firms, seeing policy-makers pushing unemployment lower and prepared to accept higher inflation, would, Lucas argued, anticipate higher price rises when making decisions about wages, hiring and investment. The Lucas critique was an important push-back against the hydraulic thinking of the 1960s but led to some economists adopting ridiculous views on the ineffectiveness of macroeconomic policy in the longer run. Taken together the 1960s and 1970s reaction against the prevailing Keynesian consensus in macroeconomics was to play an important role in Britain for the following three decades.

The incoming Labour government in 1974 was quick to repeal Heath's Industrial Relations Act, gaining itself some respite from the wave of strikes which had crippled the Heath administration. But inflation continued to rise, hitting 22.7 per cent in 1975, while the value of sterling continued to fall.

Whereas the industrial policy of the 1960s had been about creating brave new technological wonders, the industrial policy of the 1970s was defensive in nature. This was less about the government failing to pick winners and more about losers successfully choosing the government. The emblematic case was British Leyland. This car manufacturer, which operated forty plants at its peak, had been created in the late 1960s by a series of in-vogue mergers. The first Wilson government had hoped to help create a British General Motors. But by 1975 high oil prices and depressed consumer confidence had created a truly terrible environment for any car company. Awful industrial relations and frequent strikes crippled production. Rather than letting it fail, the government effectively nationalised it.

The need to keep the car industry alive was not the only drain on the public purse. Depressed tax receipts and higher benefit payments as unemployment rose began to put more pressure on the public finances, finances not in great shape after Barber's failed dash for growth. The government's deficit was above 6 per cent of GDP by 1976 while the current account deficit stood at around −4 per cent.

With inflation climbing, a large current account deficit and a government running a substantial deficit of its own, the idea that sterling would decline further did not seem an especially adventurous bet. And in this new, post-Bretton Woods era of a reopening global financial system, such a bet was not hard to make. Any currency crisis risks becoming self-perpetuating; if enough speculators believe a currency will lose value and sell it then that itself can create enough selling pressure to cause the value to plummet. And in 1976 there were plenty of reasons to sell sterling.

The government, now under the leadership of James Callaghan, believed it had little choice but to turn to the IMF for a loan to help support the currency's value. The fear was that a further steep decline would imperil Britain's ability to import her energy needs. The IMF loan of 1976 is today deeply misunderstood and mischaracterised in the political debate. For a start, it was never about the government 'running out of money' or the public finances needing to be 'bailed out'. Government debt to GDP was around 50 per cent in the mid-1970s and, while the deficit was large, the government was able to raise the money to finance it from domestic savers. The loan was required to provide some support for sterling, which otherwise could have continued its downward spiral, pushing up inflation and endangering imports. It was a circuit breaker to provide some relief by granting access to foreign currency resources. Nor was it unique: Britain had taken out an IMF loan twenty years earlier for the same purpose.

But the loan came with strings attached. The IMF were, understandably enough from their point of view, concerned that sterling was falling for a reason. This was no simple speculative attack that could be stemmed by the IMF opening its cheque book and pledging to stand behind Britain. Action was needed to stem inflation and bring down the deficit to restore confidence in the pound. That meant public spending cuts, tax rises and higher interest rates in return for a loan. 'Conditionality' attached to foreign loans is never popular with the recipient. For Callaghan's Labour Party this provoked a crisis.

A faction of the Cabinet led by Tony Benn, once a bright young technocratic minister under Harold Wilson and now the standard bearer of the Labour left, argued that accepting the required cuts in public spending would mean essentially abandoning the manifesto Labour had been elected on, which would inflame the trade unions and be a betrayal of the wider movement. Callaghan backed his Chancellor, Denis Healey, in arguing that the government had no choice. Benn's 'Alternative Economic Strategy' openly advocated a siege economy – Britain would institute import controls, leave the European Common Market and take control of savings and investment through nationalising the banks. If Wilson had experimented with Keynesian Plus in the 1960s, this was an argument for something further. That was too much for most of Benn's peers, let alone the public. The IMF conditions were accepted and the loan taken. Less than half of it was ever drawn down and it was all repaid by 1979. Sterling stabilised.

Far more important than the loan itself was the changing attitude to macroeconomic management. It was captured in Callaghan's party conference speech in 1976, in which he argued that 'we used to think that you could spend your way out of a recession, and increase employment by cutting taxes and boosting Government spending. I tell you in all candour that that option no longer exists, and that in so far as it ever did exist, it only worked on each occasion since the war by injecting a bigger dose of inflation into the economy, followed by a higher level of unemployment as the next step.' This was tantamount to a rejection of thirty-odd years of official macroeconomic consensus and it came from a Labour Prime Minister.

The fundamental problem in the 1970s was that Britain had faced a series of shocks to the supply-side economy that hit at its ability to produce output – weaker sterling and higher oil prices raised the cost base on which British industry operated. But the response, at first under Heath and later under Labour, had not been to act on supply problems but to try to stoke demand. The result was inflation on a scale never experienced before in peacetime.

High and sustained inflation, of the type Britain experienced in the 1970s, creates winners and losers. Those in well unionised jobs, where bargaining power secured higher wage rises to compensate, were relatively well protected. Savers and those in non-unionised workplaces were the big losers.

The winter of 1978–79 saw another wave of industrial unrest as unions pushed back at yet another attempt to control inflation through an incomes policy which tried to limit wage rises. The acceptance of the 1976 loan had, as Benn predicted, been greeted as a betrayal by the leadership of the trade unions. Over four and a half million workers were involved in strike action in 1979 and the number of days lost surpassed the 1972 peak. The dead did, briefly, go unburied as grave diggers refused to work. But at least this time the lights stayed on.

The Conservative government that took power in 1979 was, like the governments of both Wilson and Heath, elected on a manifesto of reform and modernisation. Like its predecessors it had grand plans for the British economy. This one, though, would see them through.

15

The Counter Revolution

The Conservative governments of 1979 to 1997 were as wide-ranging in their changes as the Attlee government of 1945 to 1951; the post-war consensus which had begun to break down in the 1970s would be swept away in the 1980s. Not only did the tools of economic policy change but the targets did too. The relationship between the government and markets would be fundamentally altered and the economic borders of the state be radically redrawn.

In the 1979 election, Margaret Thatcher defined herself as much against the Heath government as against her Labour opponents. She was running not just to be Prime Minister but to change the face of Britain. In many ways she is best understood as a product of the 1930s. Born in 1925, her formative experiences came in 1930s Grantham where, as she would often recount, her views were formed by her father, a greengrocer and alderman. For three decades from 1945 onwards the 1930s had been, in political rhetoric, the hungry 30s, a time that no one wanted to return to, a warning from history. But Grantham was not Jarrow, it was the kind of place which the marchers on the crusade had been trying to catch the attention of. Grantham was a town which had been a bedrock of support for the National Government, a part of the country for which the 1930s meant not mass unemployment and dole queues but newly built suburban housing, low interest rates, lower taxes and new industry. Viewed from Grantham, it was hard to see quite what was wrong with the economy of 1930s Britain. Or at least why it required such sweeping change. Had her father been an unemployed shipworker or coal miner her view might have differed. But he was not. He was the kind of small businessperson for whom the post-1945 state meant more bureaucracy and more taxes.

Thatcher believed that Britain in 1979 faced a stark choice: continued drift and decline or tough reform, and she was determined to take the latter path. Judged on her own terms, she succeeded. Whereas French GDP per head had been about 11 per cent higher than British GDP per head in 1979, in 1997 the gap was down to 3 per cent. Over the course of the 1980s and 1990s Britain's relative decline against Europe was reversed. Britain was no longer regarded as the sick man of the continent by the early 1990s. But that reversal and restructuring came at a high cost, a cost unimaginable to politicians of the 1960s or 1970s. Unemployment peaked at 11.9 per cent in 1984, a level not seen since the inter-war years. The conventional wisdom was that no government presiding over mass worklessness could ever win re-election, but the conventional wisdom was wrong. The child of the 1930s seemingly remembered something which most commentators forgot: the National Government had been re-elected. As long as economic policy was creating enough winners, then however loud the losers might shout, a government could be returned to power. And Thatcher's government created plenty of winners.

The 1980s were a paradigm shift for Britain's political economy. In the 1950s, the incoming Conservative government had relaxed some controls and cut some taxes, while in the 1960s Wilson had embraced indicative planning and doubled down on social democracy. Policy had shifted over the forty-odd years of the broad consensus, but the aim had remained constant: full employment. In the 1980s that target would be dropped. The control of inflation took centre stage in macro-economic policy-making while supply-side micro-level reform was embraced to foster dynamism and drive up productivity.

This broad policy stance has been described by one political economist as the free economy and the strong state, a fitting encapsulation. The Conservative governments of 1979–1997 were not nineteenth-century liberals. They sought to empower market mechanisms and get the state out of the economy as far as possible, but they kept defence spending high, re-equipped the police and believed in a state capable of taking decisive action against enemies both internal and external.

Nowadays it is conventional to brand the changes that Britain underwent – beginning in either 1979 or 1976 according to the author's taste – as 'neoliberalism'. The problem is that the term is often bandied about, usually as a form of insult, to mean 'things of which the author disapproves'. It is applied to politicians as varied as Jim Callaghan, Ronald Reagan and Angela Merkel. In a narrower sense, though, the term has some use. There was, without a shadow of a doubt, a turn towards the greater use of market mechanisms in 1980s Britain. The first question of any proposed government inter-vention in the economy shifted from 'What will this achieve?' to 'Should we be doing this?' In sharp contrast to the 1940s to 1970s, wherever possible the market was henceforth to be used to allocate resources.

On the level of macroeconomic management, the popu-lar reputation of the Thatcher years, 1979–1990, is that she handled it well, whereas John Major (her successor from

1990 to 1997) made a hash of it. This is not only unfair but untrue. Thatcher's structural reforms of the British economy were to bear fruit but her macroeconomic policy was often little short of disastrous. Major's government, by contrast, eventually stumbled into a macroeconomic framework that appeared to work.

The early years after 1979 were marked by an experiment in monetarism. Conquering inflation, it was believed, entailed getting the money supply under control. That meant deflationary budgets with public spending squeezed, coupled with higher interest rates from the Bank of England. The first problem was one of definitions: what exactly did controlling the money supply mean?

The Medium Term Financial Strategy (MTFS), which guided policy from 1979 to 1983, initially sought to control a measure known as M3 (a broad definition of money including notes and coins and bank deposits). The problem was that, in line with their free-market instincts, the government abolished capital controls in 1979, leaving British banks free both to borrow from abroad and to repatriate cash held overseas. So even with public spending being cut and interest rates high, M3 continued to outgrow its targets. The response was to double down with ever higher interest rates and more contractionary budgets.

High sterling interest rates attracted flows of foreign money, pushing up the value of the pound; by 1981 the economy was in a deep recession, the unemployment rate had passed 10 per cent and the pound looked overvalued. The Budget of 1981 nonetheless ploughed on with the strategy. A letter to *The Times* signed by 364 economists called for policy to be reversed. In common with most public letters on economic issues, it was ignored.

'Monetarism' as a concept in British politics was never solely about the money supply. Money targets moved to focus on narrower measures of money in 1985 before quietly being dropped altogether. The MTFS slowly became less explicitly monetarist and more conventional in terms of targeting balanced budgets and the reduction of debt.

The constrained demand and high unemployment of the early 1980s, together with a stronger pound (rather than any changes in the money supply) helped get inflation below 5 per cent by 1984 and towards 3 per cent by 1986. Unemployment, though, remained above 10 per cent. The price of reducing inflation had been a high one.

The government then managed to convince itself that inflation had been conquered and the fundamentals of the British economy were now sound enough to permit growth to accelerate without accelerating price rises. Tax and interest rates were cut by Chancellor Nigel Lawson, stoking the Lawson boom of the late 1980s. House price inflation hit an annual 30 per cent, which was widely welcomed by homeowners. By 1990 consumer price inflation had once again risen above 10 per cent, prompting a renewed squeeze and interest rates of almost 15 per cent to bring it back down. Stop-go was not such a distant memory after all. The recession of the early 1990s was less steep than that of the 1980s but unemployment, which had fallen to a low of 6.9 per cent in early 1990 amid the Lawson boom (notably higher than at any point in the 1970s crisis), rose once again to above 10 per cent by late 1992.

A deep recession followed by an unsustainable boom and another recession is hardly the best of macroeconomic records and yet it is the one that Thatcher's prime ministership produced. Her successor's macro policy got off to a tough start. Against the wishes of the outgoing Prime Minister, sterling joined the European Exchange Rate Mechanism (ERM) in October 1990, one month before Thatcher left power.

The ERM was a European initiative which had begun in 1979 without Britain's involvement, and was a forerunner to the euro. It represented a gold standard-esque placement on the international macro trinity. Capital markets would be left open, currencies would be pegged to the German Deutschmark and interest rates would be used, not for domestic economic management, but to defend the value of the currency. In reality this meant outsourcing monetary policy to the German Bundesbank, which had the strongest record in Europe on controlling inflation. Countries joining the ERM hoped to not only benefit from stable exchange rates but to borrow some of the reflected credibility of the German central bank in keeping inflation contained.

Britain had quietly, and unofficially, shadowed the policy of the Bundesbank in 1987 and 1988, against the wishes of Thatcher and her chief economic advisor Alan Walters. That prompted a dispute which led to Lawson's resignation as Chancellor. When Britain eventually joined the ERM it did so at a sterling–Deutschmark rate of DM 2.95 to the pound and committed itself to maintain the value within 6 per cent of that target.

German reunification after the end of the Cold War saw a sharp rise in German government spending to modernise the east. Keen to keep a lid on inflation the Bundesbank began to hike rates, and Britain, via the ERM, was forced to follow.

By 1992 it was clear that sterling's position was untenable: interest rates were plainly too high for an economy just emerging from recession. Speculators, most famously George Soros, stepped up their bets on the pound falling in value. The government initially dug its heels in, raising interest rates to 10 per cent and authorising the Bank of England to spend billions of dollars' worth of foreign exchange reserves on buying sterling to defend its value. On Wednesday, 16 September 1992, which would become known as Black Wednesday, the Bank of England raised the base rate twice in less than 24 hours, first to 12 per cent and then to 15 per cent, meanwhile spending around £3.3 billion of reserves in a futile attempt to stave off the inevitable. That evening the government admitted defeat and allowed the pound to float freely. George Soros booked a profit of over $1 billion as the pound fell to under DM 2.40 by October.

Black Wednesday was a blow to the government's pride and prestige, one that helped to fundamentally damage the Conservative reputation for economic competence for at least the next decade. But it was no bad thing for the economy. Weaker sterling and lower interest rates helped drive a recovery from 1992 onwards. By accident rather than design John Major's government had found a macroeconomic regime which appeared to work. Fiscal policy would focus on ensuring the public finances were on a sound footing, whilst monetary policy (controlled by the Chancellor but managed by the Bank of England) would seek to keep inflation in check. The pound would freely float to whatever rate the market determined. By 1997 unemployment was back below 7 per cent and inflation below 4 per cent.

The record of the Thatcher years on supply-side change bears up better in hindsight than the record on macroeconomic management. Here the costs were high but the benefits at least very visible. Productivity growth picked up and the gap in productivity between Britain and its European neighbours began to diminish. The British disease of the post-war years appeared to be cured.

Much as it annoys latter-day Thatcherites, a case can be made that the real cure for Britain's economic woes came not from Downing Street but from Brussels. Even worse for

die-hard fans of the Iron Lady, the prime minister responsible
was Ted Heath.

British entry to the common market in 1973 was ultimately
to prove a major boost to economic dynamism, although the
results would filter through only gradually. Exporters now had
access to a larger and developed market, while domestic firms
faced new forms of competition from European producers.
Britain's economy, which had been progressively closing itself
off from the rest of the global economy for three decades after
1945, began to reopen. The average tariff on imports would
fall from over 9 per cent in the late 1960s to under 5 per
cent by 1979 and just 1.2 per cent by the mid-1980s. Import
penetration, a measure of the market share of imports, in the
manufacturing sector rose from around 20 per cent in the
mid-1970s to 40 per cent by the 1990s. Thatcher herself was
a key player in the creation of the European single market in
the 1980s: an effort to create a cross-Europe restriction-free
market in goods, services and capital. Although she later
turned against European political integration, her time in
office was marked by a more positive attitude to European
economic relations. She rather appreciated the free-market
benefits of cross-continental trading, whilst resenting how the
pooling of sovereignty crimped her desire for a strong state.

Of course there was a lot more to Britain's market turn
in the 1980s than simply embracing membership of the
European Economic Community. Especially notable factors
were the changing economic borders of the state, the ending
of the trade unions' right to veto policy suggestions and the
freeing up of the jobs market, the unleashing of finance and
cuts in taxation. Each was to play a major role in Britain's
subsequent development that outlasted both Thatcher's and
Major's times in office.

Privatisation was a new word in the 1980s but not a new

idea. Despite being, in hindsight at least, a key Thatcher era policy it was mostly absent from the 1979 manifesto. Only as the 1980s moved on did the agenda come to the fore. Returning the nationalised industries to private hands not only fitted very nicely indeed with Thatcher's own instincts but it sought to achieve two distinct aims: to increase productivity by driving more competition and to build a nation of shareholders.

In Thatcher's first term, 1979 to 1983, privatisation played only a limited role: defence manufacturer British Aerospace, some shipbuilding, what was left of British Leyland and some nuclear research were sold off. Things changed in the next Parliament with privatisation being the centrepiece of an attempt to build both a popular capitalism of mass share ownership and a revitalised, more dynamic Britain. British Telecom was sold in 1984 and British Gas in 1986. Rolls-Royce, British Steel and British Airways followed, and then the water and electricity companies in 1991. British Rail in 1994 was almost an afterthought.

Nigel Lawson, Chancellor for most of this time, argued that the money raised, whilst obviously welcome, was always of secondary importance to the key objectives of increasing share ownership and boosting productivity. The spreading of share ownership by offering people the chance to buy a stake in the newly private companies at knockdown prices was, at best, a mixed success. The number of individual shareholders did increase from around three million in 1979 to ten million by 1991 but most were not in it for the long term. Instead they took the quick buck offered and sold early.

Switching companies such as British Steel or British Airways from public to private ownership was relatively straightforward, but privatising monopoly producers such as British Gas or British Telecom proved trickier. Here the government was not only attempting a change in ownership but had to essentially invent entire markets from scratch. New regulators had to oversee utility markets to prevent the private sector owners from ripping consumers off. The initial approach became known as RPI-X, with RPI standing for Retail Price Index, the then most common measure of consumer inflation. The new firms were given a formula, for example RPI–2 per cent, and only allowed to raise their prices each year by that. So if RPI inflation was 5 per cent, then a firm with RPI–2 per cent would only be allowed to raise its own fees by 3 per cent. This would both protect consumers and incentivise firms to reduce their cost bases and improve productivity.

But did it boost productivity? The official history of privatisation in Britain, written in the early 2000s, rather dodges the question, concluding that it is 'not easy' to say. It is indeed a tricky business to separate the change in ownership from wider economic changes at the time. The measured productivity of the privatised utilities was certainly higher in the 1990s than in the 1980s, but much of that reflects a change from index cards and paper filing systems to computer databases and more modern IT. One core problem that was solved by privatisation was that decisions about pricing and investment plans no longer sat with politicians. While, in theory, increasing electricity prices to fund new power stations is a straightforward choice, in reality politicians were loath to be seen to be putting up bills. Privatisation freed up the utilities to be more nimble and responsive to market forces. Politics no longer got in the way.

The newly private companies made large reductions in headcount without noticeable drops in service quality. Many of them had become overstaffed and somewhat bloated during the decades of state ownership and governments found making direct redundancies difficult. Shareholders had no such qualms.

Of course, those redundancies would have been almost impossible to carry out had the union movement been as strong as it was in the 1970s. In 1972 striking power workers could make the lights go out, but by the early 1990s the newly private utilities had shed around 20 per cent of their workforce with the unions powerless to stop them.

Union power, which had slowly risen from the late Victorian years onwards, was decisively beaten in the 1980s. The raw numbers speak for themselves: 52 per cent of those in employment were union members in 1979 but just 37 per cent by 1990 and under 30 per cent by 1997. Any talk of tripartite bargaining, of speaking to 'both sides of industry' or of British corporatism was banished.

High unemployment blunted labour bargaining power, as it always has done, but that macroeconomic factor was reinforced by six trade union acts passed between 1980 and 1993 which banned secondary strikes (strikes in support of another union rather than directly concerning workers in a given firm), restricted picketing, imposed the need for a ballot before action and reformed union governance. In 1990 the 'closed shop', an arrangement in which employers agreed to hire only union members, was banned. Taken together the measures were tougher on the unions than anything proposed since the Edwardian years.

Unions of course fought back, but the high-profile fights of the day usually ended in government victory. The Miners' Strike of 1984 to 1985 was the key turning point. The NUM were the shock troops of the British left who had beaten the Heath government twice in the 1970s. The Thatcher government's plans to close 20 collieries with the loss of 20,000 jobs provoked the NUM into action but the government was ready: coal had been stockpiled to prevent a repeat of the 1970s climbdowns. Arthur Scargill, the NUM's fiery leader, played into the government's hands by beginning the strike in spring, when coal was less in demand, and, crucially, by not holding a ballot before taking action and hence breaking the new trade union law.

The dispute lasted for a year and saw widespread clashes between picketing mine workers and police, often shipped into coalfields from other areas of Britain. The length of the dispute, together with legal action from the government, depleted the NUM's funds and caused strike pay to run out by January 1985. By the time the union formally accepted defeat in March 1985, many miners had begun to drift to back to work. If the NUM could be beaten, then any union could, and employers took note.

Alongside the restrictions on unions, labour law was loosened across the board – it became easier to dismiss employees, harder to access employment tribunals and easier to make use of temporary contracts. In the 1970s economists of both the left and the right had written of a profit squeeze on British business. Such worries disappeared in the 1980s. The bargaining power of British labour was seriously reduced.

The City of London had begun its return to global prominence in the 1960s but it really took off in the 1980s as capital controls were removed and the sector deregulated. The 'Big Bang' of 1986 saw a widespread liberalisation of the City amid a wider move from old-fashioned outcry trading on the floor of the stock exchange to electronic desk-based exchanges. The London Stock Exchange had traditionally been divided into brokers, who bought and sold shares for the public, and jobbers, who acted as market makers, buying and selling from brokers. The Big Bang allowed the two types of firm both to merge with each other and to be acquired by other financial sector actors such as banks. It rapidly kicked off a series of couplings between previously smaller firms and the entry of the old merchant banks and some high street banks into what was becoming modern full-service investment banking. Foreign companies were allowed to own firms involved in the British stock market for the first time, attracting the big American and European banks into London. Trading volumes soared from around 50 per cent of the value of all listed stocks in 1985 to 90 per cent by 1990, with the value of companies listed on the exchange rising by around 25 per cent over the same period. Privatisations, and lucrative fees to be earned in handling them, were another boost to the financial sector. Both the rewards of working in finance and the number of people involved picked up, to an extent that the City itself could no longer contain. Financial institutions spilled out into the old docklands around Canary Wharf and the Isle of Dogs. Fewer than 900,000 workers were employed in finance in 1982 but over 1.1 million by 1992.

Soaring pay in the sector was in part a reflection of sharply rising productivity, which had as much to do with the revolution in computing and communications technology as with the opportunities offered by more open global markets and domestic deregulation. The financial sector's contribution to total economic output rose from around 3.5 per cent to 5 per cent. With the benefit of thirty years of hindsight it is unclear quite how much of the seemingly ever-increasing wealth to be made in financial services reflected genuine innovation and how much was simply the capture of economic rents. Were the services available to cross-national firms in terms of capital raising and international finance radically different from those on offer in the 1910s? Payments certainly moved faster but more of the core work of raising and managing capital remained constant.

Taxes on personal income and corporations were cut repeatedly during the Thatcher and Major administrations. The top rate of income tax fell from 83 per cent in 1979 to 60 per cent in 1980 and 40 per cent – where it was to remain for twenty years – in 1988. The basic rate was cut from 33 per cent when the Conservatives took power to 24 per cent by the time they left office. The standard rate of corporation tax was 52 per cent in 1979 but 31 per cent by 1997. No British government before or since has cut taxes by so much.

And yet the picture is slightly more nuanced than the headline falls suggest. VAT was almost doubled in the government's first year, from 8 per cent to 15 per cent, and then increased again in the 1990s to 17.5 per cent. Partly what was happening was a switch from direct progressive taxation on incomes to indirect taxes on expenditure, although the extra revenues raised from VAT did not fully compensate for the revenue lost with the cuts.

The tax take as a share of GDP continued to hover around the 40 per cent mark through the Tories' years in office. The mystery of how this was achieved despite the very substantial cuts in personal and business taxes can be solved by looking at the North Sea. Crude oil was discovered there in the late 1960s but it was in the late 1970s (rather unfortunately missing the 1973–75 price spike) that production really came on stream. The UK was producing around 1.5 million barrels a day by 1979, rising to over 2.7 million by 1988. The tax revenues from this black gold were substantial, peaking in the mid-1980s at around £12 billion a year, a bonus 8 per cent of the total British tax take. One in twelve pounds that the British government received came straight from the North Sea. Norway used its oil bonanza to build a sovereign wealth fund that is now one of the world's largest pools of assets; Britain used its take to cut corporation and personal tax.

Thatcher talked a good game on cutting back the size of the state but much of it was rhetorical. Government spending, as share of GDP, was just under 40 per cent in 1990 – not too different from the 44 per cent of the mid-1970s. And while public sector employment was reduced from almost 27 per cent of all workers in the 1970s to 22 per cent by 1990, that fall came almost entirely from the sale of the nationalised industries. Local government workforces did shrink a little but the central civil service actually grew. Indeed government spending on goods, services and staff actually rose, from 18 per cent of GDP to 22 per cent, between 1973 and 1990. But real terms cuts in benefits (such as delinking the dole to earnings growth) saw government transfer payments fall from 16 per cent of GDP to 13 per cent. The broad story, as with tax, was more of shifting priorities tha a radical changing of shape.

One of the more lasting changes of the 1980s came in housing policy. Britain was already firmly on the path to being a nation of homeowners by 1979, but in the 1980s that trend was turbocharged. The Housing Act of 1980 gave council tenants who had been in their property for more than three years the right to purchase it from their local authority at a discount. As the minister responsible was to later note, 'no single piece of legislation has enabled the transfer of so much capital wealth from the state to the people'. Around six million people now had the chance to purchase their home at an average discount of over 40 per cent on the market price and more than a third of them did so. The mortgage market was deregulated further, with more buyers able to pull themselves onto the first rungs of the housing ladder. Between 1980 and 2000 the share of households living in socially provided accommodation fell from around 30 per cent to 20 per cent, while owner occupation rose from 55 per cent to closer to 70 per cent.

One factor which made Black Wednesday such a political disaster for the Major government was that interest rates increasing by five percentage points in a day was now something that a mortgaged nation cared deeply about.

House prices more than doubled over the course of the 1980s and, despite a steep drop amid the high interest rates and unemployment of the early 1990s, were still some 2.2 times their 1980 level by 1997. Persistent house price inflation appeared to be here to stay. The governments of the 1980s and 1990s were keen to talk up their structural reform agenda and bravery in taking on vested interests when the interest involved was organised labour. When it came to homeowners, that courage appeared to desert them. The Green Belt, a series of planning restrictions dating back to the 1950s designed to contain the growth of urban sprawl, was left unchanged by housing and planning acts in the late 1980s and 1990s. The planning system as a whole left existing residents with a great deal of power to resist new developments in their neighbourhoods. In effect, existing homeowners had, and still mostly have, the ability to prevent new supply which would damage the prices of their own assets. One might have naively assumed this was just the kind of thing a free-market government would fix.

Unemployment was persistently higher in the 1980s and 1990s, and real wage growth persistently weaker, than in the 1970s and 1960s. The bust, boom, bust pattern of macroeconomic performance that characterised the period from the early 1980s to the early 1990s was hardly an improvement on the old stop-go. But by the 1990s inflation finally did seem to have been tamed. What is more, Britain was clearly a more dynamic and competitive economy. The decline in income per head relative to western Europe appeared to have been ended. Britain, in terms of output per hour actually worked, still had productivity well below that of France or Germany, but the situation was at least not getting worse. Few international observers talked any more of a British disease. Indeed British officials and experts were now much in demand globally to talk about how to turn an economy around. The absence of competition that had hampered the economic performance of the 1940s to 1970s had been ended. The ending of the union veto enabled, in many cases, the more rapid introduction of new technologies which allowed firms to cut back on less productive workers.

But all the positive changes came with consequences. The undercutting of labour bargaining power and the slashing of progressive tax rates brought a material increase in inequality. The Gini coefficient, the standard measure of inequality across incomes, rose by 40 per cent over the 1980s. The income share of the top 10 per cent of earners increased from 27 per cent in 1979 to 35 per cent by 1997, while that of the top 1 per cent rose from 7 per cent to 12 per cent. Unsurprisingly enough the largest cuts in income tax in any decade since the industrial revolution were accompanied by the largest rise in inequality of any decade since the industrial revolution. The poverty rate, defined as the percentage of the population living on less than two thirds of the median wage, doubled from under 10 per cent to over 20 per cent over the course of the 1980s.

The regional impact of these national changes also varied widely. London's long post-war decline in population was reversed in the early 1980s as the greater southeast, where the newly successful service industries were concentrated, began to pull, once more, away from the rest of Britain.

High interest rates, the overvaluation of the pound in the early 1980s and the recessions of the early 1980s and 1990s cut deeply into British manufacturing. The number of people employed in the sector fell from 6.6 million in 1979 to 4.4 million by 1997. The word deindustrialisation entered the British economic lexicon just as decline left it.

Just as in the 1930s or the post-war years, divergent sectoral performances had differing regional impacts. While the GDP per head was some 10 per cent above the national average in the southeast by 1997, it was 20 per cent below it in the northeast, Northern Ireland and Wales, and some 10 per cent below it in Yorkshire and the previously prosperous west midlands.

Those differing sectoral performances also had a gendered effect on the labour market. The employment rate of men aged 16–64 fell from 87 per cent in 1979 to 82 per cent in 1990 and 78 per cent in 1997. But that of women of the same age rose, from 57 per cent when the Tories took office to 63 per cent by 1990 and 64 per cent by 1997. The gender employment gap was falling sharply.

In the old industrial heartlands of Britain the reputation of the Thatcher years is somewhat different from the view held in the Home Counties. And yet just like the National Government the Thatcher and Major governments proved that high unemployment was no bar to re-election. The landslide victory of 1983 can perhaps be explained away by a combination of the victory in the Falklands War, a split opposition and Labour's move further to the left. But the victories of 1987 and 1992 were each in their own way substantial.

The Conservatives dominated the middle-class vote throughout the period, as might be expected for a party that was conquering inflation, cutting taxes and putting the unions back in their place. But the coalition of Conservative voters was wider than that.

The comedian Harry Enfield's 1980s TV character Loadsamoney is a useful example of the new strand in the Thatcher coalition. A caricature of materialist 1980s culture who waves around wads of cash, he was not a stockbroker or a banker but a painter and decorator. Across broad swathes of the country, tax cuts and the right to buy won the Tories working-class friends. While the state was sharply pared back, its most cherished assets (such as the NHS) continued (albeit with cuts). The Conservatives' noisy Union Jack-waving patriotism certainly helped win over a few votes, but any Marxist analysis (as some on the Labour left were wont to indulge in) which attributed working-class Conservative voting to some form of 'false consciousness' was very wide of the mark. For many working-class voters, voting Conservative appeared to be in their economic interest.

The breakdown of Bretton Woods and the reopening of global capital markets was bound to eventually help reorientate Britain towards greater economic openness, as was joining the EEC in the early 1970s. But the Thatcher government embraced these changes with a new vigour. The ending of the Cold War and the opening of whole new markets for Western firms simply added another kicker. Foreign investors were welcome in the UK, as long as they brought their cash. Inward investment rose from around 1 per cent of GDP in the late 1970s to almost 3 per cent by the late 1980s. Imports rose too, especially from Europe. As the old British car industry died a long death a new one arose, led by the Japanese. Britain's newly flexible labour markets and market access into western Europe attracted Nissan to open a plant at Sunderland in 1984. Toyota and Honda followed. By the 1990s the City of London was once again a premier global financial centre although few of the leading firms were British owned. The official attitude had shifted – ownership now, it seemed, mattered less than location. The British economy was becoming akin to the Wimbledon tennis championships: hosted domestically but dominated by foreigners.

Eighteen years after Britain's turn back towards market liberalism much had changed. The state had stepped back from many of its previous roles, and the very concept of what economic policy was trying to achieve had shifted. Full employment no longer seemed to be the desired outcome. The welfare state was much less generous but taxes on income were sustainably lower. Competition was back and economic dynamism had increased. The country's global reputation was turned around. The nature of British capitalism seemed to have been transformed, although there were questions by 1997 over quite how British the capitalism which then existed in the UK actually was.

Thatcher and her successor had achieved many of the targets they had set themselves: Britain by 1997 was no longer beset by high inflation or a sense of perpetual crisis. But the government was running out of steam. Support for better quality public services – especially health and education – was beginning to trump demands for more tax cuts. The government appeared rudderless with no big ideas, tarnished by allegations of sleaze and divided over the question of Britain's relationship with what had by then become the European Union. After eighteen years of Conservative rule the Labour Party won a landslide victory in 1997. But this would be a very different kind of Labour government than in the past.

16

New Dawn, NICE Decade

The Labour Party would never love Tony Blair but by the mid-1990s they disliked the idea of losing general elections more than the idea of being led by him. It is hard to imagine him becoming leader in a world in which the party had not been beaten four times in a row. The 1980s had not been an especially enjoyable decade for the British left, to say the least. While Thatcher's governments were rolling back the frontiers of the state, the Labour Party spent much of its time fighting against itself. The party swung sharply to the left after defeat in 1979; the Callaghan government had failed after all and so economic policy was now to be driven more by Benn's Alternative Strategy than by the record of 1974–79. Neil Kinnock tried to play the old Harold Wilson ploy of being elected from the party's left but slowly moving it into the political centre – with decidedly mixed results. Along the way, bitter internal battles were fought over the meaning of socialism, the extent to which ideological desires had to be compromised with electoral reality, and the rules of the party on everything from the power of the annual conference to how leaders were elected. The instinctive distrust of the leadership felt by those on the left of the party had its roots in the late 1970s, when the party's elite appeared happier to listen to IMF officials and Treasury mandarins than to union leaders and members of the party's National Executive Committee. The grass roots wanted more control over the politicians and the politicians were not keen to give it to them. Finally, after the fourth defeat in 1992, the party settled on John Smith as leader, a competent former Shadow Chancellor and very much a middle of the road social democrat in the Wilson mould. Only after his untimely early death did Tony Blair get his chance.

The Blair-Brown governments of 1997 to 2010 worked within the framework they had inherited from Thatcher and Major. It briefly seemed that change was on the horizon. In the mid-1990s Blair flirted with talk of a 'stakeholder economy', drawing on the work of the economics writer Will Hutton with his admiration for the Rhine capitalism and social market economy of Germany. But in the end the real model was found across the Atlantic rather than the Channel. Many of New Labour's thinkers, especially in economic policy, had spent time in the United States. The Clinton presidency coupled with the latest developments in macroeconomic theory proved more of a roadmap than anything happening on the continent.

The trade union laws of the 1980s and 1990s were not rolled back and union membership continued to fall. The privatisations were not reversed. The top rate of income tax was not touched until the crisis of 2008 and the basic rate was cut further to 20 per cent, the lowest in almost a century. Full employment did not replace stable inflation as the goal of economic policy and in many ways the Thatcher paradigm shift was left in place.

But to see Blair and Brown as mere sons of Thatcher is to miss the wood for the trees. Their governments aimed for a delicate balancing act of effecting progressive change wherever possible without ever frightening the electorate of the semi-mythical Middle England too much. Inequality, as measured by the Gini coefficient, was not reduced, but its rise was stopped. Poverty fell, especially child poverty and pensioner poverty, through targeted government spending. Britain got its first national minimum wage in 1998. The tax credits system which grew through Brown's years at the Treasury, inspired (of course) by an American innovation, the earned income tax credit, topped up the wages of low earners and those with children. Public spending on health and education was stepped up after an almost two-decades-long squeeze. NHS waiting lists came down and pay across the public sector rose. Britain had not had a non-Tory government that served two or more terms since before the First World War, yet Labour now won three elections in a row.

There was a definite sense in 1997 to 2010 that the economists were in charge. The ethos was very much one of 'light touch', of intervening in microeconomic policy only where there was a clear 'market imperfection', that is to say a structural impediment to the market working effectively. The kinds of interventions favoured were exactly those recommended by leading economic journals: the effective exercise of anti-trust policy to challenge market power, subsidising of research and development, and focus on improving human capital. The scale of competition policy was beefed up with the authorities better able to investigate monopolists and so too were the powers of the regulators of the privatised utilities.

Nowhere was the influence of the latest economic thinking more visible than in the macroeconomic framework the government adopted. Ever since the 1970s macroeconomic academia had been debating the merits of rules versus discretion in managing the economy. By the 1980s a broad consensus was building on the benefits of giving an independent central bank the task of controlling inflation. Such a bank – for example the US Federal Reserve or the German Bundesbank – if granted control of monetary policy and set a target for inflation would, it was thought, be a more credible actor than a democratically elected government. Governments would always have an incentive to keep one eye on the electorate when setting overall macroeconomic policy. The academics' fear that politicians might often be tempted to ease up a bit ahead of elections was borne out in practice by the British experience of the 1950s to the 1980s. In theory, giving an independent agency, one not subject to public pressure, the power to set interest rates would help control inflation through the influence on expectations. If firms, wage bargainers and financial markets all believed that the central bank was prepared to raise interest rates if needed in order to keep inflation low, they would work on the assumption that inflation would indeed remain low. The very fact that an independent central bank had the power to raise interest rates would hopefully mean that in practice they had to be raised less frequently.

Britain had adopted an inflation target in the early 1990s, in the aftermath of the ERM debacle, but in 1997 the Bank of England was made operationally independent of the government and mandated to hit the target. Interest rates, and wider monetary policy, would now be set by a nine-person Monetary Policy Committee (MPC) rather than the Chancellor. The broader macro framework adopted in 1997 can be thought of as one of 'constrained discretion': government had the capacity to act but had chosen to bind its own hands in most cases. The newly independent Bank of England would have the primary responsibility for managing the business cycle, and its first duty would be to ensure stable inflation. Fiscal policy was bound by a 'golden rule' to keep government debt to GDP at or below 40 per cent and to balance the budget over the course of the economic cycle. The old Butskellite settlement had been reversed: monetary policy would now manage the economy on a day to day basis while fiscal policy concerned itself with the management of government debt. The government's own economic agenda would focus on the supply-side drivers of longer-term growth: boosting competition, incentivising investment, and improving human capital. Membership of the European Union's single market placed further limitations on policy: in order to ensure fair competition across the economic bloc, subsidies to firms and policies which favoured domestic over European companies were outlawed.

As one senior Treasury official of the time was to later note, the whole arrangement was surprisingly familiar to students of British economic history. The combination of membership of the European Union, the independent Bank of England controlling interest rates and targeting inflation, and the golden rule on the government's budget acted in many ways like the knave-proof system of pre-Great War Britain. There was more than a touch of the old Lloyd George domestic reform agenda in the policies Brown pursued at the Treasury.

Ten years, and two general elections, after the new framework was put in place things appeared to be going very well indeed. The contrast with the turbulence of the early 1990s and 1980s, the crises of the 1970s and the stop-go disappointments of the 1960s and 1950s appeared stark. Labour's re-election posters in 2005 essentially plastered much of the country with dry lists of economic statistics – the longest period of continuous economic growth in two centuries, the lowest interest rates in five decades, the highest employment in four decades. Few post-war governments seemed to have as much to boast about.

The expansion which had begun in 1992 was to last for fifteen years. Inflation remained remarkably stable, unemployment continued to fall, and productivity growth rose to be the strongest, over the decade to 2007, of any major developed economy. Gordon Brown, in a statement he would come to regret, announced that 'boom and bust' had been abolished. He was not the only policy-maker in an exuberant mood. Mervyn King, the then Governor of the Bank of England, marked ten years of Bank independence with a speech looking back on what he called the 'nice decade', with nice in this case standing for Non-Inflationary, Continuous Expansion, which is not bad as economics puns go.

There are several theories as to why inflation, which had bedevilled policy-making for three or more decades, no longer appeared to be the, or even a, major problem of macro policy by the late 1990s and 2000s. The explanation on which central bankers tend to be the keenest is that policy-making became more effective, that is to say it was outsourced to them. Certainly, the removal of direct political influence from rate setting and the higher credibility of central bank governors compared to finance ministers with the financial markets played a role. Inflation targeting, as opposed to 1980s experiments with money control, aligned the tools of monetary policy with clear objectives and allowed them to get on with it in a spirit of disinterested technocratic management. But that is not the whole story. The structural reforms of the labour market that took place, at a high cost in terms of worklessness, over the 1980s and early 1990s were also a large factor. The breaking of union power meant that a repeat of the 1970s self-sustaining wage–price spirals was extremely unlikely. And just as important as more focused policy-making and domestic labour changes was the reglobalisation of Britain's economy (another parallel with the Edwardian era). The deepening of Europe's single market throughout the 1980s and 1990s was followed by the end of the Cold War and China's entry into the global economy. The pool of labour available to Western capital essentially doubled over the course of two decades. Britain, as in the first great wave of modern globalisation, was at the forefront of the second. Imports, as a share of national income, rose from around 20 per cent in 1990 to almost 30 per cent by 2008. All of which acted to dampen down inflation.

High street staple Marks & Spencer is perhaps the emblematic case study of the changes Britain was undergoing in the 1990s and 2000s. As late as 1995, around 75 per cent of the slightly dowdy clothes it sold were still proudly badged as 'made in Britain'. But in the late 1990s it made the decision to outsource production to lower-cost countries. The proportion of British-made clothes fell below 20 per cent by 2005 and some 30,000 domestic textiles jobs were lost. But for consumers this meant cheaper goods and, for the country as a whole, materially lower inflation. Globalisation was lowering prices and, importantly, companies could access the benefits of cheap labour without that labour moving to Britain.

The global economy of the 1990s and 2000s, despite serious bumps such as the dot com boom and bust and the Asian crisis of 1997, was generally a more benign one than that of the 1970s or 1980s. Fast growth in the emerging economies of Asia helped the pace of global GDP growth to pick up. Good luck, as well as good design, played a large role in the early success of the New Labour years.

But while the traditional variables of GDP growth, employment rates, inflation and productivity all pointed towards some kind of British economic miracle in the decade to 2007, underneath the surface all was not well. Although it was little noted at the time, something of a disconnect had emerged between the headline growth of the macroeconomy and the actual real incomes of the typical worker. Median real wages, the after-inflation earnings of those in the middle of the distribution, began to slow in the 2000s. Median real wages stagnated for five years from 2003 until 2008 even as GDP grew by around 11 per cent. The deregulation of the labour market in the 1980s had boosted employment rates by the 2000s but also recreated an older world of lower-paying jobs. Some one fifth of workers found themselves earning less than two thirds of the median wage, compared to closer to one in ten in much of western Europe. While the minimum wage had put a floor on pay, it remained a fairly low one. In the sectors where unions remained stronger, such as transport, wage growth tended to be stronger. Indeed by the mid-2000s transport workers, with their ability to create what the tabloids would brand 'commuter hell' by going on strike, appeared to be one of the last bastions of union power in the private sector.

One reason that increasingly stagnant median earnings were generally missed was the ability of credit to fill the gaps. Britain's liberalised banking system was very happy to fill the gaps left where wage packets should have been. By the mid-2000s the growth rate of consumer credit was running at over 10 per cent annually. Household balance sheets were becoming more leveraged and at risk if the flow of finance were ever to dry up or if interest rates were to spike higher. But, dangerous as this was, the real action was happening in the housing market. Between 1997 and 2007 house prices more than doubled. House prices moved from being just over four times average earnings in the mid-1990s to more than eight times average earnings in 2007. The owner occupation share of the market, which had been rising since the First World War, peaked at 71 per cent of households in 2003. For those who had bought before the 1990s boom the house prices of the 2000s acted as a spur to confidence and consumption.

The late 1990s to late 2000s saw a credit boom in Britain. The total value of loans to the household sector and non-financial firms rose from around 170 per cent of GDP to over 230 per cent of GDP in a decade, the fastest growth in private indebtedness that Britain had ever experienced.

Frothy asset markets helped to fill the Treasury's coffers as a buoyant market for homes boosted stamp duty receipts, and financial sector bonuses and profits increased the income and corporation tax takes. But, in the last four years before the crisis of 2007, the government debt to GDP ratio began to rise. Gordon Brown's early years at the Treasury had been marked, in his own preferred term, by prudence. Labour had stuck to the Tories' spending plans for the first two years of the Parliament and, even as spending began to rise after 2000, was reluctant to raise the major rates of tax to keep pace. National Insurance was increased in 2001 with the money earmarked for the NHS, but that was the exception that proved the rule. Higher taxes seemed to reek of 'old Labour', not something either Blair or Brown wanted to be associated with. The public, they rightly judged, quite liked higher spending but was less keen on paying for it. Government debt to GDP crept up from around 30 per cent at the turn of the millennium to 40 per cent by 2007/08, still of course lower than for most of the previous century.

The government made something of a push on regional policy to narrow the gaps in regional performance that had opened up in the 1980s and 1990s. New Regional Development Agencies were set up but their impact varied across the country. The budget attached to regional growth initiatives never approached what it had reached in the 1960s or 1970s and the policy approach was inconsistent. The booming financial service sector in London acted as a motor to help pull the capital and its surroundings further ahead.

The basic building blocks of New Labour's political economy worked well enough from the late 1990s until 2007 – a relatively hands-off approach to macroeconomic management and very light touch regulation of the City seemed to be producing a strong and stable economy coupled with tax receipts that could be funnelled into anti-poverty measures. Low earners and the worst off in society benefited from a minimum wage, tax credits and large increases in spending on core public services. Public sector workers saw chunky real terms rises in their pay. Higher earners were left to their own devices without increases in their marginal tax rates. And any discontent from those in the middle was papered over by a rising volume of credit.

But the game could only go on as long as the financial markets did not deliver a nasty shock, and in 2007 they did.

Britain had not been alone in experiencing a credit boom; the United States and southern Europe had enjoyed their own binges. Financial regulators, both in Britain and overseas, had become complacent. In 2007 and 2008 much of what had previously been hailed as financial innovation would be exposed as nothing of the sort.

In the United States the height of the credit boom had seen a major growth in what were politely termed subprime mortgages and what are better thought of as 'mortgages given to people who could not really afford a mortgage'. What allowed the boom was the expansion of the so-called 'originate and disseminate' model of lending. Whereas a conventional mortgage was extended by a bank to a household and then held on its balance sheet until it was either repaid or defaulted on, this did not have to be the case. Instead the bank could extend a mortgage and then sell it on to some other part of the financial sector. At this point a bit of alchemy could be used to slice and dice up the individual mortgages into new securities. A bundle of subprime loans secured on properties in Florida could be added to some from the MidWest and a handful from the

West Coast. In theory, the resulting composite bond should be safer than the sum of its parts. Sure, some individual mortgage holders might default but each individual borrower was only a small part of the package as a whole. By the mid-2000s mortgage-backed bonds built on subprime lending were regularly being granted the top AAA credit rating. This theory was elegant, so too was the notion that it actively reduced risks in the financial sector by moving the risk of default away from individual lenders and towards those better able to manage it. Elegant though it was, the theory also turned out to be entirely wrong.

If national house prices began to decline in the US, as they did in 2006, then the incentives for subprime borrowers to default would all rise at the same time. A bundle of loans might be worth even less than the sum of its parts. And because the risk had been, in theory, spread around the financial system as a whole, no one knew exactly where it was at any given time. Banks, insurance companies and asset managers were by the summer of 2007 eyeing each other with suspicion, trying to judge if their counterparty would be the next institution to blow up. Trust evaporated and the rate charged to borrow for even short-term periods spiked. Overall credit growth fell into reverse with real consequences for the economy as credit-reliant firms failed and households pulled back on spending.

In Britain the first casualty was Northern Rock. The Newcastle-based lender had been a rather sleepy provincial building society until the early 1990s, when it transformed itself into a bank and seized on the opportunities offered by the originate and disseminate model with a vigour almost unmatched in Britain. By 2007 it was responsible for around one in five new mortgages in Britain, some of them offered at a loan to value ratio of 130 per cent (otherwise known as 'negative equity on day one'). This was despite having a branch network numbered in the dozens and a small base of deposits. The bank funded itself through short-term borrowing in the money markets and through selling its loans on to a special purpose vehicle cunningly named Granite (a northern rock). Fundamentally its business relied on borrowing cheaply for short periods of time to fund more lucrative loans with longer maturities. When short-term interest rates spiked, that model died. By September 2007 the Rock was receiving emergency funding (secured against its assets) from the Bank of England. The BBC learned of this development and it led the *Ten O'Clock News*. Next day depositors were rushing to withdraw their cash. At that point the small branch network, which had helped keep costs low in the good old days, became a serious problem: in the rush, queues formed quickly. Few things make a deposit holder more nervous than television pictures of other people queuing up to withdraw their cash. Britain soon had its first retail run on a bank since the 1860s. The firm was nationalised in February 2008.

There is still, over a decade later, a tendency to equate the collapse of Lehman Brothers, a US investment bank, in September 2008 with the onset of the global recession – usually nowadays termed the Great Recession. But that is to mistake a consequence of the recession for its cause. The freezing up of global money markets and the credit crunch of 2007 were enough to tip Britain, the United States and much of Europe into recession by early 2008; that recession then brought about more serious financial stress which resulted in a round of further banking failures in late 2008.

By the time Lehman failed Britain had been in recession for two quarters and unemployment had already risen about one percentage point to just under 6 per cent. If the British authorities had been somewhat blindsided by the outbreak of this financial crisis they can least claim some credit for devising the solutions that helped to end it. For much of 2007 and early to mid-2008 global policy-makers had treated what was happening in financial markets as an issue of liquidity rather than solvency. The problem, they believed, was a lack of readily available funds, which could be solved by central banks lending freely (in return for collateral), much as had been attempted with Northern Rock. By September 2008, the Treasury and the Bank of England had come to grasp that the distinction between a liquidity problem – in theory a temporary cashflow issue – and a solvency problem, in which the total value of liabilities outweighs the total value of assets, is irrelevant at a time of acute crisis. As mutual trust collapsed the financial institutions were calling in their loans to each other, forcing many to try to sell the very same assets at the same time – which depressed the price of those assets, leading to further demands for repayment as balance sheets deteriorated. To break the cycle the government embarked on a programme of recapitalisation that would eventually be followed by Europe and the United States. Alongside extraordinary measures to extend liquidity from central banks, the government gave banks two options: either they should raise fresh capital privately, to improve their balance sheets and build confidence, or the government would inject its own funds in return for a stake in the business. Within weeks the government owned large stakes in the Royal Bank of Scotland and the newly merged Lloyds-Halifax Bank of Scotland Group. The financial crisis that had begun in 2007 was petering out by early 2009, but the economic crisis was just beginning.

Many were quick to point out that for almost thirty years the government of the day had been arguing that its role was not to bail out private sector firms. When British Leyland had needed cash in the 1980s or its successor Rover in the early 2000s they were simply allowed to fail. When Lloyds or RBS needed the money, though, it was found. The key difference was that a bank failure risked, as Lehman's demonstrated, a much larger secondary effect as savings were lost and the money supply contracted. That may be true economically, but it was scant comfort to those working for failing firms in 2008 and 2009 which were not on the receiving end of government largesse. The failure to rapidly clamp down on pay in the newly publicly supported financial sector created an impression that bankers had caused the crisis but were not being held accountable.

Gordon Brown, Prime Minister since 2007, was instrumental in creating what became known as the G-20, a rather hodgepodge group of leading economies that included, for example, Argentina and Turkey but excluded the much larger economies of Spain and the Netherlands except through their EU representative. The idea was to co-ordinate fiscal stimulus and ensure that the world did not respond to this financial crisis in the same way it had to that of 1929 – with a move to protectionism and attempts at national self-sufficiency.

British fiscal policy, which had only years before been relegated from the role of active demand management, now stepped up. VAT was cut to 15 per cent (from a previous 17.5 per cent), capital spending brought forward and various smaller stimulatory steps (such as the cash for clunkers scheme which offered a bounty to anyone trading in an old car) taken to try to boost demand. The government's deficit leapt from 2.9 per cent of GDP in 2006/07 to 7.5 per cent in 2007/08 and over 10 per cent in 2009/10. Nothing like these numbers had ever been experienced in peacetime. The actual value of the fiscal stimulus, though, was far smaller than this suggests. Discretionary support for the economy, in the form of spending increases and tax cuts, amounted to more like 2.5 per cent of GDP in 2008/09; the bulk of the deficit was simply the result of collapsing tax receipts and rising welfare spending, the so-called 'automatic stabilisers' that kick in in any recession. In Britain's case they were unusually large in the late 2000s as the tax base had become increasingly dependent on the asset markets and financial sector, which were now in acute crisis.

Thirty years after James Callaghan had declared that a government could not spend its way out of recession, the Brown government appeared determined to try to do just that. The big difference was in the nature of the two recessions. In the 1970s Britain had faced a series of shocks to the supply side of the economy, the kind of shocks to which fiscal policy is ill suited to respond. Cutting taxes and increasing spending to boost demand is of no help if the problem is that industry is crippled by suddenly higher energy prices and a wave of strikes. In 2007 to 2009, the financial crisis was primarily a demand shock – suddenly tighter credit availability was pulling down household and corporate spending – and seeking to increase demand to compensate was entirely the correct response from the government.

The return of the spirit of Keynes to the Treasury dominated much of the political debate in 2008 and 2009, but even larger shifts were happening at the Bank of England. The Bank was slower to respond to the crisis in 2007 than its peers at the Federal Reserve and European Central Bank. In August 2007, whereas the ECB was extending billions of euros of emergency lending to its banking system, the Governor of the Bank of England was lecturing the markets on the 'moral hazard' of being too reliant on state support. But once the scale of the crisis in the real economy was clear, the Bank acted quickly. By early 2009 interest rates had been cut from 5 per cent to just 0.5 per cent. That was the end of the road for conventional monetary policy; the Bank believed that the base rate had hit its effective floor. Nonetheless, with the economy likely to remain in recession, more had to be done to prevent demand collapsing and inflation falling further below its target of 2 per cent. The answer was quantitative easing or QE. QE is what was once called 'unconventional monetary policy' but has become increasingly common since 2009.

While QE is sometimes called 'money printing' as a form of shorthand, that is a misleading notion. The Bank did not fire up the printing press. Instead it electronically created new 'money' (or bank reserves) at the stroke of a key and used this to purchase government bonds from the private sector. This extra demand for government bonds should push their price up and the interest rate on them down. Government debt is the benchmark on which other assets are priced, so lower interest rates there should mean lower interest rates on commercial bonds and long-term loans. If conventional central bank policy is about moving short-term interest rates, then QE is more concerned with affecting longer-term rates. A helpful side effect for the government is to reduce the cost of its borrowing, which eases fiscal pressure and helps it to finance its own deficits. QE should also have a second-round impact through what is known as the portfolio rebalancing channel: the banks, insurance companies and pension funds that sell their holdings of government debt to the Bank of England receive cash in return, which they can then spend on new assets, pushing up the prices of non-government bonds and shares.

The Bank's decision to launch £200 billion of QE in 2009 provoked concern in some quarters that high inflation would follow; debasing the currency seemed to be some sort of Rubicon that central banks had previously dared not cross. But in a world still reeling from the financial crisis, where firms and households were keener to save and repair their balance sheets than to spend, such fears proved to be very wide of the mark.

By mid-2010 the acute stage of the financial crisis was over. Britain's banks no longer looked at risk of collapse. But the

economy had contracted by more than 6 per cent before bot-
toming out in 2009, its deepest recession since the inter-war
years, and unemployment had risen to close to 8 per cent,
its highest level since the mid-1990s. Sterling lost around 20
per cent of its value. Media commentary now increasingly
focused on the government's sky-high deficit and how it would
be reduced.

The Conservative electoral campaign in 2010 alleged that
Brown had brought Britain to the brink of bankruptcy and
now was the time to start to start 'fixing the mess'. Some
prominent economists agreed, whilst others urged the government to concentrate on fixing the economy rather than
the public finances by maintaining stimulus, even at the cost
of higher debt. In the end the debate amongst economists was
fascinating but irrelevant. Enough of the public agreed with
the Conservatives to put them back in power. Macroeconomic
policy was set to be changed once again.

17

After Shock

The financial crisis was essentially over in Britain by 2009 but its lingering impacts would dominate the nation's political economy for the next decade. The economic performance and the turbulent politics of the 2010s all took place in the shadow of the crisis.

The election campaign of 2010, which Labour unsuccessfully sought to characterise as being a choice between investment and cuts, was not the one David Cameron had expected to fight when he became Conservative leader in 2005. Cameron, much like Blair, found himself leading a party that had lost three general elections in a row and which needed to somehow rehabilitate itself with middle-ground opinion. His answer was to emphasise his own social liberalism and to demonstrate that he led a party in touch with and at ease with modern Britain. In the early years of his leadership, economics (once central to the party of Thatcher) were downplayed. Aping a decision Labour had made in the mid-1990s, the so-called 'heir to Blair' went as far as to pledge to match Labour's tax and spending plans for the first two years of a new Parliament.

The crisis changed all that. Rather than matching Labour's spending plans the Conservatives rediscovered their Thatcherite preference for a smaller state. In the event the 2010 election result was closer than many had expected and the Conservatives found themselves in coalition with the Liberal Democrats.

The new government inherited an economy that was growing, but slowly. The government's deficit, which was to dominate politics for the next five years, stood at over 10 per cent of GDP and the government debt ratio had jumped from around 35 per cent of GDP on the eve of the crisis to closer to 75 per cent by 2010, which, while low by comparison with the 1920s or 1940s, was the highest since the mid-1960s.

There were three related but distinct arguments for the policies that followed. The first was a simple belief in the virtues of a smaller state. It was twenty years since Margaret Thatcher had led the Conservative Party but many of its members remained committed Thatcherites. A smaller state, they believed, would mean lower taxes and a more dynamic, faster growing economy. Another argument focused less on the size of the state and more on the level of debt. The economists Carmen Reinhart and Ken Rogoff had in 2010 published an extremely influential paper in a leading US journal entitled 'Growth in a Time of Debt'. This paper argued, on the basis of an empirical historical study, that once debt to GDP passed the 90 per cent mark, annual GDP growth began to sag considerably. It would later emerge, in 2013, that their paper contained a spreadsheet error which, when corrected, removed the correlation. That, though, was still in the future in 2010, and George Osborne, the new Chancellor, was just one of many politicians around the world citing Reinhart and Rogoff in justification of a need to cut deficits. With the deficit and debt levels where they stood in mid-2010, the 90 per cent threshold seemed to be only 18–24 months away.

The third, more nuanced argument could be termed the balance of risks approach. Even with a debt to GDP ratio of 75 per cent and a deficit of 10 per cent of GDP, Britain was not experiencing a real issue with selling enough bonds to fund itself. The interest rate on ten-year gilts at the time the coalition took power was around 3.9 per cent, one of the lowest any government had faced since the 1950s. But that could, in theory anyway, change quickly. The worry was that investors might take fright at Britain's continuing deficit and begin to demand a higher return on their purchases of government debt. Any spike in interest rates would not only put more pressure on the government budget by raising the annual interest bill but impact firms and households as the mechanism pushed rates higher across the economy. By that logic, one could accept that cutting back on fiscal support for the government might mean some short-term pain but it would lower the risk of an even more damaging rise in borrowing costs. Nervousness was certainly in the air in 2010. S&P, one of the major credit-rating agencies, had warned in 2009 that Britain's AAA rating was at risk, while Bill Gross, a leading US bond fund manager, had rather apocalyptically argued that gilts were resting 'on a bed of nitro-glycerine'. Sterling had already fallen by 20 per cent since 2008, and the country's large current account deficit appeared to leave it vulnerable to any swings in international opinion.

In the end Britain did lose its AAA rating but, despite it regularly overshooting its targets for borrowing, interest rates did not soar. Quite the opposite. The yield on gilts fell below 3 per cent in 2011 and below 2 per cent in 2012. However loudly financial market types warned about the risk of spiralling British debt, in practice the markets were generally happy to keep buying up gilts at ever lower yields. The global picture in the 2010s was that, despite soaring government deficits, the global financial system faced a shortage of 'safe' assets. The kind of mortgage-backed bonds that had been regarded as safe only a few short years earlier had been shown to be in fact quite dangerous, while many of the top-rated companies that had previously issued supposedly safe bonds were now also struggling. Question marks were now being raised over the safety of the government debt of countries across parts of the eurozone such as Italy and Spain. British gilts, no matter the state of the deficit or the level of the debt, appeared to offer a relative haven. Picking global bonds in a crisis is somewhat akin to picking the least dirty shirt out of the laundry basket, and gilts did not seem to be too badly crumpled. Whatever merit there had been in cautiously attempting to cut the size of the deficit in 2010 in order to guard against a spike in borrowing costs evaporated as rates collapsed in 2011 and 2012.

Much of the debate in the 2010–2015 Parliament focused not on the raw deficit figures but on the concept of the structural deficit. The structural deficit is one of those parts of modern macroeconomics which are an excellent idea in theory but a hard one to use in reality. The core principle behind it is a sound one: to strip away all the parts of the deficit that relate to the economic cycle and focus on the fundamentals, to ask not 'What is the deficit today?' but instead 'What will the deficit be once the economy has returned to normal?' In 2010 the British economy was still clearly emerging from the Great Recession; as unemployment fell the welfare bill would too. And as employment rose so would tax receipts. Much of the headline deficit of more than 10 per cent GDP would be dealt with through an economic recovery, but not all of it. The structural deficit attempts to isolate the proportion of government borrowing which is 'structural', or permanent, in nature. That is a sensible enough approach but working out exactly what is structural and what is just cyclical, or the impact of the current stage of the economy cycle, is a tricky business. It depends on estimates of the future level of productivity growth, on how far unemployment can fall before inflation begins to rise and ultimately on an estimate of the trend in the level of growth of the economy. The structural deficit is something that can only be estimated, rather than a variable that one can actually measure. Those sorts of estimations are hard enough at the best of times, let alone in an uncertain environment such as 2010. In 2010, the newly formed Office for Budget Responsibility (OBR), an arms-length body established to produce forecasts for the Treasury and to monitor progress, reckoned that the structural deficit inherited by the coalition was set to be 2.3 per cent of GDP in the 2014/15 financial year on the basis of the outgoing Labour government's plans. That was the gap which would have to be closed through what became known as austerity.

The first coalition budget hiked VAT from the pre-crisis level of 17.5 per cent to 20 per cent, cut back on welfare spending and outlined a tight squeeze on departmental budgets. There were some supporters of the coalition who went as far as to believe in what they called 'expansionary fiscal contraction', the notion that the very action of the government cutting back its spending would itself cause growth to pick up. They hoped that the confidence of firms would be increased by the government taking action to prevent any future spike in interest rates and that households, knowing that future debt levels would be lower, would be boosted by the knowledge that their future tax bills would be lower too. That, however, was putting rather too much faith in the power of expectation over the reality of the government cutting spending in a still weak recovery. Fiscal contraction turned out to be, as the name suggests, contractionary.

Osborne was an ambitious Chancellor: his own agenda was

not just to reduce the deficit or shrink the state but to rebalance the British economy itself. The dependence on government and public sector consumption would be replaced by a growth model based on rising exports and rising investment. In the early 2010s, as the world emerged from recession, export-led growth was a very popular idea, one so popular that most governments globally wanted to pursue some version of it. In the absence of intergalactic exports, though, that was impossible. The hoped-for boom in investment failed to materialise despite cuts in corporation tax, the rolling back of bureaucracy and red tape and the low borrowing costs available to corporates. In the end the outlook for economic demand is a major determinant of decisions around business capital expenditure, and that appeared to be pretty soggy. Osborne did do his bit when it came to the government's own capital spend, which was generally shielded from the wider squeeze on government spending.

Before becoming Chancellor he declared himself to be a 'fiscal conservative but a monetary policy radical'. Over the next few years he would be true to his word. Even as budget after budget saw deficit target missed and he responded by further tightening policy, the Bank of England was encouraged to be ever more inventive in finding new ways to effect monetary easing.

QE, which had stood at £200 billion in 2010, was increased to £375 billion in 2012. Under the Funding for Lending scheme, which also began in 2012, the Bank further supported around £70 billion of lending to households and firms via cheap funding to commercial banks. Mark Carney was headhunted from the Bank of Canada to take over at Threadneedle Street in 2013 and arrived with a reputation as 'rockstar economist', although no one was quite clear exactly what that meant. His great innovation was 'forward guidance', essentially a pledge to keep monetary policy extremely easy and rates ultra-low for the foreseeable future in order to build confidence.

Assessing the impact of the ultra-easy monetary policy from 2010 onwards is far from straightforward. It certainly proved unable to generate a robust, self-sustaining recovery, but it is likely that the counterfactual world, in which tight fiscal policy had been coupled with tight monetary policy, would have been worse. One side effect was booming asset prices, as investors faced with the prospect of miserly returns from traditionally safe assets were forced into bidding up the prices of alternatives. House price inflation began to take root once again in late 2012.

The recovery from the 2008/09 recession was painfully slow. It would not be until 2014 that the economy reached its previous peak, making it the slowest recovery since the early 1800s. Tight fiscal policy played a large part in that, although so too did the damage to the financial sector endured in the crisis. The recoveries from financial crashes tend to be fraught and slow. The coalition were also unlucky in the international environment they faced. The first half of their term in office coincided with the Eurocrisis of 2010–2012, which not only depressed growth in Britain's largest export market but also kept alive the risk of a renewed financial crisis following a potential break-up of the single currency. That acted as a constraint on lending as well as holding back business confidence. The combination of an easing of eurozone tensions and a slowing of the pace of fiscal tightening, together with the impact of Funding for Lending, saw growth begin to pick up somewhat in 2013 and 2014.

Austerity reshaped the British state but not in a deeply uneven manner. Money was still found for tax cuts, often quite large ones; corporation tax was slashed from 28 per cent in 2010 to 20 per cent by 2015. More dramatic still was a series of hikes in the size of the personal allowance which an individual can earn before paying any income tax. The Liberal Democrats had campaigned on taking the low-paid out of the tax system and the Conservatives were not only happy to oblige but totally adopted the policy as their own. The personal allowance rose from £6,475 for under 65s in 2010 to £10,000 by 2015. Subsequent Tory governments would increase it further to £12,500. While the Liberal Democrats had argued this was a policy aimed at cutting the tax bill for the low paid, what Tory strategists quickly cottoned on to was that it has the impact of cutting taxes for everyone. Indeed, raising the threshold from, say, £9,000 to £10,000 has precisely zero impact on the take-home pay of someone earning £8,500 a year, who is already below the threshold for paying tax, but it cut the tax bill of anyone earning £10,000 or more by £200 a year (of course some of that could be clawed back by moving other tax bands, but such changes rarely happened). The number of income tax payers fell by half a million over the 2010s, the most sustained fall on record. The top rate of income tax, which Labour had briefly raised from 40 per cent to 50 per cent, was cut back to 45 per cent. Fuel duty on petrol was frozen at each passing budget rather than being increased.

Taken together, the cutting of the top rate of income tax, the large rise in the personal allowance, the cuts to corporation tax and the freezing of fuel duty amounted to a drop in revenue of around £30 billion a year by 2015 compared to the tax take in 2010. These were substantial tax cuts for a government committed to the notion of balancing the budget, even if they were partially offset by the VAT rise and some other smaller revenue-raisers, which together brought in an additional £25 billion or so.

The bulk of austerity's burden was to be borne in the form of spending cuts rather than tax rises. Even here, though, the pattern varied. The NHS budget continued to rise in real terms, and spending on state pensions was not only protected but increased through the adoption of the 'triple lock' – a commitment that the basic state pension would henceforth rise by whichever was the highest of three rates: inflation, earnings growth or 2.5 per cent. Spending on schools and overseas aid was 'protected'.

Public sector pay, the welfare system and the 'unprotected departments' took the brunt. Universal credit, the new payment which was supposed to merge six existing benefits into one, was slow to be rolled out and frequently cut beforehand, leaving a system less generous than its predecessors. Local authorities saw their real terms budgets cut by a quarter, with the number of employees of local councils falling from 2.9 million in 2010 to 2.2 million by 2015.

After five years of public sector restraint and cutbacks, the headline deficit had fallen from over 10 per cent of GDP to 4.1 per cent by 2015/16. But most of that reflected a cyclical recovery; the structural deficit – the supposed target of five years of austerity – was still over 2 per cent of GDP, just about where the OBR had predicted it would be in 2015, before Osborne had even unveiled his agenda.

With the public sector shedding workers and demand constrained, one might have expected unemployment to remain high. Indeed that was a near consensus view in 2010. The OBR forecast at the time of Osborne's first budget that unemployment would be over 7 per cent for most of the next five years before finally dropping down to a still elevated 6.1 per cent around the time of the next election. Growth was to undershoot what turned out to be optimistic projections and yet, from 2012 onwards, unemployment fell rapidly. It was around 5.5 per cent by the time Cameron sought re-election. Not only did unemployment fall but the employment rate actually rose;

previously inactive people re-entered the workforce. By 2015 the percentage of 16- to 64-year-olds in work had risen from its mid-recession low of 70 per cent to 74 per cent, the highest rate in British economic history. This was what the Conservatives, uncertainly, called their jobs miracle.

The 2008/09 recession and the recovery from it were the first real stress test of the liberalised labour market created in the Thatcher and Major years. Both the 1980s and 1990s recessions came while reform was in progress rather than complete. Firing was made easier, but so too was hiring. Taking on a worker was less of a commitment for a firm now it had the power to quickly reverse its decision. In the early 1980s a 5 per cent fall in GDP pushed up unemployment by seven percentage points, while in the 1990s a 2.5 per cent drop in output saw the unemployment rate rise by 4 per cent. By contrast a 6 per cent fall in 2008/09 was accompanied by a rise in worklessness of three percentage points. The relationship between lost output and lost jobs appeared more favourable and firms were quick to begin hiring again once the downturn ended. That said, there were legitimate concerns about the nature of some of the new roles – more were part-time or had limited hours, and pay and conditions were often worse than the pre-recession norm.

The macroeconomic trade-off meant that the silver lining of rapid jobs growth came with quite the cloud. The counterpoint to the jobs miracle was a productivity disaster. Rapid growth in the number of hours worked coupled with a slow expansion in overall economic output added up to a historically weak productivity performance. Whereas output per hour worked had grown at a steady rate of around 2.2 per cent per year for the three decades up until 2008, in the decade afterwards it collapsed to a growth rate of more like 0.5 per cent. That might not sound like much, 2.2 per cent and 0.5 per cent are after all both small numbers. But over the course of a decade it is the difference between output per hour worked expanding by 24 per cent and output per hour worked growing by 5 per cent. In fifty or sixty years' time, when the conclusive economic histories of the early twenty-first century are written, the productivity collapse after the financial crisis will be a major theme.

The problem quickly became branded as 'the productivity puzzle' due to its lack of an obvious cause. Poor productivity growth was certainly not just a British problem – the slowdown could be seen in the United States, in China and across Europe – but it was particularly acute in Britain. And given Britain had an existing productivity gap with western Europe, even if growth there slowed there should have been no reason why Britain could not continue to catch up. A global slowdown in the frontier of productivity growth should matter less to a country further back from that frontier.

Possible explanations varied from the drop in North Sea oil production (an incredibly high productivity field now in terminal decline) to mismeasuring financial services output in the years before the crash (perhaps what had been recorded as a productivity miracle was simply a mirage created by excessive risk-taking, pondered one Bank of England policy-maker). Weak corporate investment did not have help, and it is possible that the destruction of labour bargaining power in the 1980s, helped by strong jobs growth, encouraged the hiring of people for low productivity jobs that once would have not been worth the hassle. And, although poor productivity is usually thought of as a supply-side issue, it may be that weak aggregate demand amid austerity also played a part by weakening incentives to investment.

A fundamental macroeconomic fact of the 2010s was that labour was cheap and widely available. For all the fretting about the role of technological change in the jobs market, there was very little evidence that robots were indeed stealing people's jobs. If anything, the opposite was happening. In the fifteen years to 2018 the number of automated car washes, the kind of thing that used to be attached to most petrol station forecourts, fell by half, while the number of manual car washes – usually a bunch of men with a bucket – soared. By the late 2010s, some 80 per cent of car washes were manual. This was obviously less efficient and less productive. But the incentives for the owners were clear. Buying an automatic roller washer meant spending tens of thousands of pounds. Setting up a manual car wash cost only a few hundred pounds. And if demand for car washes fell then the workers could simply be dismissed with few sunk costs. In an era of cheap labour, technological progress seemed to have sometimes gone into reverse.

Whatever the reasons for the slowdown in productivity, the real-world consequences were felt immediately through a sharp fall in real wages. The norm in the late 1990s and 2000s had been for average weekly wages to grow by around 4 per cent a year and, with inflation usually around the Bank of England's target, that translated into real wage growth of about 2 per cent a year. But in 2008 wage growth fell below inflation and the real pay of British workers began to fall. By 2015 more Britons were in work than ever before but real pay was enduring its longest squeeze since the Napoleonic Wars. Average weekly earnings would not regain their 2008 levels, in real terms, until the very end of 2019, just before the COVID-19 pandemic hit.

By the time of the 2015 election, although real wages were still well below their previous peak, and indeed their 2010 level, they had been growing reasonably solidly for the past year. A collapse in the price of oil coupled with a rebound in the value of sterling caused inflation to fall sharply in 2014 and 2015. The 2015 election turned out to be extremely well timed indeed for the Conservatives, although less so for their coalition partners.

David Cameron won a surprise majority in that year's general election despite a squeeze on real incomes and cutbacks in state service provision. Cameron's party reduced their Liberal Democrat partners to a rump, taking 18 seats from them, and gaining overall 38 more than in 2010. In Scotland, which had only narrowly voted to stay part of the UK in a referendum the year before, the Nationalists now controlled 56 of the 59 seats; it appeared that 45 per cent of the vote was not enough to win a binary referendum but was more than adequate to sweep the parliamentary board against a divided opposition.

The usual focus on weak headline growth and the consequences of austerity together with the long squeeze on real wages would suggest that the Conservatives should have struggled in 2015. But the bedrock of the Conservative support-base was relatively well looked after. Homeowners saw the value of their assets rise, businesses received tax cuts and the impact of the broader reduction in income tax through the rising personal allowance should not be underestimated. The parts of the state which older voters, who were not only more likely to vote but voted Conservative in even greater numbers than usual, relied upon, such as pensions and the NHS, were shielded from cuts. The collapse in inflation in the year before the election created a mini feel-good factor. Substantial increases in the minimum wage, now rebranded as the National Living Wage for the over 25s, were announced in the run-up to the election.

There was another aspect to the campaign that does not quite fit with the usual economics textbooks. One reason for moving away from politicians' discretion to rules-based policy-making had been to guard against 'deficit bias', the idea that the public would usually like more spending and fewer taxes in the immediate future and for this to be paid for by later generations. And yet in 2015, and to an extent in 2010, the public appeared to be hostile to the very notion of public debt and public borrowing. The middle of the decade would see the somewhat odd spectacle of independent central bankers essentially asking the supposedly reckless politicians to spend a bit more to boost demand and make their own jobs easier.

Labour's leader from 2010 to 2015 was Ed Miliband, the Oxford-educated son of a Marxist intellectual, who had served as an advisor to Gordon Brown. Much of the press never forgave him for having the audacity to beat his brother David, an Oxford-educated son of a Marxist intellectual, who had served as an advisor to Tony Blair, to the leadership. Miliband's pitch was somewhat to the left of that of Brown and Blair and closer to where the party had been in the early 1990s. He offered a broadly social democratic prospectus of active industrial policy, fiscal expansion and, in what was dubbed Marxism at the time, a price freeze in domestic energy markets. British business, and the business press, decided this was all distinctly anti-enterprise and that they would have to stick with the Conservatives. Surprisingly few people paid attention to the Conservative pledge to hold an in or out referendum on Britain's membership of the European Union. The Tories were likely to be in coalition with the Liberal Democrats who would surely nix the idea, and even if it happened, Remain was bound to win. That was the lesson of the fiercely fought Scottish referendum of 2014.

Europe had been a festering sore in the Conservative Party since the 1980s. Margaret Thatcher had been generally pro-European in office but turned against the notion in the 1990s, and her disciples followed her. The Major government had been deeply split over the ratification of the Maastricht Treaty that transformed the old EEC into the EU. But Europe-focused campaigns in 2001 and 2005 had failed to cut through with the public. Fewer than one in ten Britons named it as a major issue facing the country as late as 2015. Immigration, which had picked up sharply in the mid-2000s with the entry of formerly communist states into the EU, had ruffled many feathers but it seemed people still tended to vote on the older core issues of public services and taxes rather than the fact the country had more foreigners in it.

Cameron's post-election honeymoon was a short one, and by early 2016 he found himself heading up the Remain side in the much-promised referendum. The leadership of the Conservative, Labour, Liberal Democrat and Nationalist parties backed Remain. As did the major trade unions and the major employers' organisations. And yet Leave won on a 52–48 per cent split and a high turnout.

Some tried to cast this as the result of a great revolt by the supposed losers of globalisation against the elites. Those who had seen their real earnings stagnate even before the crisis of 2008 and then endured six years of austerity. But that simply does not fit the pattern of voting; the young – who had experienced the highest unemployment during the crisis and the deepest falls in wages afterwards – voted overwhelmingly to remain. The old, who had been protected from the worst impacts of austerity and were the most likely to own the buoyant assets of the past few years, voted to leave. Many northern towns did indeed back Leave, but so did many southern towns. The largest cities of the north voted for Remain. The median Leave voter was more likely to be found in a Kent golf club than a Manchester working-men's club. Old-fashioned class analysis does not fit the pattern of the 2016 vote any more than a worry about the supposed perennial deficit bias of the public fits the pattern of 2015.

The key to understanding the somewhat strange politics of

the 2010s is to look beyond the older divides of the twentieth century and into the newer cleavages of the twenty-first. Age has always been a factor in general elections, with older voters, who are broadly speaking more secure and more likely to own assets, tending towards the political right. But in the 2010s age came very obviously to the fore, and the decisions of older voters determined the outcome of both the Brexit referendum of 2016 and the Scottish vote of 2014.

A comparison of the general election results in October 1974 and 2017 is instructive; one can be explained by class and the other by generation. In 1974 the Tories beat Labour by 56 per cent to 19 per cent amongst voters in the sociological groups ABC1 (white collar professionals) whilst losing by 16 per cent to 49 per cent among C2 (skilled manual workers) and by 22 per cent to 57 per cent among DE (unskilled workers and the unemployed). That was a vote decisively on class grounds even at a time when the left's intellectuals were fretting about a decline of class-based politics. By contrast the class breakdown of the vote in 2017 was broadly flat. The Tories won ABC1 by just 44 per cent to 40 per cent, tied with Labour at 40 per cent each for C2 and lost DE by just 41 per cent to 44 per cent.

The pattern of age-based voting was the direct inverse. In 1974 the relative likelihood of a 30- to 70-year-old voting Labour or voting Conservative was roughly similar, with a tilt to the Conservatives as the voter aged. In 2017 age was the decisive factor, with a 30-year-old twice as likely to vote Labour as a 70-year-old.

That trend of older voters turning increasingly to the political right no doubt is partially driven by cultural factors – such as a dislike of immigration and the changes the modern world has wrought – but it also reflects diverging economic experiences. Older people in Britain in the 2010s were not only protected from the worst squeezes of austerity but were more likely to own their own homes and so benefit from house price inflation rather than be squeezed by rising rental costs. The real disposable incomes of retired and working-age households, after adjusting for housing costs, reveal a surprising pattern. Not only did the retired enjoy stronger income growth through the decade than those in work, but by 2012 their post-housing cost income was already actually higher. For the first time in British economic history a higher standard of living was enjoyed by the typical retired household than by the typical working one.

Political economy tends to examine the interaction of different interest groups and how they can shape economic policy in their favour. The new development in twenty-first-century Britain is the rise of an almost post-economic voting bloc: the retired and those nearing retirement who are insulated from the day to day gyrations of the economic cycle by guaranteed pensions and asset ownership. And what is more they are a group whose share of the population is rising and who are much more likely to vote.

In the immediate aftermath of the Brexit vote economic confidence was damaged and sterling fell by around 20 per cent, acting as a shock absorber for the wider financial system. The Bank of England cut interest rates to a record low of 0.25 per cent and increased the volume of its QE programme to £445 billion.

The economy took a hit as corporations put investment plans on hold while they waited to see the final outcome, and spiking inflation, caused by the weaker currency, put a new squeeze on real incomes. Growth fell from being one of the highest among the G-7 group of leading economies in late 2015 and early 2016 to the lowest within a year. But an immediate recession, which the Treasury had tied itself in knots to predict before the vote, failed to materialise. Brexiteers were quick to call such warnings of impending doom 'project fear'.

Membership of the EEC and then the EU had been a crucial component of Britain's economic model since the 1970s. It had expanded the markets available to exporters, exposed domestic firms to new types of competition, helping to boost dynamism and productivity, and it had acted as an anchor to policy-makers through the rules of the single market constraining their actions.

The immediate problem in 2016 was that Leave had won but no one quite knew exactly what that meant. Sure it meant leaving the European Union, but could Britain stay in the Single Market or the Customs Union? Or might there even be a second referendum to reverse the decision? Those questions were to dominate David Cameron's successor Theresa May's rather miserable three years in office.

Seeking her own mandate, she risked an early election in 2017, three years before it was due – though at the time it did not seem to be an especially risky venture. Having failed to win under Ed Miliband, despite his efforts to appease the right-leaning press, many Labour members in 2015 had decided they might as well be hung for a sheep as a lamb and voted for the real thing. Jeremy Corbyn was the party's most left-wing leader in modern times. Miliband had offered some tinkering with markets and a dash of economic expansion. Corbyn offered a major expansion of state spending, the ending of austerity and the renationalisation of the privatised utilities. At the time the election was called, May held a commanding 20 per cent lead in the polls.

But as the campaign wore on that lead evaporated. Corbyn proved to be a surprisingly adept campaigner and May a dreadful one. And while the 2015 election was opportunely timed for the Conservatives amid a bounce in real wages, the 2017 one came as wages were once again being squeezed. May lost her majority and endured two years of purgatory trying to negotiate an exit deal with the European Union. Under increasing pressure from the right of her own party to deliver a clean break, the terms of the exit became harder and harder. Traditional Conservative allies across business found themselves without a strong voice in government. Whether it was the car manufacturers reliant on easy cross-border logistics for their supply chains or the banks who needed cross-border regulation to sell their products in Europe seemed to matter little. But then the Conservative voter base was itself increasingly walled off from what was happening in the economy.

While Brexit dominated British politics, the deficit, which had been the primary issue in the two previous elections, moved to backstage. Philip Hammond, May's Chancellor, continued to pledge to eliminate it, but the heat was draining from the issue. More significantly the aims of fiscal policy began to shift. Osborne had spent six years not only pledging to eliminate the structural deficit but also hoping to return the debt to GDP ratio from its elevated level of around 80 per cent back down to the pre-crisis 40 per cent. That implied tight spending restraint for decades ahead. Slowly but surely that target was dropped in favour of merely stabilising the debt ratio at its current level. A much less onerous proposition.

May's failure to find a deal that was acceptable to her party, her former European partners and Parliament ended her unhappy premiership in stalemate. Boris Johnson, her successor, talked a tough line in rhetoric to keep his own backbenchers onboard whilst agreeing an exit package with Europe that was essentially little different from what May had managed.

He then sought the backing of the British public in a snap general election in 2019. Unlike 2017, Corbyn's campaign – by now more an ever-growing list of economic pledges than a compelling narrative – flopped rather than fizzling. Johnson by contrast stayed focused on his simple message of 'Get Brexit done'. The result was a landslide, with the largest Tory majority since 1987.

Most striking was the wave of Conservative gains from Labour across the north of England and the midlands. Ex-industrial seats that had returned Labour MPs for decades fell to the Conservative advance. Even former mining towns that had spearheaded resistance to Thatcher's changes fell to her successors. Of course working-class support for Toryism was nothing new, it certainly would not have surprised a Baldwin or a Salisbury. But, as throughout the 2010s, age mattered more. Age had been the dominant factor in 2017 and was to prove even more decisive in 2019. It turned out that the baby boomers of Blyth Valley, a former mining town in southeast Northumberland, were not that different from the boomers of the Medway towns in Kent.

Johnson won a strong enough majority to easily pass his Brexit deal which would see Britain leave the European Union at the end of January 2020 but remain in the Single Market and Customs Union until 2021. The bigger question of what Britain's economic model would look like without the anchor of membership of the European Union was left unanswered.

Epilogue

Pandemic

In his New Year message as 2020 dawned Boris Johnson promised Britain that Brexit would deliver a new roaring twenties. In the end, economically at least, 2020 was surprisingly similar to 1920, with the deepest recession on record.

The global pandemic of 2020, and the associated economic fallout, has the potential to be a larger political economy event than the global financial crisis of 2007–2009. Some of the left saw the early days of the pandemic as a form of proof that 'Jeremy Corbyn was right' after all. Certainly, the big state proved vital in 2020, just as it had in 2008. But after the 2008 crisis passed, the state found itself being aggressively shrunk.

Britain's economy and political economic structure have been being reshaped by crisis for decades. The crisis of the 1940s ended with Attlee's New Jerusalem; the crisis of the Great War ended with the miserable 1920s.

Economic change is shaped by what has gone before – things are after all usually path dependent – but nothing is inevitable. Attlee and Thatcher both pushed the country in radical new directions, as in his own way did Peel. But most governments of the past two hundred or so years have been content to muddle through. The path of least resistance is usually the easier one and there is something very British about a 'make do and mend' approach to economic problems.

Even if the pandemic had not hit in 2020, 2021 was going to be a potential turning point for Britain: the year Brexit became a reality. In the years since 2016, both the left and right of British politics set out grand new visions of what the future might hold. For the Corbynite left a Britain freed from troublesome European rules on state aid to firms and obligations under the Single Market could see a revitalised system of industrial policy, with state-owned banks channelling funds to new technologies while state-owned utilities oversaw a revolution in green energy generation. A sort of Harold Wilsonian vision of the role of a modernising state coupled with a Bennite approach to an Alternative Economic Strategy. But while the left wanted to replay the 1960s and 1970s, much of the right thought the 2020s could be a repeat of the 1980s. 'Global Britain' would be a free trading, deregulating economic powerhouse, a sort of 'Singapore on Thames'.

Neither vision was realistic. For all the talk of getting Brexit done, with Europe set to remain Britain's largest trading partner for the foreseeable future the nature of Britain's relationship with the EU will continue to dominate trade policy for decades. A more likely outcome than either the guiding activist state of the left or the deregulatory dreams of the right is a middle path: Europe continues to dominate British trade but on less favourable terms, with a knock-on impact on productivity growth. But what should have been the key economic debate in Britain in 2020 was quickly relegated to a distant second place.

As the Johnson government geared up for its first budget in March 2020 the emphasis was supposed to be on what it called 'levelling up'. The new Tory majority was a different manner of beast to anything that had come before, dependent on forty-odd ex-Labour seats across the older industrial areas of Britain. Diverging demographics, especially of age, were driving a political realignment. Canterbury, which had elected a Conservative MP even in Labour's 1997 landslide, was now Labour-held, whilst the Tories held Dudley and Leigh. Boris Johnson's party had won a solid majority on the back of older voters but had two assets in 2019 that were unlikely still to be present in 2024: Brexit as a rallying call and Jeremy Corbyn as his opponent. Something needed to be done to cement his new majority and the easiest answer seemed to be a lot of cement. Johnson pledged an infrastructure revolution, one focused on the midlands and the north, which have received less in the way of government capital spending than London and the south. Public sector net investment would rise to 3 per cent of GDP, its highest level in decades, to build a wave of new rail lines and roads to connect up the north and, it was hoped, drive productivity higher.

Behind this sat an almost entirely new fiscal strategy. Gone was the old Osborne era target of reducing debt to GDP and gone too was the Hammond approach of austerity-lite. Public borrowing would rise to fund the agenda. The structural deficit was quietly dropped as a fiscal target in favour of a debt interest rule. The government would now aim to keep debt service costs below 6 per cent of tax revenues rather than working towards any absolute level of debt. This had the advantage of taking into account the record low borrowing costs the government faced in a world still short of safe assets. Indeed, while the level of government debt was by early 2020 the highest it had been in five decades, the cost of servicing it, at just 1.7 per cent of GDP, was now the lowest it had been since the Second World War. A formal statement of the new rules was expected at Rishi Sunak, the new Chancellor's, first budget.

But by the time Sunak rose to his feet in the chamber in mid-March, the world had moved on. As the pandemic arrived in Britain the Bank of England cut interest rates back to their post-Brexit low of 0.25 per cent and the Chancellor announced what seemed like a generous package of fiscal stimulus worth some 1.3 per cent of GDP. This was the single biggest giveaway budget since the early 1990s, coupled with a co-ordinated cut in interest rates. Fiscal and monetary policy shock and awe to see Britain through the coming crisis. Within weeks it would seem to be but a drop in the ocean.

In the early days of Britain's first lockdown, commentators were quick to compare the crisis to the total wars of the twentieth century. But that was wide of the mark. In fact the crisis was almost the direct opposite: in the wars the challenge government had faced was how to maximise production and generate resources to sustain a total military effort. In 2020 the challenge was one of demobilisation, of how to cut back on economic activity in order to reduce social contact and prevent the spread of the disease. The one thing that was similar was the price tag. As tax revenues plummeted and spending increased, the deficit hit the 20 per cent of GDP mark not seen since the early 1940s.

The obvious answer on how to demobilise an economy was to pay people to remain at home. The furlough scheme, drawn up in a matter of days with input from both the TUC and the CBI in a ghostly echo of the year of consensus, originally paid employees some 80 per cent of their previous salary to remain off work. It was initially planned to run for a matter of weeks but was continually extended. By July it was the single largest item of government spending and costing more than the NHS to run. Some 11 million workers found themselves furloughed at its peak. Government-backed loans worth around £66 billion were extended to tide firms over.

QE was extended again to help manage the sheer volume of government bond issuance. Once again, interest rates collapsed so that by the end of the year, despite debt to GDP leaping above 100 per cent, the actual interest bill the government paid had fallen.

In the initial phase of the crisis, when it was hoped that restrictions would last for just a few weeks, the emphasis was very much on freezing the economy in place. The hope was that the furlough scheme would keep workers attached to their jobs and the cheap loans would allow firms to stave off insolvency. When things reopened everyone could pick up where they had left off. But as the crisis dragged on and as reopening become a gradual process which sometimes went into reverse, the hopes of a return to normal began to fade, and with it the cross-party, and cross-industry, consensus that had emerged. By the winter of 2020 a traditional left/right divide over how the crisis would be paid for and the role of the state in the recovery was evident.

Closing the non-essential retail and hospitality sectors alongside the schools whilst encouraging people to work from home had a catastrophic impact on GDP, which fell by more than 20 per cent over the course of March and April. Never before had the British economy contracted so quickly, but of course never before had closing down economic activity been such an explicit aim of policy. The rebound that began in May picked up steam in July and August and then began to peter out in September as cases of COVID-19 once more rose in number.

Overall, GDP looked set to be down by around 10 per cent in 2020 as a whole, the worst year since the post-war bust following the Great War.

The one legacy that will certainly remain is a much higher level of debt to GDP than before the crisis. The success of the vaccine rollout in 2021 offers the hope of a relatively rapid recovery but how much lasting damage the economy suffers will very much depend on how structural the changes induced by the pandemic prove to be.

Even with furlough schemes and cheap loans, some existing trends accelerated in 2020 and proved too much for many firms. The jump in the market share of online retail, to around 30 per cent of all purchases by value, proved too much for many high street names. And even though people are unlikely to want to drink and eat less in 2021, the length of the lockdowns forced many hospitality firms to close their doors permanently. In all, 20,000 retail stores closed in 2020 and almost quarter of a million jobs were lost in the sector.

The differential impact on the north – where lockdowns have lasted longer and been stricter – will make any levelling up agenda much trickier in post-pandemic Britain than pre. Not only is the starting point harder, but if the rise in working from home proves to be lasting then the investment case for many of the transport projects which lay at the programme's core will be undermined.

Whatever direction it may take, how Britain's economy develops in the 2020s will be shaped by what came before and it will be moulded as much by political choices as by economic notions. In the end, political economy matters at least as much as macroeconomics. A government reliant on the votes of retired households will take different decisions from one based on a coalition of workers. The Johnson majority, with its three score or so former Labour seats in the north and midlands of England, rests on a different basis from Cameron's. The government does not simply have to get the economy moving again after the pandemic, it has to get it moving in a way which benefits enough of its own coalition of voters to get itself re-elected. If it succeeds in that, then quite a lot of pain can be tolerated elsewhere.

John Maynard Keynes got many things right over the years but he always overestimated the role of ideas and down-played brute political reality. 'It is ideas, not vested interests, which are dangerous for good or evil,' he wrote in *The General Theory*. 'Indeed the world is ruled by little else.' He was wrong. Ideas played an important role in the paradigm shifts Britain underwent in the 1840s, the 1940s and the 1980s, but in each case those ideas could only ever be implemented by a shifting balance of political forces. There are plenty of ideas about how Britain's economy should be reshaped after COVID-19 and Brexit but implementing any of them means assembling the right political coalition.

A Note on Data

Almost all the data in this book come from the Bank of England's mammoth dataset 'a millennium of macroeconomic data for the UK', which is freely available on their website and covers Britain from roughly the time of the Domesday Book until 2016. It is truly an excellent resource for which I am deeply thankful. The Office for National Statistics' website is nowadays a much more user-friendly experience than it once was and was also extremely useful.

Further Reading

The books listed here are, I am afraid, not a full bibliography but a list of those texts which I have found most helpful. In most cases they contain extensive notes and references which the truly inspired can happily delve further into.

David Cannadine's *Victorious Century, Britain 1800 to 1906* and Peter Clarke's *Hope and Glory; Britain 1900–2000* serve as an excellent introduction to modern Britain; both cover economics as well as politics and society.

Power and Plenty: Trade, War, and the World Economy in the Second Millennium by Ronald Findlay and Kevin H. O'Rourke is, as the name suggests, much broader in its coverage than the Britain of circa 1750 onwards that I have sketched out here. But it is the best single volume on economic history I have ever read and cannot be recommended highly enough. Daron Acemoglu and James Robinson's *Why Nations Fail* is also a much broader work that is highly recommended.

The two volumes of the *Cambridge Economic History of Modern Britain* covering 1700–1870 and 1870–present, expertly edited by Roderick Floud, Jane Humphries and Paul Johnson, are superb. I also still enjoy the earlier three-volume edition edited by Roderick Floud and Deirdre McCloskey, first published in the mid-1990s, from which I first learned British economic history.

On the industrial revolution, Robert Allen's *The Industrial Revolution in Global Perspective* and Joel Mokyr's *The Enlightened Economy, Britain 1700–1850* are both indispensable.

Stephen Broadberry's *The Productivity Race: British Manufacturing in International Perspective 1850–1990* is a little dry at times but well worth reading. Nicolas Crafts' *Forging Ahead, Falling Behind and Fighting Back* covers the development of Britain from the industrial revolution to the financial crisis in a broad international perspective and with excellent detail.

From the Corn Laws to Free Trade by Cheryl Schonhardt-Bailey is especially good on the political economy of a key British turning point, while Euan Green's *The Crisis of Conservatism: The Politics, Economics and Ideology of the Conservative Party 1880–1914* and Frank Trentman's *Free Trade Nation* are equally good on a potential turning point avoided.

David Edgerton's *The Rise and Fall of the British Nation* is a wonderful read on the politics and economics of the twentieth century, quietly explaining why the author thinks almost everyone else has got it wrong. George Peden's *Arms, Economics and British Strategy: From Dreadnoughts to Hydrogen Bombs* is an excellent read and especially good on the two total wars. Richard Toye's *The Labour Party and the Planned Economy 1931–51* is a very useful read on the wider Attlee period.

Alexander Cairncross's *Sterling in Decline* and his co-authored book with Kathleen Burke *Goodbye, Great Britain* are fantastic on the international context of the 1950s to 1970s, while Glen O'Hara's *From Dream to Disillusionment: Economic and Social Planning in 1960s Britain* is superb on Wilson. Andrew Gamble's *The Free Economy and the Strong State* is a fascinating analysis of the Thatcher years.

The autobiographies of the various post-war Chancellors have been very useful; Denis Healey's *Time of My Life* and Nigel Lawson's *The View from Number Eleven* are especially good. Robert Skidelsky's three-volume biography of Keynes is both a pleasure to read and a fantastic source on the life of the twentieth century's most important economist.

Finally, when George Osborne created the Office for Budget Responsibility he probably did not have authors in mind, but the OBR's twice-annual economic and financial outlooks are a superb resource. As are the Bank of England's quarterly Inflation Reports, now renamed Monetary Policy Reports.

Sources

Clement Attlee, quoted in *New Jerusalems: The Labour Party and the Economics of Democratic Socialism*, Elizabeth Durbin (Routledge and Kegan Paul, 1985)

Winston Churchill, Hansard, https://api.parliament.
uk/historic-hansard/commons/1925/apr/28/
return-to-gold-standard

Gregory Clark, 'The Great Escape: The Industrial
Revolution in Theory and in History', http://faculty.
econ.ucdavis.edu/faculty/gclark/papers/IR2003.pdf

Gregory Clark and Marianne E. Page, 'Welfare reform,
1834: Did the New Poor Law in England produce significant economic gains?', *Cliometrica*, Spring Cliometrica
Society (Association Francaise de Cliométrie), vol. 13 (2),
pp. 221–244, May

John Darwin, *After Tamerlane: The Rise and Fall of Global
Empires 1400–2000* (Allen Lane, 2007)

Ronald Findlay and Kevin O'Rourke, *Power and Plenty:
Trade, War, and the World Economy in the Second Millennium*
(Princeton University Press, 2007)

John Hajnal, 'European Marriage Patterns in Historical
Perspective', edited by D. V. Glass.; D. E. C. Eversley,
Population in History (Edward Arnold, 1965)

Michael Heseltine, Hansard, https://api.parliament.uk/
historic-hansard/commons/1980/jan/15/housing-bill

Thomas Hobbes, *Leviathan* (Andrew Crooke, 1651)

Eric J. Hobsbawm, 'Artisan or Labour Aristocrat?', *The
Economic History Review*, New Series, Vol. 37, No. 3,
August 1984, pp. 355–372

Eric J. Hobsbawm, 'The Forward March of Labour
Halted?', *Marxism Today*, September 1978

Paul Krugman, 'Mr. Keynes and the Moderns' speech, 18
June 2011. Prepared for the Cambridge conference com-
memorating the 75th anniversary of the publication of
The General Theory of Employment, Interest, and Money

Paul Krugman, *The Age of Diminishing Expectations* (MIT
Press, 1994)

James Loch MP, quoted in Eric J. Evans, *The Forging of the Modern State: Early Industrial Britain 1783–1870*, Third Edition (Routledge, 2001)

Karl Marx, Capital: A Critique of Political Economy, Volume 1 (Verlag von Otto Meisner, 1867)

John Maynard Keynes, 'The economic consequences of Mr Churchill' (The Hogarth Press, 1925)

John Maynard Keynes, *Economic Consequences of the Peace* (Macmillan and Co. Ltd, 1919)

George Orwell, 'Charles Dickens', *Inside the Whale and Other Essays* (Victor Gollancz Ltd, 1940)

George Orwell, *The Road to Wigan Pier* (Victor Gollancz Ltd, 1937)

George Osborne, *Financial Times*, November 2008

David Parker, *The Official History of Privatisation*, Vols 1 and 2 (Routledge, 2009 and 2012)

Henry Parris, *Government and the Railways in Nineteenth-century Britain* (Routledge and Kegan Paul, 1965)

Cheryl Schonhardt-Bailey, *From the Corn Laws to Free Trade* (St Augustine's Press, 1996)

Adam Smith, *The Wealth of Nations* (W. Strahan and T. Cadell, 1776)

Charles Tilly, 'War Making and State Making as Organised Crime', edited by P. Evans, D. Rueschemeyer, and T. Skocpol, *Bringing the State Back In*, pp. 169–191 (Cambridge University Press, 1985)

John Tomlinson, 'Inventing "Decline": The Falling Behind of the British Economy in the Postwar Years', *The Economic History Review*, New Series, Vol. 49, No. 4, November 1996

Max Weber, *The Protestant Ethic and the Spirit of Capitalism* (Penguin, 2004)

Acknowledgements

Richard Beswick has been everything I could have asked for in an editor. This book is many times better than it would have been without his input and I am eternally grateful for his initial commissioning decision. I also owe many thanks to Tamsyn Berryman at Little, Brown and Elizabeth Dobson for the copy edit. Readers have hopefully been spared most of my occasionally adventurous approach to spelling. All mistakes remain my own.

This book would simply not have been written were it not for my agent, Kate Barker. The five-year gap between us initially going for a coffee to discuss book ideas and the manuscript eventually being turned in was a long one. Sorry, Kate.

Colleagues at the *Economist*, *Prospect* and the BBC have, over the years, sharpened my writing. Especial thanks are due to Emma Duncan at the *Economist*, Tom Clark of *Prospect* and my old *Newsnight* workmate Chris Cook, who while never officially the editor of my BBC blog posts, certainly appointed himself to the role.

Gavin Kelly and Nick Pearce commissioned me to write a chapter on Britain's changing political economy in the sixty years or so before Brexit for the *Political Quarterly* in 2018. They were excellent editors and got me seriously thinking about many of the themes that make up the latter chapters of this book. Similar thanks are due to Richard Vadon of the BBC for championing *World War Two: The Economic Battle* and to Lizzie McNeil for producing it superbly.

I am a journalist rather than a historian. This book would not exist without the years of scholarship from which I have drawn. The notes on further reading at the end provide a starting point for anyone else wanting to delve further into the topics discussed here.

Twitter, and the people I follow on it, are also due a hearty thanks. Social media can be a useless time sink but it can also function as an excellent way of building connections with people who really know their stuff. In particular, the anonymous economic history expert known only as @ Pseudoerasmus has been a great help to me over the years with his encyclopaedic knowledge of the academic literature and links to relevant papers.

Social media is all well and good, but real friends are much better. Many friends have been forced to listen to me drone on about British economic history for far too long. You all known who you are, Some of you, like Vino Sangrapillai, Pete Morton and Rob Vance, have been putting up with this for twenty years.

Last but by no means least, I owe much to my family. I imagine living with me is never easy. Living with me while I am writing a book is probably even harder. Living with me while I am writing a book, a global pandemic has trapped you in the house and you are also pregnant must have been a chore. Thank you, Natalie.

Index